DØ790151

## More Praise for *The Power of Latino Leadersl*

"Latinos have advanced because of the activist tradition of our leaders who organized people to address social injustice. As the Latino community comes into its power, our future leaders can learn from *The Power of Latino Leadership* as they create their own history. 'Si Se Puede—Yes We Can' is a call to action. This book captures this spirit."

—**Dolores Huerta, President, Dolores Huerta Foundation; cofounder, United Farm Workers; and recipient of the Presidential Medal of Freedom**

"Latinos are part of the fabric of America. Our culture and values are perfectly consistent with the American Dream that has made and continues to make the United States great. *The Power of Latino Leadership* explores a leadership model to maximize the role of Latinos in America's future growth and prosperity."

—**Julián Castro, Mayor of San Antonio, Texas**

"*The Power of Latino Leadership* is a must-read for Latinos who want to integrate their history and culture into their future contributions, whether just starting on their leadership journey or already recognized leaders."

—**Carlos F. Orta, President and CEO, Hispanic Association on Corporate Responsibility**

"At Western Union, I have the opportunity to see leadership in many ways. The most impactful are the hardworking, everyday heroes that make a difference in their communities. Bordas celebrates this type of leadership in this inspiring book. *The Power of Latino Leadership* brings to life the contributions US Latinos are making to invigorate our communities, culture, and economy."

—**Hikmet Ersek, President and CEO, Western Union**

"It is now that Latino political and social strengths are being realized. This is attributed to leadership within the Latino community that has singularly focused on ensuring that our voices are heard and that we influence all sectors of American life. In *The Power of Latino Leadership*, Bordas offers a model for future leadership that draws on our strengths and leverages our enormous potential."

—**Lisa Garcia Quiroz, Senior Vice President for Corporate Responsibility and Chief Diversity Officer, Time Warner, and Founding Publisher, *People en Español***

"This book is a must for anyone who wants to know how leaders develop their practices within a community context. Bordas has pulled together illuminating examples with great lessons for anyone working to create an equitable and truly diverse society."

—**Rinku Sen, President, Applied Research Center; Publisher, Colorlines.com; and author of *The Accidental American***

"To the joy of some and the panic of others, America grows more diverse by the day. Leaders want to understand and motivate those they lead but may feel intimidated by the complex history and culture of Latinos in America. Native-born and immigrant…newly arrived and in the country since before there was a United States, Spanish-speaking, bilingual, English-dominant, with roots in countries running from Mexico all the way to the tip of South America…it's a lot to master! Juana Bordas has written a handbook for making sense of it all. *The Power of Latino Leadership* helps the reader decode the coming America and the changing workforce."

—**Ray Suarez, Senior Correspondent,** *PBS News Hour,* **and former host,** *Talk of the Nation,* **NPR**

"As one of the foremost experts on leadership in the Latino community, Juana Bordas has mentored generations of young Hispanics throughout her distinguished career. In her acclaimed new book, *The Power of Latino Leadership,* she presents a compelling case for how the strengths Hispanics bring to the table—deep roots, strong values, and our multifaceted culture—can infuse new life into and bring a fresh perspective to leadership development for all our country's current and future leaders."

—**Janet Murguía, President, National Council of La Raza**

"Juana Bordas's exploration into the traits of contemporary Latino leaders arrives at an important moment for our country. Latinos are the nation's second largest population and, as the 2012 election demonstrated, have become a decisive force in American politics. Bordas provides timely insight into Latino contributions to our nation's future and why their influence will continue to increase."

—**Arturo Vargas, Executive Director, National Association of Latino Elected and Appointed Officials**

"Juana Bordas is a highly credentialed champion of diversity in leadership and organizational change. Her new book, *The Power of Latino Leadership,* is a welcome reminder of Juana's lifelong passion to support and empower young Hispanic leaders. To develop a deeper appreciation for the countless contributions the Latino community is making to America's multicultural leadership journey, read this book!"

—**Ken Blanchard, coauthor of** *The One Minute Manager* **and** *Great Leaders Grow*

# THE POWER OF

# Latino
# Leadership

*Juana Bordas*

Also by the author:

*Salsa, Soul, and Spirit: Leadership for a Multicultural Age*

THE POWER OF

# Latino
# Leadership

## CULTURE, INCLUSION, AND CONTRIBUTION

**JUANA BORDAS**

Berrett–Koehler Publishers, Inc.
San Francisco
*a BK Business book*

Berrett-Koehler Publishers, Inc.
235 Montgomery Street, Suite 650
San Francisco, CA 94104-2916
Tel: (415) 288-0260    Fax: (415) 362-2512    www.bkconnection.com

**ORDERING INFORMATION**

Quantity sales. Special discounts are available on quantity purchases by corporations, associations, and others. For details, contact the "Special Sales Department" at the Berrett-Koehler address above.

Individual sales. Berrett-Koehler publications are available through most bookstores. They can also be ordered directly from Berrett-Koehler: Tel: (800) 929-2929; Fax: (802) 864-7626; www.bkconnection.com

Orders for college textbook/course adoption use. Please contact Berrett-Koehler: Tel: (800) 929-2929; Fax: (802) 864-7626.

Orders by U.S. trade bookstores and wholesalers. Please contact Ingram Publisher Services, Tel: (800) 509-4887; Fax: (800) 838-1149; E-mail: customer.service@ingrampublisherservices.com; or visit www.ingrampublisherservices.com/Ordering for details about electronic ordering.

Berrett-Koehler and the BK logo are registered trademarks of Berrett-Koehler Publishers, Inc.

Printed in the United States of America

Berrett-Koehler books are printed on long-lasting acid-free paper. When it is available, we choose paper that has been manufactured by environmentally responsible processes. These may include using trees grown in sustainable forests, incorporating recycled paper, minimizing chlorine in bleaching, or recycling the energy produced at the paper mill.

Library of Congress Cataloging-in-Publication Data

Bordas, Juana.

The power of Latino leadership : culture, inclusion, and contribution /

Juana Bordas.

    pages cm

Includes bibliographical references and index.

ISBN 978-1-60994-887-0 (pbk.)

1. Hispanic Americans. 2. Leadership. I. Title.

E184.S75B6724 2013

973'.0468--dc23

                              2013002381

First Edition

18  17  16  15  14  13         10  9  8  7  6  5  4  3  2  1

Cover designer: Barbara Haines

Interior design, illustration, and composition: Seventeenth Street Studios

Proofreader: Laurie Dunne

Indexer: Janet Perlman

Cover art: istockphoto.com and Jorge Enciso: Design Motifs of Ancient Mexico (Dover).

*For the hundreds of thousands of Latino leaders who are uplifting their communities and building an inclusive society that cares for its people. For our young and emerging leaders who will fulfill the vision of Latino destino.*

# Contents

# Preface

I GREW UP IN THE early 1950s, when Latinos were in a cultural no-man's-land. These were the days when the sign No Mexicans, No Dogs hung in the windows of Texas restaurants and my mother was embarrassed by her broken English. In fact, the term *Hispanic* as an official designation occurred only from the 1980 census on. If my mother were alive today she would marvel at how far Hispanics have come. *Un milagro*—a miracle! Then she would make the sign of the cross in gratitude for divine providence.

Many people believe that the rising Latino influence is a recent phenomenon fueled by our exploding demographics. It's true that the Latino population in the United States grew by 43 percent in the last decade, accounting for more than half of the population gain.[1] Today one in six people in the United States is Hispanic. Our numbers are fifty million strong.[2] And tomorrow? By 2050 one in three Americans will be Hispanic.[3]

Most Latinos, however, understand that our advancement has taken centuries. Our roots go back to before the United States was a nation. Hispanics were born of conquest and colonization. We are a fusion people—mainly the offspring of the Spanish conquistadores and the indigenous people of this hemisphere. But many Hispanics have African as well as European ancestors, such as those from Germany and France, who also settled the Americas. Hispanics are a mixture of cultures, languages, races, and nationalities.

And yet today, we are emerging with a strong identity. Latinos are embracing their culture and language, gaining economic and political clout, and expanding their global connections. These gains have been possible because of the vision, contribution, and relentless activism of our leaders. They have built a legacy of inclusive community leadership, based on cultural values and traditions, that has as its purpose to uplift people. And yet the story of how Latino leaders have guided their people has not been fully told.

I aspire to make that contribution. *The Power of Latino Leadership* is the first book squarely focused on describing the principles and practices of how Latinos lead. It will help Latinos to be effective and powerful by leading from their cultural core and will infuse mainstream leadership with an inclusive community spirit that fosters contribution and service.

The concept of *Latino power*, however, warrants a new definition. Historically, power has been hierarchical, the domain of the influential few, and associated with control and dominance. Most often power has been found in the hands of White males. Latino power, on the other hand, has evolved from the community—it is the power of *We*—the power that people have to change their lives for the better.

Latino power is accessible to many people. Diffused power means leadership is not concentrated in one voice or only a few. Instead, Latino power is leadership by the many—the thousands of Latino leaders working every day in communities across the country. Leaders encourage people to tap into their own power. Julián Castro, the young mayor of San Antonio, follows this tradition: "I think that what our young people should understand is that they can be leaders in their own right in their own community—in their neighborhood, church, college, job, or career, wherever it is. That is more empowering than looking up to one person as the Latino leader."[4]

Moreover, *Latinos are diversity*—they are a cultural and ethnic group, not a race. Latinos are Brown, Black, White, Yellow, and all the beautiful hues in between. Some Latinos have ancestors who were here before this country was the United States. Others have recently immigrated. Our extended families are composed of multiple generations. These differences drive an *inclusive* leadership form rooted in the culture's expansive diversity. Latino leadership is one of coalition building, bringing people together, working across sectors, and embracing a consciousness of partnership. Latino leaders leverage the power of inclusion.

Latinos maintain close ties to their twenty-two nations of origin and are culturally linked with people in North, Central, and South America. Over one-third of the continental United States was historically part of México, and these cultural roots remain strong. Latinos' power, therefore, is global in scope. Furthermore, until the last decade, over 40 percent of Latino growth was fueled by immigrants who bring hope, determination, and replenish the cultural core.[5] Unlike previous waves of immigrants, Latinos are acculturating, not assimilating. They are bringing their gifts into the mainstream and infusing the United States with a Latin flavor.

*Latino power is rooted in history and tradition*, an understanding that the past is the rich soil that nourishes tomorrow. Latinos owe a great debt to the leaders who have paved the way for our community to blossom. *The Power of Latino Leadership* acknowledges their legacy and contributions and delineates a path for continued Latino advancement.

*Latino power is ahora—now.* The road to the White House runs directly through the Latino community. In the 2012 presidential election, 71 percent of Latinos supported Barack Obama, ensuring his victory.[6] Latinos voted their values: a compassionate immigration policy, education for our children, care of the elderly, greater economic and social equity, and advancing a diverse society.

And *Latino power is our future*, the promise and potential of youth. For the first time, the US census reports that the majority of babies born in 2011 were a warm color of brown, chocolate, or latte. They are ethnic and racial minorities, and the majority is Latino. Today, one in five schoolchildren is Hispanic, as is one in four newborns.[7] Never before has an ethnic group made up so large a share of the youngest Americans. This speaks to this urgency of this book, which will support young Latinos who wish to keep their cultural ties operating in a way that reflects their values and chart the future of our community.

Sustained by a culture of celebration, faith, and hope, Latino power is *destino* (destiny). It is the collective contribution Latinos will make. Based on their people-centered values, inclusiveness, and *bienvenido* (welcoming) spirit, Latino leaders are building a diverse and humanistic society.

And for those who are not Latino, a special welcome.

## *Bienvenido*—The Power of Latino Inclusiveness

MY FAMILY IS A sundry variety of Latinos, like a delicious box of assorted chocolates. My seven brothers, sisters, and I emigrated from Nicaragua, and those older than I speak with a Spanish accent. Our children were born and raised in the United States and have a more blended Latino experience. Many of them married into different cultural groups, so now we have Latinos by marriage. My brother-in-law Karl, who is of German descent, and my niece Lorrie's Anglo husband can both attest that if you hang around Latinos long enough *the rhythm is going to get you.* Then there are the wonderful *amigos* who have been part of our extended family for so long that they are now Latinos by affinity, or *corazón* (heart).

This tradition of welcoming people into the tribe or culture has ancient roots. Native Americans acknowledge that a person can have an Indian heart or spirit. African tribes have ceremonies to initiate people who have become one of them. African Americans have honorary aunties and uncles and "other mothers." Likewise, Latinos have elastic and expansive extended *familias*. People who have a special affinity are invited to become *comadres, compadres, madrinas, padrinos, tías,* or *tíos.* (More on this as we continue.)

If you are not a Latino by birth, this book is an invitation to do likewise: To become part of the familia. To experience our dynamic culture. To tap your feet to the salsa beat and become a Latino by corazón! To join with us in creating a new America that is inclusive and heals the divisions that have separated us.

## Let's Talk about Latino Leadership

INTEGRATING A MODEL ON Latino leadership is a work in progress. Just as Latinos are immensely diverse, so are their leadership forms. This book's purpose is to *start a conversation on how Latinos lead.* I humbly understand people may not always agree with the concepts. I acknowledge the wisdom and experience of the many leaders in the Latino community and welcome their perspectives and insights. So what are my credentials for writing this book?

I am Pan-Hispanic. Perhaps more simply said, my destino, which is a person's unique life path, opened doors for me to experience the many facets of my Latina familia. This allows me to put forth a comprehensive leadership model that brings together the nuances of the culture yet at the same time reflects our rich diversity.

Florida, where I was raised, is a cauldron of Latino culture. My extended family includes Mexicans, Colombians, and Cubans. My great-grandmothers were from Peru and British Honduras. I trained for the Peace Corps in beautiful Puerto Rico and served in Chile. Finally, I have lived in Colorado forty years among my cherished Mexican American *hermanos,* which has instilled a deep love for these politically oriented and mariachi-loving people.

My first book, *Salsa, Soul, and Spirit: Leadership for a Multicultural Age,* contained nine leadership principles from Latinos, Blacks, and American Indians in the United States. This multicultural model enriched American leadership by including the enormous contributions of communities of color. My goal was to inspire a core of multicultural leaders who recognize that diversity and inclusiveness are indispensable to crafting an equitable democracy and a global community.

I also wanted to honor the points of convergence from the common history and experiences shared by communities of color who despite racism and discrimination continue to focus on mutual advancement, people-centered leadership, and responsible social action. Communities of color must identify the common ground and work together to bring their immense potential to fruition.

As a Latina, however, I want to further this work by highlighting the values and experiences that flow from my own culture and integrate these into a unique leadership model. *The Power of Latino Leadership* offers additional dimensions to the multicultural leadership principles in my first book. I hope by reading this book, other leaders will develop a deeper appreciation of the connecting points in our myriad cultures and further the conversation about multicultural leadership forms.

Many mainstream leadership books are written by scholars who have a theoretical framework and who may base their conclusions on research. When it is applicable, I reference and connect their work with current Latino leadership practices. A book about Latino leadership, however, if it is to accurately reflect its topic, requires a person who has practiced leadership in a proven and productive way.

My mainstream credentials include teaching at the Center for Creative Leadership, the most highly utilized corporate center in the world. I served as an adviser to the Kellogg National Leaders Program, as a vice chair of the Greenleaf Center on Servant Leadership board, and as a trustee of the International Leadership Association.

I have worked with the Hispanic community since I was twenty-one in the barrios of Santiago, Chile. I later served as the executive director of Mi Casa Resource Center, as the first president of the National Hispana Leadership Institute, and as the founder of the Circle of Latina Leadership in Colorado. In partnership with many organizations and talented Latinos, I have designed and implemented Latino leadership programs in Arizona, Colorado, Ohio, Illinois, the District of Columbia, New Mexico, Florida, and Texas. My article "Latino Leadership: Building a Humanistic and Diverse Society" was published by *The Journal of Leadership Studies* in 2001 and is one of the first conceptual frameworks on Latino leadership.

While these experiences are important in establishing my credibility, it is the many Latinos who I have worked with in countless endeavors that prepared me to write this book. I am immeasurably grateful to have spent my life with thousands of Latinos who have advanced our community and nation. Today as an elder, I wish to integrate this knowledge into a viable theory of leadership based on our practical and collective experiences and woven from the beautiful culture that connects us. My *abuela* (grandmother) would simply have said, "Es tu destino."

And speaking of destino, what luck that you are reading this book! Ah, perhaps it is not luck; perhaps it is your destino that your past and present have led you to this point of learning about the powerful leadership forms in the Latino community. Latinos can take pride in the immense contributions our leaders have made. Non-Latinos can become more culturally adaptive and start using the principles in this book to lead with a more inclusive spirit. We can all infuse our leadership journeys with a renewed sense of purpose and a vibrant Latino flavor!

## *¡Ahora!* Latino Excellence

OK, I ADMIT IT—I love *mi cultura* (my culture), and as you read on you will see that I am a Latina convert! I assimilated back in the late 1950s. But I knew I had lost a brilliant aspect of my cultural soul, and by serving in the Peace Corps in Chile, I reintegrated the beauty and power of my culture. So I am a Latina by birth and a convert by choice!

In this book, I present Latino culture, values, and leadership in the very best light. Hopefully, by recognizing our cultural zenith, leaders will emulate these values. Young Latinos will embrace the traditions of their *abuelos* and learn that keeping their culture will make them more powerful and successful. (This is not to deny the inconsistencies and less-than-desired aspects present in all cultures. For Latinos, discrimination and colonization are historical traumas. Remnants of these difficult circumstances endure in higher rates of poverty, lower educational levels, and diffuse identity.)

I would like the reader to consider that mainstream leadership books routinely emphasize the ideal. Books such as *Good to Great* or *In Search of Excellence* put forth the possibilities when visionary leaders take the

helm. Authors do not spend much time on topics such as "From Bad
to Worse" or "In Search of Mediocrity," although there are plenty of
middle-of-the-road leaders and organizations. By stressing the ideal—the
best of the best—and by having positive models to emulate, leaders and
organizations expect to improve and move closer to that ideal.

And may reading about the Latino ideal nurture understanding and
respect in other people who wish to share in our wonderful culture and
powerful forms of leadership.

### ¡Que Viva el Español!

NOW ABOUT THE SPANISH words sprinkled throughout this *libro* (book)
. . . Spanish is used when the meaning of a word is obvious or when it
adds flavor and cultural zest. The first use of a Spanish word in a chapter
is italicized and translated in the glossary. If the context cannot be
understood without translation, the *palabras* (words) will be in parentheses
or set off by a dash. The intent is to have readers get into the rhythm of
*español* and to learn new ways of communicating. For Spanish speakers
this makes the libro closer to their hearts. But being familiar with español
is a good skill for leaders across the board. Many a politician or business
leader has won over a Hispanic crowd by starting his speech in español.

Using a few Spanish words can facilitate positive work relations
and promote culturally effective management with the fastest-growing
segment of the workforce. Spanish fosters a business's ability to tap into
the lucrative and growing Latino market. Teachers can connect with
a growing percentage of their students. Spanish words are also being
integrated into the mainstream. As evidence of this, the March 3, 2012,
*Time* magazine cover was titled "*Yo decido:* Why Latinos will pick the
next president." Taco Bell's slogan is "Live *Más.*"

Because of immigration and migration the global community is right
in our neighborhood. The Internet is connecting people from across the
world like next-door neighbors. A great global passport is being able
to communicate with people by saying a few words in their language.
Spanish is a good start since it is spoken in twenty-two countries and is
the language spoken by most people in the Western Hemisphere.[8]

So ¡*Ándale—vámonos!* Let's get started!

# Acknowledgments—*Gracias*

G RATITUDE IS A CHERISHED Latino trait. Thank you to the many, many *gente* (people) who have helped and guided me in my leadership journey, especially my familia. A special gracias to my talented and dedicated *amigos* for reading and making suggestions on the manuscript: Richard Couto, the people's professor; Cynthia Evans, the compassionate editor; Eric Fransen, the Millennial whiz kid; Lynette Murphy, the brilliant strategist; Sylvia Puente, the spiritual activist; Art Ruiz, the reflective thinker; and Karen Seriguchi, the talented copyeditor. Their insights, leadership experience, and contributions have enriched these words. To Steve Piersanti, the most inspiring editor in the world, and the Berrett-Koehler staff: thank you for your guidance in shaping this work. I am blessed with an extended familia like this and am forever grateful.

# Special Contributions:
# Profiles of Latino Leaders

T HE ROOTS OF LATINO leadership run deep. Our leaders have transformed the tribulations of being deemed a minority to the incredible influence Latinos are having today. Leaders are building on a tradition of people-centered, socially responsible, and community-based leadership. This was revitalized in the 1960s, when César Chávez and the United Farm Workers marched for fair pay and decent working conditions.

Today, leaders are stepping forth in unprecedented numbers and are guiding the Latino community with a deep sense of purpose. I have been privileged to include the voices of nine of these outstanding leaders in this book. You will be inspired by their stories and learn from their experiences and wisdom. (Unless otherwise noted, all the quotations from these special contributors in this book come from personal interviews conducted with them, which were transcribed verbatim and then coded for common themes and patterns.)

**Anna Escobedo Cabral** was treasurer of the United States from 2005 to 2008. Previously, she directed the Smithsonian Institution's Center for Latino Initiatives and served as president of the Hispanic Association on Corporate Responsibility, a nonprofit coalition that advances Hispanic representation in corporate America. From 1993 to 1999, she was deputy staff director for the US Senate Judiciary Committee and executive staff director of the Senate Republican Task Force on Hispanic Affairs. Currently, Cabral holds a leadership position at the Inter-America Development Bank, which supports economic development throughout South America and the Caribbean.

**Julián Castro** became, at the age of twenty-six, the youngest elected city council member in San Antonio, Texas, history. He was elected mayor in 2009 and became the youngest mayor of a top 50 US city. He handily won reelection in 2011, with nearly 80 percent of the vote. Castro has focused on attracting well-paying jobs in twenty-first-century industries, positioning San Antonio to be a leader in the new energy economy, raising educational attainment, and revitalizing the inner city. In 2010, he was named to the World Economic Forum's list of Young Global Leaders. *Time* magazine placed him on its "40 under 40" list of rising stars in American politics. He was tapped for the keynote address for the 2012 Democratic Convention.

**Janet Murguía** is president and CEO of the National Council of La Raza, the largest Hispanic advocacy organization in the United States. In this role she addresses issues affecting Hispanics, such as education, health care, immigration, and economic equity. Murguía is on the board of the American Heart Association, the Partnership for a Healthier America, and the Leadership Conference on Civil and Human Rights. She is board chair of the Hispanic Association on Corporate Responsibility. Murguía was one of *Washingtonian* magazine's "100 Most Powerful Women in Washington" and *People en Español's* "100 Most Influential Hispanics."

**Carlos Orta** is president of the Hispanic Association on Corporate Responsibility, whose mission is to advance the inclusion of Hispanics in corporate America at a level commensurate with their economic contributions. He has worked in external affairs, corporate philanthropy, and government affairs at three Fortune 500 companies: Anheuser-Busch, Ford Motor Company, and Waste Management. Orta was selected by *Latino Leaders* magazine as one of the "101 Most Influential Leaders in the Latino Community."

**Antonia Pantoja** described herself as an institution builder. Though she passed away in 2002, her legacy continues through ASPIRA (to aspire), a leadership program for Puerto Rican youth. Pantoja was the first Puerto Rican woman to receive the Presidential Medal of Freedom and the John W. Gardner Leadership Award. It was my honor to work with her on the curriculum for the National Hispana Leadership Institute and to review interviews for the film *Antonia Pantoja: Abriendo Caminos* (Opening Pathways, 2006). Her autobiography, *Memoir of a Visionary*, was published by Arte Publico Press in 2002."

**Federico Peña** served as cochair of the historic 2008 and 2012 Barack Obama campaigns. He was elected mayor of Denver in 1983 and 1987, the first Latino mayor of a city with a minority Hispanic population. He revitalized Denver's economic health by initiating such projects as Denver International Airport, a new convention center, and Coors Baseball Stadium. A civil rights lawyer, Peña served in the Colorado House of Representatives and was tapped by the Clinton administration as the US secretary of transportation and US secretary of energy. Peña is currently the managing director for Vestar Capital Partners.

**Hilda Solis** was the twenty-fifth US Secretary of Labor, and the first Latina to serve in a president's cabinet. She served in the US House of Representatives from 2001 to 2009, representing the 31st and 32nd congressional districts of California. Early in her career she was elected to the Rio Hondo Community College Board in 1985 and the California State Assembly in 1992. In 1994 she was the first Hispanic woman elected to the California State Senate. She is known for her work with environmental justice, immigration, education, and workers' rights. Solis was the first female recipient of the John F. Kennedy Profile in Courage Award, in 2000.

**Arturo Vargas** is executive director of the National Association of Latino Elected and Appointed Officials. Previously he was vice president for Community Education and Public Policy for the Mexican American Legal Defense and Educational Fund. He also served as senior education policy analyst at the National Council of La Raza. Vargas serves on the boards of Zero Divide, the Independent Sector, and the Alliance for a Better Community. He received *Hispanic* magazine's Hispanic Achievement Award for Community Service and for five years was named one of its 101 most influential Latinos. Twice he has been chosen one of "100 Hispanic Influentials" by *HispanicBusiness* magazine.

**Raul Yzaguirre** was cochair of Hillary Clinton's valiant bid for the presidency in 2008. He was president of the National Council of La Raza for more than thirty years, building it into the largest Hispanic advocacy organization in America. He is a founder of the Hispanic Association for Corporate Responsibility, the New American Alliance, and the National Hispanic Leadership Agenda. Yzaguirre was the first Hispanic to receive a Rockefeller Award for Outstanding Public Service from Princeton University and the John W. Gardner Leadership Award. He was appointed the ambassador to the Dominican Republic by President Barack Obama in 2010.

## Thoughts for Young Latino Leaders

The leaders interviewed for this book, like the majority of Latino leaders of the last century, have come from the public and nonprofit sectors. These leaders provided needed services to people, empowered them, and built community capacity. They have brought the Latino community to where we are today.

This book's purpose is to secure that legacy by describing the powerful ways these leaders have served their communities. I recognize that in this century young Latinos will expand the scope and power of Latino leadership. They will lead in every sector of society: as savvy entrepreneurs and successful corporate executives, college professors, writers, and school superintendents. Latinos will broadcast the news, direct movies, and produce TV shows. They will be America's doctors, US senators, and Supreme Court justices. And yes, we will elect the first Latino president.

It is my hope that as young Latinos move forward, they will honor the collective efforts it took for us to advance and never forget where they came from. By building on the legacy of the leaders who came before, young Latinos can continue advancing our community and integrate the contributions, cultural assets, and power of Latino leadership into the American mainstream.

~~~~~~

# Leading Latino Style

**B**EYOND ITS CULTURAL INFLUENCE, Latino power will drive the American economic engine in this century. In 2017, Latinos will be the majority of the people entering the US workforce.[1] They are the fast-growing small-business sector. US Latino spending power represents a trillion-dollar market and the eighth-largest gross national product in the world.[2]

On a more practical level, by the middle of this century, when Latinos become the dominant workforce, organizations will need to cultivate Latino talent and benefit from their dynamic work ethic. Companies who are part of the bilingual market economy will grow and prosper. The future success of organizations and businesses, then, is closely linked to the growing Latino population and market. *The Power of Latino Leadership* offers an exciting, hands-on, and test-driven way to connect with and leverage Latino assets, energy, and values. It puts forth ten *culturally specific leadership principles* rooted in Latino history and tradition.

What is important to note is that, just as women left their imprint on the twentieth century and changed every institution in their wake,

1

so too will Latinos be the dominant force in these times. Women started the last century as 18 percent of the workforce. Today, they are a majority of workers and make up over a quarter of managers. They are the majority of students in colleges and universities, including law and medical schools. Women have made leadership more collaborative and relationship oriented.[3]

*The Power of Latino Leadership* describes how Latinos will have a similar transformative effect in this century. The book validates the leadership practices that have held Latinos together through the tribulations of being conquered, colonized, and deemed a minority. Their resiliency, contributions, and cultural vibrancy are a testament to the wisdom and perseverance of their leaders.

During the twenty-first century the Eurocentric influence of the past five hundred years will be transformed into a diverse multicultural form. Jorge Ramos, an award-winning Univision news anchor, notes that the Latinization of America is the fundamental influence that will change the monocultural nature of our society and replace ethnocentric tendencies with a multiethnic, multiracial, and multicultural nation.[4] Ramos is observing that the melting pot is being converted into a delicious paella and that Latinos are a vital ingredient adding color and flavor to our emerging rainbow nation.

## Hispanic and Latino

Almost four decades have passed since the US government mandated the use of the term *Hispanic*. *Latino* was not added as a choice until the 2000 census.[5] Hispanic and Latino are used interchangeably in this book. A 2012 study by the Pew Hispanic Center, *When Labels Don't Fit: Hispanics and Their View of Identity*, noted that 51 percent of Latinos have no preference between Hispanic and Latino. Thirty-three percent still prefer Hispanic, which is more traditional. (Most Hispanic organizations formed decades ago use this designation.) Fourteen percent now prefer Latino.[6] We will learn more about the multifaceted Latino identity as we explore this dynamic culture and its distinctive leadership forms. It is important to note that Hispanics may be of any race.

# Part I: *La Historia*: Latino Fusion and Hybrid Vigor

T HE POWER OF LATINO *leadership* begins with the complex history that birthed the Latino phenomenon. Be prepared for an exciting roller coaster ride that starts in ancient Rome, traverses the conquest of the Americas, and continues to Manifest Destiny in the nineteenth century. Why, you might ask, do we have to unearth these historical skeletons? How will this shed light on the dynamic leadership that sustained and advanced Latinos?

Well, consider that the word *Latino* comes from its connection to *Latin America*, which has its antecedent in the Roman conquest of Spain in 200 BC. Part I, "*La Historia*: Latino Fusion and Hybrid Vigor," starts with the footprints of the Spanish conquistadores—one of the precursors of today's Latinos. To understand how far we've come and the powerful legacy of our leaders, young Latinos must know their history. Non-Latinos will learn about the long-standing presence and contributions of Latinos in this hemisphere.

Chapter 1, "Ancient Roots and Mestizo Ancestry," considers the racial and cultural blending in Spain that was transported to the "new world." These antecedents resulted in a type of encounter very different from that which occurred in North America. Mestizos—the mixed-blood offspring of the Spanish and the indigenous people of this hemisphere—became the dominant population and are the ancestors of today's Latinos. We will explore a "creation" story of the Mestizo birth almost five centuries ago that prophesied the cultural fusion that would occur and gave hope for the future.

Chapter 2, "The US Latino Legacy," describes the annexation of the US Southwest from México and the designation of Latinos as minorities. This was abetted by Manifest Destiny in the nineteenth century, proclaiming that Indians, Blacks, and the ancestors of today's Latinos needed to learn the ways of White civilization. Manifest Destiny swept in a belief in cultural superiority and laid the groundwork for the segregated society that continued until the civil rights movement of the 1960s.

# Part II: Preparing to Lead: A Latino Perspective

**B**ECOMING A LEADER IN the Latino community requires pondering questions such as: Why do I desire to lead? What will be my unique contribution? How will I stay on the path I have chosen? Part II offers three culturally based principles that prepare a person to become a leader and to tap into his personal power.

Chapter 3, *"Personalismo:* The Character of the Leader," explores the belief that every person has inherent value and must be treated with respect. While many cultures espouse this, it is *an actual expectation* of Latinos, not just a cultural nicety. Personalismo prescribes that leaders establish personal, genuine, and caring relationships.

Second, the leader must become the type of person other people will follow. The essence of personalismo is the leader's character—her persona. The leader embodies traits that earn respect and trust.

To become this type of person requires a deep connection with the leader's inner self—the rock on which character formation rests. This implies understanding one's roots and family heritage, staying culturally connected, and understanding history. This is discussed in chapter 4, *"Conciencia*: Knowing Oneself and Cultivating Personal Awareness." A leader must also deal with the aftermath of exclusion and discrimination, both on him personally and on Latinos as a whole.

*The essence of personalismo is the leader's character—her persona. The leader embodies traits that earn respect and trust.*

The belief that every person has a distinct life path and purpose is explored in chapter 5, *"Destino:* Personal and Collective Purpose." Knowing one's destino requires the insight of conciencia. Individualistic cultures believe a person is in charge of and determines his own future. Many Latinos believe it is impossible to control chance, fate, or unplanned events. (Having to deal with discrimination is a case in point.) Life presents certain opportunities, experiences, and challenges. Destino is a dance with the currents of life.

# Part III: The Cultural Foundations of Leadership

L ATINO LEADERSHIP FLOWS FROM the cultural spring. Part III considers the values that unify Latinos and their emerging collective identity.

Chapter 6, "*La Cultura*: Culturally Based Leadership," looks at how the Latino culture is bound together by a common history, heritage, spiritual tradition, and language. *Most importantly, the culture is integrated by shared values such as respect, honesty, service, and generosity.* We will note seven key values from which culturally based leadership has emerged.

The Latino culture is a blended one, with roots in countries where the Spanish once ruled. The US Census Bureau's code contains over thirty Hispanic or Latino subgroups.[7] When speaking of culture, I am referring to the *US Hispanic culture*. However, because 47 percent of Hispanics are immigrants, they have close cultural ties to Latin America.[8] US Latinos share a language, similar values, and traditions with both Latin America and Spain.

It is important to consider that US Latinos are undergoing a unique *acculturation* experience. A new Pan-Hispanic culture is emerging that integrates the many Latino subgroups and the newly immigrated. Cultural synthesis began with the Spanish and continues to be a distinguishing characteristic of US Latinos. Because 63 percent of Hispanics are of Mexican descent and historically one-third of the United States was México, the US Latino culture is influenced by and reflects these origins as well.[9]

Throughout this book we will learn about Latino values through *dichos* (adages or proverbs). In most cultures, adages convey the important and valuable. The Anglo adage "The early bird gets the worm" advises, "Be there first and be ready to act." "Don't make a mountain out of a molehill" means "Take things in stride and have perspective." Similarly, *Mi casa es su casa* encourages generosity and sharing. *Mi casa es su casa* frames leadership as service and as caring for people. It counsels leaders, "Give of your time and ideas. Be generous. Value people and tend to their needs."

Dichos are a way for Latinos to remember the wisdom of their *abuelos* and understand the foundations of leadership. For non-Latinos, learning dichos invites them to increase their cultural adaptability and become Latinos by corazón.

*Latinos are diversity.* Their multifaceted identity and inclusiveness is reflected in "*De Colores*" (Of Many Colors)—a traditional song about life's incredible diversity. In chapter 7, "*De Colores:* Latino Inclusiveness and Diversity," we will learn more about this cherished song and how it invites people to be part of the culture.

"*De Colores*" starts with the official US census designation of Hispanics as a category in 1980. However, while the census brought together the multiple categories of "Latino," these subgroups continue to maintain their distinct identities and nationalities. Bringing diverse communities together and building a shared identity has been the ongoing work of Latino leaders. In today's multicultural and global community, this indispensable ability is a special contribution of Latino leadership.

Inclusiveness is also evident in the intergenerational spirit. Latinos venerate age and experience. At the same time, young people are the promise of tomorrow. This intergenerational model is even more imperative today: the 2010 US census indicated that 23 percent of children under eighteen are Hispanic.[10]

# Part IV: Putting Leadership into Action

L ATINOS ARE A *WE*, collective culture, where the familia and *comunidad* (community) take precedence over the individual. Leadership, therefore, is not driven by individual success or credit but by contributing to the group welfare. Chapter 8, "*Juntos*: Collective Community Stewardship," discusses four action-oriented principles that support this process.

*Juntos* (we are together) signifies the collective and collaborative nature of leadership. Latino leadership is the power of many. Leaders are community stewards who promote *dispersed, shared, and reciprocal* power. The leader as equal—where the leader works side by side with others—facilitates people's belief that they too can contribute. Traditionally, people power (not money, influence, or extensive resources) was the fuel for advancement.

Four practices foster community stewardship: (1) the power of a shared vision, (2) the power of history and cultural traditions, (3) *compartir*—the power of participation and shared responsibility, and (4) *paso a paso*—the power of a step-by-step approach where each success reinforces abilities and self-confidence. By linking the past, present, and future, leaders leverage the power of history and culture so that a sense of continuity and wholeness emerges.

In chapter 9, "*¡Adelante!* Global Vision and Immigrant Spirit," we see how Latinos are connected through español to twenty-two countries and through a special kinship with Brazil, Portugal, Italy, and the Philippines.[11] Latinos are also an integrating force of the Western Hemisphere—bridging North, South, and Central America. Moreover, in the United States there are three dominant subgroups: Mexican, Puerto Rican, and Cuban, but in the last twenty years Latino diversity has expanded. Today there are substantial populations of Dominicans, Guatemalans, Nicaraguans, and Colombians.[12]

*Juntos (we are together) signifies the collective and collaborative nature of leadership. Latino leadership is the power of many.*

These international connections make Latinos a prototype for global leadership. In 2010 over 50 percent of all US immigrants were from México and South or Central America.[13] Immigration has contributed 40 percent of Latino demographic growth in the past decade.[14] Immigrants seek opportunity, work hard, and bring an entrepreneurial spirit evident in the Latino workforce participation and small-business sector growth— both of which are the highest in the nation.[15]

Immigration presents a conundrum for Latino leaders—any organization or business experiencing a 40 percent growth must scramble to find the resources to integrate this expansion. Furthermore, leaders must constantly help the newly arrived with education, English classes, and basic services. The fair and humane treatment of immigrants remains fundamental to the Latino agenda and was evident in the Latino vote in 2012 presidential election.

Chapter 10, "*Sí Se Puede:* Social Activism and Coalition Leadership," frames leadership as social activism, a natural evolution for Latinos whose concern for the community good necessitated challenging social inequities. *Sí se puede!* (Yes, we can!) was a rallying cry for the farm workers who marched with César Chávez in the 1960s advocating fair pay, decent working conditions, and adequate housing. Chávez was following the Latino tradition of advocacy and social action that was reignited during the civil rights movement. Dealing with immediate issues while providing the skills and knowledge to address the institutional barriers that perpetuate injustice is core to Latino leadership.

The struggle for social and economic equality has endured because of *consistencia*—fierce determination, commitment, and reliability. While these are widespread leadership traits, for Latinos consistencia is a lifelong commitment—an understanding that social change takes generations. Consistencia is the reason leaders put in the long hours and hard work needed for community progress. Consistencia has been the nucleus of the growing Latino power today.

Social change requires a critical mass of organized people with a unified agenda. The most powerful Latino organizations are coalitions that bring the diverse Latino groups together around a whole array of issues.

Coalition leadership is sorely needed today in a divided America. Latinos offer viable models of reaching across differences, promoting partnerships, and working for the common welfare.

*"Sí Se Puede: Social Activism and Coalition Leadership,"* frames leadership as social activism, a natural evolution for Latinos whose concern for the community good necessitated challenging social inequities.

So how do leaders motivate people to do the hard work of community building *and* commit to the long-term struggle of creating a more equitable society? In chapter 11, *"Gozar la Vida:* Leadership That Celebrates Life," we discover that leadership has to reflect a *social, family-oriented, and celebratory nature.* Check out most Latino events, and you will see music, dancing, good food, and socializing.

*Gozar la vida* means "to enjoy life." For the 70 percent of Latinos who are working class, or who have dealt with discrimination, enjoying life replenishes their spirit and resolve. Since the culture prescribes that *people come first,* celebration strengthens relationships. What better way to enjoy people than to have a fiesta where the music is blaring and everyone contributes something?

And what do people do when they get together? Well, Latinos love animated conversation, storytelling, and expressing *cariño* (affection). When Latinos greet each other they give each other *abrazos* (embraces). They hug their leaders, too, because they have personal attachments to them.

Chapter 12, *"Fe y Esperanza:* Sustained by Faith and Hope," explores the abiding faith that grounds the power of Latino leadership. How could Latinos have otherwise survived the five hundred years since the conquest of this hemisphere and kept advancing with their values and communities intact? The revered dicho *Está en las manos de Dios* (It's in the hands of God) acknowledges protection and guidance on a daily basis. It anchors Latino optimism.

Faith, or *fe*, is a living current prescribing that people take care of one another. Leaders can tap into this sense of social responsibility and inspire the hope that by working together people can change their lives. César Chávez recognized that spirituality upheld the activist nature of leadership. "I don't think I could base my will to struggle on cold economics or on some political doctrine," he said. "I don't think there would be enough to sustain me. For the basis must be faith."[16]

## Part V: Latino *Destino*

IN 2030 LATINOS WILL be one-third of our nation's people—certainly a critical mass that can influence the twenty-first century. What are the lasting contributions Latinos will make to our country? How will they achieve this? What actions are needed to coalesce the growing numbers, for them to work with other groups, and to actualize Latino power?

Chapter 13, "Building a Diverse and Humanistic Society," discusses how the humanistic values of the Latino culture can help create a compassionate society—one that values people and community before material wealth or individual achievement. Second, we see how, as a fusion people from many races and nations, Latinos are cultural adaptives who have the ability to connect across differences. Due to their inclusive nature, Latino leaders can help fashion a society that embraces our great diversity.

I propose that Latinos put forth an expanded definition of inclusiveness—one that leaves an open door. This final chapter invites non-Latinos to become part of the familia (with the responsibilities this entails). Non-Latinos can experience and incorporate valued aspects and *become Latinos by affinity, or corazón.*

And there is more good news: becoming a Latino by corazón is a springboard to experiencing other cultures, to becoming a *cultural adaptive*—a person who adopts beneficial behaviors, values, and reference points from a variety of cultures.

There is a hurdle to overcome, however. Historically, when White immigrants came to the United States, they were urged to assimilate.

Due to racism, segregation, and exclusion, Latinos and other people of color kept their cultures and communities intact and *acculturated* to the mainstream. We will look at acculturation as key to becoming cultural adaptive. When mainstream leaders learn to acculturate, they can foster diversity in their organizations and in our society as well.

The final section in chapter 13 summarizes ten steps to actualize Latino power, foster a higher level of collaboration among Latino organizations, and build bridges with mainstream groups.

 *Non-Latinos can experience and incorporate valued aspects and become Latinos by affinity, or corazón.*

## *La Bendición*

Our venture into Latino history, culture, and leadership ends with an ancient spiritual tradition. When people embarked on a journey or a new stage of life, during times of change or challenge, they would ask for a *bendición*, or blessing, from their *abuela* or another respected person. This protected them and prepared them for a good outcome. The ending of this book actually heralds a new beginning: Latinos are ready to integrate their assets and unique leadership forms into the US mainstream and to create a diverse and humanistic society. As we embark on the good work of creating this noble future, a special bendición protects and guides us. We will contemplate a vision about today's increasing multicultural people and the contribution Latinos will make to this evolution.

Latinos are becoming an influential cultural group in the United States and are already the predominant population in the Western Hemisphere. *The Power of Latino Leadership* will clarify and claim Latino advancement as the next positive wave of American evolution. It will propose a leadership model uniquely suited to the multicultural Latino-flavored century that is rising.

The management guru Tom Peters, addressing the National Association of American Architects, was *right on* when he said, "Hispanics are just wonderful. They are the next wave of people who will revitalize America . . . if you took away Texas, Florida, Arizona, and California, we'd lose 85 percent of our national vitality."[17] You heard it from the man! Latino destino is to revitalize and reinvigorate the American spirit. We are living proof of how embracing culture, relishing in diversity, and making a contribution to others enlivens the human spirit and enriches life. This is the essence of the growing Latino power today!

> *Welcome to the Latinization of the Americas.*
> *We are all going to have a very good time!*

## 10 Latino Leadership Principles

| Principle | Overview | Leadership Application |
|---|---|---|
| **1. Personalismo** <br> *The Character of the Leader* <br> *(pages 57–66)* | • *Every person has inherent worth and essential value.* <br> • *The leader's character earns trust and respect.* <br> • *Personalismo secures the relational aspects of leadership* <br> • *Leaders nurture other leaders and build community capacity.* | • *Treat each person with respect regardless of status or position.* <br> • *Never forget where you come from.* <br> • *Connect to people on a personal level first.* <br> • *Always keep your word.* |
| **2. Conciencia** <br> *Knowing Oneself and Personal Awareness* <br> *(pages 67–77)* | • *A leader must engage in in-depth reflection and self-examination.* <br> • *Integrity requires paying close attention to one's intuition, impulses, and motives.* <br> • *The psychology of oppression and "white privilege" are barriers to inclusion.* | • *Examine your personal intention: Why do you do what you do?* <br> • *Listen to your intuition and "inner voice."* <br> • *Resolve discrimination or exclusion issues.* <br> • *Develop a secure cultural identity and know your cultural assets.* |
| **3. Destino** <br> *Personal and Collective* <br> *(pages 79–95)* | • *Every person has a distinct life path, purpose, and life pattern.* <br> • *Destino is not fatalism.* <br> • *Tapping into one's destino brings clarity, alignment, and sense of direction.* <br> • *Powerful leaders are in sync with their destino.* | • *Know your family history and traditions.* <br> • *Explore your heart's desire.* <br> • *Identify special skills and talents.* <br> • *Reflect on your legacy and personal vision.* <br> • *Open the door when opportunity knocks.* |
| **4. La Cultura** <br> *Culturally Based Leadership* <br> *(pages 99–111)* | • *Latinos are a culture and an ethnic group, not a race.* <br> • *Seven key values are fastening points for the culture.* <br> • *A humanistic orientation (people come first) and diversity/inclusion are cultural mainstays.* | • *Have a "We" orientation.* <br> • *Be simpatico—congenial, likable.* <br> • *Exercise respect, honesty, and generosity.* <br> • *Establish personal ties and be part of the familia.* |

| Principle | Overview | Leadership Application |
|-----------|----------|------------------------|
| **5. De Colores**<br>*Inclusiveness and Diversity*<br>*(pages 113–128)* | • Latinos are connected to 26 countries.<br>• Hispanics were added to the US census in 1980.<br>• Hispanics are the only group that "self-identifies" on the census.<br>• Latinos embrace all ages with an intergenerational spirit. | • Practice bienvenido (welcome).<br>• Realize that because culture is learned, people can become Latino by corazón, or affinity.<br>• Help forge a collective identity from diversity.<br>• Create allies, circular relationships and participation through intergenerational leadership. |
| **6. Juntos**<br>*Collective Community Stewardship*<br>*(pages 135–149)* | • Juntos means "union, being close, joining, being together."<br>• Latinos are servant leaders and community stewards.<br>• Leadership is conferred by the community.<br>• Leaders build a community of leaders and community capacity. | • Work as part of the group and side by side with people.<br>• Follow the rules.<br>• Anchor collaboration with four practices: sharing a vision; integrating history and cultural traditions; sharing responsibility; and working paso a paso. |
| **7. ¡Adelante!**<br>*Global Vision and Immigrant Spirit*<br>*(pages 151–166)* | • The US is a nation of immigrants who bring initiative, hard work, optimism, and faith.<br>• Latino growth has been fueled by immigration.<br>• Latinos are acculturating, not assimilating. A cultural revitalization is occurring.<br>• Latinos are a prototype for global leadership. | • Integrate the newly arrived and provide multiple services.<br>• Be aware that 51% of Latinos identify with their nations of origin and that this diversity must be brought together.<br>• Address immigration as a civil rights and advocacy issue.<br>• Strengthen cultural self-awareness. |
| **8. Sí Se Puede**<br>*Social Activism and Coalition Leadership*<br>*(pages 167–181)* | • Economic discrepancies and social inequalities drive a social activist agenda.<br>• Sí se puede is community organizing, coalition building, and advocacy leadership.<br>• The Latino model is leadership by the many.<br>• The inclusive Latino agenda speaks to the welfare of all Americans. | • Build people's faith that they can take action.<br>• Practice consistencia—perseverance and commitment<br>• Build networks, be inclusive, and forge coalitions.<br>• Be a cultural broker and build partnerships with other groups. |

| Principle | Overview | Leadership Application |
|---|---|---|
| **9. Gozar la Vida**<br>*Leadership That Celebrates Life!*<br>*(pages 183–195)* | • *Latinos have a celebratory, expressive, optimistic, and festive culture.*<br>• *Celebration strengthens bonds, a collective identity, and people's resolve.*<br>• *Latinos are stirring the salsa and gusto into leadership.*<br>• *Communication is key for getting things done through people.* | • *Allow time to socialize.*<br>• *Communicate with carisma (charisma), cariño, (affection), and corazón (heart).*<br>• *Speak the "people's language" and be a translator for the mainstream culture.*<br>• *Always serve food.*<br>• *Keep a "cultural balance" and exercise strategic thinking and problem solving.* |
| **10. Fe y Esperanza**<br>*Sustained by Faith and Hope*<br>*(pages 197–208)* | • *Optimism is esperanza, or hope—an essential Latino quality.*<br>• *Gracias (being grateful) allows people to be generous and give back.*<br>• *Latino spirituality centers on relationships and responsibility.*<br>• *Spirituality is a moral obligation to ensure others' well-being and the collective good.* | • *Be bold—have the faith and courage to make unpopular decisions.*<br>• *Practice humility, modesty, and courtesy, the foundation for the leader as equal.*<br>• *Be clear on your purpose and serve something greater. This lessens self-importance.*<br>• *Tap into optimism, gratitude, and faith to inspire and motivate people.* |

# PART I

# *La Historia:* Latino Fusion and Hybrid Vigor

L ATINOS WHO LIVE IN THE Southwest are keenly aware that less than 170 years ago—a historical hiccup—one-third of the continental United States was México. Other people sense this when they traverse states like New Mexico, or states with Spanish names like Arizona (arid zone), Montana (the land of mountains), or Nevada (the place where it snows). Cruising the California freeways, passing city after city named in the Spanish tradition for patron saints (San Diego, Santa Ana, Santa Monica, Santa Barbara, San Jose, San Ramon, San Francisco, and San Rafael), any driver might find it almost impossible to ignore their Hispanic roots—not to mention the *bendición* that comes from having so many *santos* presiding over cities or watching over us as we drive.

It is perhaps in El Pueblo de Nuestra Señora la Reina de Los Angeles del Río de Porciúncula (the Village of Our Lady, the Queen of the Angels of the River Porziuncola), now known as Los Angeles, that the United States' Spanish-Mexican heritage is most apparent. Surfacing like fog lifting off the California coast, the past is etched into street names, historical monuments, the profuse mission architecture, the faces of the brown-skinned children, the Spanish exchanged on street corners, and the whiff of warm tortillas. The only city with more residents of Mexican descent is Mexico City.[1]

The truth of the matter, however, is that most Americans don't acknowledge these historical roots. Even with these antecedents splattered like graffiti on freeway bridges, city walls, and street corners, the past is tucked away, forgotten.

In the spring of 2005, PBS made a documentary about the Hispanic settling of Colorado (the land of red earth), where I live. The Spanish-Mexican-Indian people, whose progeny are the modern-day Hispanics, herded the cattle and ran the ranchos, planted the *maíz, frijoles,* and squash, carved out the mines, laid the railroad tracks, and constituted the economic muscle of the state. The usual whitewashed history of Colorado makes scant reference to these contributions. When the PBS special aired, therefore, there was much celebration among Hispanics.[2] Finally our story was being told. Yet a good friend who is Latino told me that his Anglo wife truthfully said, "I don't know anyone besides you who would be interested in this."

Contemporary America is speeding into the future and not looking in the rearview mirror. Like the great cottonwood trees that grow in the arid Southwest, however, people and societies have roots that anchor them. Roots ground us, holding us firm when the winds of change howl, offer perspective about what is lasting and significant, and nourish growth and future discovery. The past safeguards the values, traditions, and wisdom of previous generations. History gives birth to the present and is the foundation for the future. If Latinos are integral to America's past, then surely they will be a powerful force influencing our future.

## *Mucho Gusto*—An Introduction to Latino Origins

T HE STORY OF HISPANIC origins begins centuries before the founding of the United States and even before the conquistadores made their tumultuous journey across the vast Atlantic. Spain, considered the mother country of Hispanics, etched a unique landscape that blended many races, cultures, and nations. This *cultural permeability* is a distinctly Spanish characteristic and is still evident today in the expansive diversity of the Hispanic people.

Chapter 1 begins with Columbus landing in Hispaniola[3] and the conquistadores penetrating the Americas. The Spanish conquest could have washed away the footprints of the indigenous people. Instead, racial blending produced a resilient progeny—the genetic origins of today's Latinos. The first chapter reveals a beautiful creation story and myth that prophesied the birth of the Latino people and the advent of the Mestizo, or multicultural race.

It is important to note that Latinos are not just a US phenomenon; like the resilient sparrow that flies across many lands to find a home, Latinos are scattered across this hemisphere and many other parts of the world. *The evolution of US Latinos is intertwined with the history of their indigenous and Spanish ancestors.*

In chapter 2, we first look at how Spanish influence profoundly affected our nation's development. This is followed by a slice of US history, including Manifest Destiny, which proposed that Latinos and other people of color had to learn the superior ways of White civilization. While today this may seem like a historical anomaly, it raises the concept of *destino*—the belief that a country or a people may have a distinct contribution to make. The current state of US Latinos and the cultural explosion that heralds the *Latinization of America* is certainly predicting a new landscape for our country. Latino destino, explored in the final section, presents an intriguing concept about the distinctive contribution this dynamic and diverse people will make. Chapter 2 ends with an overview of the tremendous influence US Latinos have today and their potential for shaping a new American future.

## CHAPTER 1

# Ancient Roots and Mestizo Ancestry

OST PEOPLE TODAY ARE genetically mixed. Our blood has intertwined through ongoing migrations—our genetic streams run together from unknown sources. The difference for Latinos is that the fusion of races, nationalities, and cultures was so pervasive that it spread across our entire hemisphere, producing a people traditionally known in Central and South America as Mestizos, the offspring of the indigenous people and Europeans, primarily the Spanish.

The *mestizaje,* as the process was termed, is not a commonly embraced concept by Latinos in the United States. There are advantages, however, to including it as part of the complex Latino identity. What is important to note is that the Mestizo experience is a precursor to the Latino culture and the bedrock of its inherent diversity.[1] (Although México is technically part of North America, in this book it is considered part of Central America due to cultural and historical antecedents.)

The lineage of many Hispanics comes from Indian mothers and Spanish fathers. Mothers traditionally preserve—and transmit—tradition, values, spiritual practices, and customs. Much of the culture, consequently, reflects this indigenous background. The integration of the Spanish and native cultures can be seen at the family dinner table. Rice and beans is a primary dish for all Latino subgroups. The Spanish introduced rice, while beans are indigenous, or American Indian. Corn tortillas come from native cultures, and flour for white tortillas comes from Europe. The many varieties of chilies and salsas are from the Americas. Ham, or *jamón*, and chorizo, now Latino favorites, were brought by the Spanish.

Whether the term *Mestizo* is used or not, much of the Latino culture reflects this blended ancestry. Since US Latinos were identified as a group only from the 1980 US census on, and their roots go back more than five hundred years, *Mestizo* is a more accurate historical reference. Taking a look at the mixing of culture and races in Spanish history will shed light as to why the mestizaje occurred in this hemisphere.

## The Spanish Are the Mestizos of Europe

L ET'S BEGIN IN 200 BC, when the Romans commenced their seven-hundred-year occupation of Spain. Roman influence is visible today in the aqueducts that stand like centurions across the Spanish plains. The term *Latino* comes from *Latin*, the language spoken in the Roman Empire (and painfully studied in the Catholic high school I attended). The major Latin-based languages are Spanish, French, Portuguese, Romanian, and Italian.[2] *Latin* also refers to Latin America, which includes México, Central and South America, and the Caribbean islands.[3] Because of these global, historical, and cultural connections, *Latino* is becoming a preferred designation for many people.

After the decline of the Roman Empire, the Visigoths, or modern-day Germans, began invading Spain in the fifth century. German rulers converted to Christianity and maintained much of the legal system and institutions developed by the Romans.[4] The *melding of cultures* rather than the imposition of one over the other was a trademark of Roman occupation and would carry over when the Spanish came to the Western Hemisphere in 1492. (This was very distinct from what happened in North America, as the Anglo-Saxons did not integrate their culture with that of the native people.) This tendency to meld cultures is still integral to Latinos today.

Geographically, Spain is the southernmost part of the European continent and the crossroads between Europe, Africa, and the Middle East. In the eighth century, the Moors invaded Spain and remained for eight hundred years. During this period the Spanish became the most culturally blended people in Europe. The Jews, Christians, and Moors ushered in a golden age of learning while the rest of Europe grappled with the Dark Ages. More than eight thousand Spanish words are derived from Arabic; and over a thousand villages with Moorish names dot the Spanish countryside.[5]

In 1469, when Isabella of Castile and Ferdinand of Aragon married, they set out to unify Spain and spread Catholicism as the official religion. Thus began a period in history where Jews and Muslims were forced to convert or leave the country. Many Jews were subjected to the Inquisition, which purged Spain of so-called infidels. It is estimated that at this time one-third of Spain was Jewish. Thus, the Jewish exodus to the "new world" began, and therefore, many Latinos have Jewish ancestry. The similarities of Latinos as an ethnic group to the Jewish community have cultural, historical, and genetic antecedents.[6]

When delving into Latino diversity, it is useful to consider that the Spanish heritage comprises Moorish, Arab, and Jewish lineages. The blood of Romans, Germans, and Celts had already mingled in Spanish veins. Thus, the Spanish were the Mestizos of Europe when Queen Isabella authorized the expedition of Christopher Columbus. Paradoxically, as Spain was becoming a more homogeneous and united Catholic country, the fusion of cultures was being transported to the new world. Diversity was already integral to the budding Latino soul.

 *The melding of cultures was a trademark of Roman occupation and would carry over when the Spanish came to the Western Hemisphere in 1492.... This tendency to meld cultures is still integral to Latinos today.*

# The Prophesy and the Promise

A S IN MANY CULTURES still connected to their ancestry, there is a Mestizo creation story. Creation myths speak to a group's essence and foreshadow the special contribution they will make to humanity. The US story, for instance, includes the resiliency of the immigrant spirit, the settling of the West, and the emergence of a new nation. The fight for independence and journey to freedom frame our national identity.

The Mestizo creation story begins with a painful birth almost one hundred years before the founding of Jamestown, the first colony in North America. When Hernán Cortés set foot on the expansive land that is now México, Tenochtitlan, which today is Mexico City, was larger than any city in Europe, with more inhabitants than London or Seville. The conquistadores found a radiant island metropolis laced with canals, opulent marketplaces, beautiful palaces, and mountains of gold and silver.[7] Starting in northern México, maneuvering across the tiny isthmus to South America, over the high Andes, and into Peru, magnificent cities were built by indigenous people, and spectacular temples rose to the sky like the great condor. The conquistadores traversed these lands and made them their own.

It took only twenty-two years for the armies of the Spanish conquerors—mounted on horses, protected with steel breast plates and armor, and using firearms as formidable weapons—to reach across Central and South America. Francisco Pizarro marched into Peru, and the great Inca Empire fell in 1522. The extent, speed, and permanency of this military adventure were as devastating as the great plagues and diseases the foreigners brought.[8]

Unlike the Anglo-Saxons to the north, who were fleeing religious persecution, the Spaniards were overwhelmingly Catholic and united in the belief of the "one true faith." The church issued an edict declaring that Indians and Black slaves had souls and should not be enslaved. To be sure, the Spanish oppressed the indigenous people, but they wrapped their mission around a holy grain. The Spanish would baptize the Indians and bring them into "the everlasting faith."

Life for the Indians conquered by the Spanish, however, was not guided by a Christian conversion experience. An oppressive cloak was thrown over the Indians, who lost their land, wealth, and gold. Dominance and colonization resulted in desecration. Their gods were stripped from them, and their temples were in ruins. The Indian immune systems could not repel the invaders—85 percent died from diseases.[9] The rest were shackled in mines, sweating in *fincas* (farms) and haciendas, or building the missions where the Spanish lived.

The Indians were losing their will to live and contemplated racial suicide. "If it is true that our gods don't exist and have abandoned us, then let us die."[10] Even though this desolation began in México, this is not a story about the Spanish conquest of México but of the plight of the indigenous people across the Americas. During this time, the Indians needed a spiritual infusion, a reason to live and to hope for the future. They needed *un milagro*—a miracle.

 *When Hernán Cortés set foot on the expansive land that is now México, Tenochtitlan, which today is Mexico City, was larger than any city in Europe, with more inhabitants than London or Seville.*

## *El Milagro at* Tepeyac

ON A COOL DECEMBER sunrise in 1531, an indigenous elder wrapped in a traditional *tilma* (poncho) and wearing a straw hat was walking in the foothills of what is now Mexico City. Juan Diego, on his way to church, suddenly hears celestial music and wonders, *Am I dreaming? Am I already in heaven?* Looking up, he sees a radiant brown woman with distinct Indian features arrayed as the Madonna, with stars in her mantle and a crescent moon at her feet. An angel lifts the folds of her azure dress. The mesquite bushes, thistles, and nopal cactus sparkle like fine turquoise. The earth glistens like the mist of a rainbow.

"Where are you going, the smallest of my children?" she sings in the Nahuatl Indian language. "I am the perfect and perpetual Virgin Mary, Mother of the True God through whom everything lives. I am your merciful mother, yours and all the people who live united in this land and all the other people of different ancestries. I want very much to have a church built for me. Here I will hear their weeping and heal all their sorrows and hardships and suffering."[11] Like a mother, she is offering solace. She acknowledges that the different races have clashed, but in spite of the horrendous upheaval this has cost, they are now inhabiting this land together.

The radiant lady asks Juan Diego to take a message about building the church to Bishop Juan de Zumárraga, who to the Spanish is the most important man in México. Well, that is like asking a peasant to speak to a king. Juan Diego goes and waits patiently for many hours. The bishop finally listens but does not believe him.

Juan Diego returns to the hill at Tepeyac to find the Madonna waiting. He laments, "Forgive me, but send a nobleman who would be held in high esteem. I am not important, and you are sending me to a place I do not belong." Insisting that he is the one she has chosen, she asks him to return. Dutifully, after many difficulties, Juan Diego kneels down before the bishop, who has many questions and then asks for a sign to prove the story is true. Juan Diego returns and recounts this to the Madonna, who says she will give him a sign in the morning.

The miracle, some would say myth, at Tepeyac, has many hurdles. As in any great quest, obstacles are put in the way of this humble servant. The bishop is suspicious and has him followed, only to have Juan disappear into the hills.

When Juan Diego arrives home, his dear uncle is dying. Juan Diego leaves before dawn to fetch a priest to give the last rites. Ashamed and fearful because he has failed the beautiful Lady, he takes a different route, hoping to avoid her. But of course that it impossible! Here she comes as if floating on a cloud. "My dearest and youngest of my sons," she says, "where are you going?"

He explains he is going to fetch a priest because his uncle is dying, but he promises to return. The Lady responds with compassion: "Let nothing trouble you, or in any way disturb your countenance, your heart. For I am here—your Mother—your foundation of life. You are in the cool of my shadow. I am your source of contentment. You are cradled in my arms. Is there anything else for you to need?"[12] She then says his uncle has been healed.

"Now go to the top of the hill, cut the flowers that are growing there, and bring them to me." The hill is stony, full of thistles, thorns, and mesquite. It is December, the time of frost and brown grasses. Yet it looks like paradise! Exquisite flowers are blooming, sparkling with morning dew. Gathering them in his tilma, he goes to the heavenly Mother, who arranges the flowers and sends him to the bishop, saying, "Trust in me. Am I not your merciful mother?"

It is still twilight at the bishop's house. The servants ignore him. And so he waits for a long, long time, patient and steadfast, his head lowered, as silent as stone. The sweet fragrance inspires their curiosity. Looking inside his tilma, they see exotic flowers that do not grow on the cactus hillside. Amazed, they hurry to find the bishop.

Prostrating before the bishop, he opens his tilma. Beautiful crimson Castilian roses that grow only in Spain tumble to the floor. The bishop falls to his knees, making the sign of the cross and praising heaven. For there, embedded in the simple tilma worn by all the Indians across the southern continent, is the brown-faced image of the Holy Mother of Creation known today as Our Lady of Guadalupe. She is not a Spaniard; she is a Mestiza. Her image is still preserved five hundred years later in the church that was built at Tepeyac—one of the most venerated and visited religious shrines in the entire world.

 *"I am your merciful mother, yours and all the people who live united in this land and all the other people of different ancestries."*

—Our Lady of Guadalupe

## Our Lady of Guadalupe

UR LADY OF GUADALUPE is perhaps the most influential and prophetic spiritual voice of the Americas and a revered religious symbol of indigenous people. She has been an icon since the conquest of our hemisphere. Her familiar image can be found on wall hangings, paintings, key chains, jackets, baseball caps, and T-shirts. She was named empress of the Americas and patroness of the Western Hemisphere by a papal proclamation in 1998.[13]

The significance of her apparition in December 1531, even if understood as a myth, must be seen in the context of the time she appeared and in the message she brought to the Indian people. At this time, México was a huge land mass that extended north to the Colorado Rockies and across to the Pacific Northwest. Furthermore, the Spanish conquest commenced in México but quickly engulfed the entire Southern Hemisphere. The legend of Guadalupe, therefore, is pertinent to the Indian holocaust that was occurring across these lands. She appears just twelve short years after the conquest. She hears weeping and sorrows and wants to alleviate suffering.

For the Indians who worshiped the sun there was great symbolism in her image. The rays of sun circling her meant she came from their god. Her Nahuatl name, Tlecuautlapcupeuth, means "the one who comes from the region of light on the wings of an eagle."[14] The eagle represents vision and the future. Her hands are in the Indian style of offering—she was bringing them hope, protection, and acceptance at a time of desolation. The eyes are cast down in quiet composure, a stance many Indians would take to survive.

Her exquisite mantle was turquoise, a color sacred to the Indians. On her dress were gold flowers in the cross shape of Nahuatl glyphs symbolizing the four sacred directions and indicating that new life was coming.[15] The Maya, Aztec, and Inca were great astronomers who looked to the sky for guidance and divination of the future. Her mantle was covered with exquisite silver stars.

Juan Diego was not a lofty Spanish official but a humble Indian. As the story is told over and over, the Indians recognize that by choosing one of their own and by speaking in their language, the Madonna affirms their worth and goodness. She looks like a Mestiza, like many children after the conquest. The Indians embrace her: "She is one of us." As a conquered people, they were losing pride in their great civilizations and becoming ashamed of their ancestry. She was restoring their dignity and belief in themselves.

Our Lady of Guadalupe symbolizes the integration of the indigenous faith with the Catholic Church; this would be the spiritual fount from which the cultural mixing would flow. The place where she wanted her church was a sacred site to the Indian people. Unlike Protestant religions, which do not have a litany of saints or a strong devotion to the mother of Jesus, the Catholic Church had a strong dedication to Mary. This followed the traditions of the Nahuatl, Mayan, Inca, and Aztec religions, which honored the female aspects of God. As a result of Guadalupe's apparition, the Church began incorporating native symbolism and rituals. The power of this integration is evident—eight million Indians were baptized into the Catholic faith in the next seven years.[16]

On December 12, the feast day of Guadalupe, Catholic churches across the hemisphere are littered with red roses. For the Aztec, flowers symbolize truth, beauty, authenticity, and divinity. Our Lady of Guadalupe's message told the Indians that as perennial as the flowers, they would survive. Why? Because the black sash she wore was the Aztec symbol of a pregnant woman.[17] The Catholic Church always referred to Mary, the mother of Jesus, as a virgin. To the Indians, on the other hand, their spiritual mother was of the earth and had children. This was a message tailor-made for them.

*Our Lady of Guadalupe symbolizes the integration of the indigenous faith with the Catholic Church; this would be the spiritual fount from which the cultural mixing would flow.*

But who was the child she was carrying? To understand this we must take a short detour. Rest assured that the inception of the Mestizo people began on that small rocky hill at Tepeyac. Everything that has emerged since the apparition—the culture, the leadership traditions, the prominence of today's dynamic Mestizo and Latino people—rests on the black sash of the Our Lady of Guadalupe, who was first known almost five hundred years.

## La Madonna in Las Americas

Almost every Central and Latin American country has a special Madonna who is revered as protector and patron saint and who forms part of the national identity. Because the Spanish conquest began in México, Our Lady of Guadalupe was the first of these. The Madonna stories reflect people's hopes, sorrows, and historical journeys. They connect the Catholic faith with indigenous people who had female deities. The Spanish had a great devotion to the mother of Jesus. In fact, Columbus's largest ship was named the *Santa María* (Holy Mary). Let's briefly look at two of the Madonnas of the Americas.

### Cuba—The Black Madonna

In 1608 two Indians and a Black slave are sent out to sea to fetch salt for the slaughter houses in the mine of El Cobre, Cuba. A fierce storm arises, violently rocking their little boat. The slave wears a medal with the Virgin Mary. So they beseech her to save their lives. Miraculously, the storm subsides. Then a statue of the Virgin Mary fastened to a board suddenly appears, floating on the waves. Surprisingly, she is completely dry and has an inscription: "I am the Virgin of Charity."

The Madonna is dressed in a cloth garment, has real hair, and seems to have Black ancestry. African slaves, who were brought to Cuba as early as 1531, beseeched the Virgin of Charity for their emancipation.[18] In 1630, when the mines were closed and the slaves freed, the statue from the storm was placed on the high altar of the El Cobre Church, replacing Saint James, the powerful patron saint of the Spanish conquest. She therefore symbolizes the triumph of the people over oppression. Many miracles have been attributed to her intervention.[19] On her feast day, September 10, Cubans from Miami to Havana march in procession with their beloved patroness.

## Brazil—The Patroness and Protector

A similar story is told in Brazil: In 1717 the governor of the providence of São Paulo is visiting Guaralinguetá. The people want to throw a feast in his honor. Three fishermen are sent out to sea but aren't able to catch any fish. They begin to pray to Our Lady of the Immaculate Conception—but the hours go by and still no fish! Ready to give up, they cast their nets once more and haul up a heavy statue of a Black Madonna. Now the fish are so plentiful they have to return to shore as the boat is almost sinking.

The statue is named Our Lady of Aparecida (the lady who appeared) and has been credited with many miracles. It would take more than a hundred years for the people to win independence from Portugal. During that time, Our Lady of Aparecida stood as an icon of the emerging Brazilian identity, giving people hope and solace. She is the patroness and protector of Brazil—the largest Catholic country in the world. Her feast day, October 12, is a national holiday, and her basilica is the largest Marian temple in the world, second only to Saint Peter's in Vatican City.[20]

Just as Guadalupe personified the Indian ancestry of México, so do the Cuban and Brazilian Madonnas reflect the Afro-Cuban and Afro-Iberian heritage of these countries. All three represent the mixed racial heritage that would become a defining characteristic of Central and South America. Likewise, these Madonnas embodied the cultural and religious integration that would occur. They gave hope to colonized people and were adopted as symbols for emancipation and liberation.

The characteristics embodied by these Madonnas are still evident in the expansive diversity, the integration of spirituality and social activism, the inclusivity, and the hopeful spirit of US Hispanics. The marches of César Chávez and the United Farm Workers drew people from many cultures and walks of life and were always led with a tapestry of Our Lady of Guadalupe.

## The Mothers of the Mestizo Race

I NEVER MET MY MATERNAL grandfather. As a child it never occurred to me to ask why my mother's last name was the same as *mi abuela's*— my grandmother's. The first child of a beautiful Mestiza who had eyes like blue water and long raven braids, my grandmother had my mother when she was a young girl. Often they seemed more like *hermanas* (sisters) than mother and daughter. No one ever mentioned my mother's father. These ancestral roots withered away and remain in the family closet, which shut tight when my parents died. Recently I was sharing this story with a Hispanic leader who said, "My wife just figured out the same thing, but it was *never* talked about."

The Spanish commonly used Indian women as concubines or as common-law wives. The Anglo settlers did not procreate on a mass scale with the indigenous people. Western European concepts of racial separation and superiority, as well as religious beliefs, prevented this. But, as noted, the Spanish were already the Mestizos of Europe, with Roman, African, Arab, Anglo, and Celtic blood. (As previously noted, eight hundred years of cultural and racial integration ended in 1478 with the unification of Spain through the marriage of Ferdinand of Aragon and Isabella of Castile.) From the Sierra Nevada to the tip of Tierra del Fuego, the mixing of indigenous people with the Spanish conquistadores was so widespread that today Mestizos, or mixed-race people, are the majority population in Central and South America.

The progeny of this forced union were ashamed of their indigenous selves—for integral to any conquest is the denigration and subjugation of the culture of the conquered. Their Spanish fathers often did not recognize them as legitimate offspring, which denied the very talents and attributes they inherited from their European ancestors. This trauma carved a deep psychological scar. The resolution of the internal battle between their indigenous selves and their Spanish heritage would take generations to mend.[21] (The emergence of the complex Latino identity is discussed in the next chapter.)

Just as roses unfold in their time, so did Indian grandmothers transform the pain of the conquest through loving and nurturing their Mestizo children. The anchor and salvation of the Mestizos were the indigenous culture, values, and hope passed on by their mothers and grandmothers. They could taste it in the tortillas, the black beans, and fried plantains they ate. Day after day they were told to hope for the future. Hard work and faith would bring a better life.

The flourishing of the Mestizo people would be a miracle, one prophesied by Our Lady of Guadalupe. The black belt foretold of a nativity—a new race of mixed-blood people—the proud descendants of many nations. During the conquest thousands of Indian women had been desecrated. Many felt ashamed and in great pain. Yet here was the mother of God, saying, "I am pregnant and I am holy." This was a great benediction to the Indian women who carried the seed of the oppressor. It gave them a sense of destiny, of divine intervention, and most of all *esperanza*, or hope, for their children.

 *The mixing of indigenous people with the Spanish conquistadores was so widespread that today Mestizos, or mixed-race people, are the majority population in Central and South America and the antecedents of many of today's Hispanics.*

And yet, Our Lady of Guadalupe had a message for all of us who live in these times, because she said, "I am truly your merciful mother, yours and all the inhabitants of this land."[22] She appears as woman of mixed race, the face of the future who speaks of universal acceptance and portrays humanity as brothers and sisters. Guadalupe is not just the mother of the Indian Mestizos but also the mother of diversity—of the European and other immigrants who are part of this land. Perhaps because of this, people of all ages, races, and nationalities have embraced her message and honor her today.

## The Birth of *la Raza*

I
T WOULD TAKE GENERATIONS, but the Mestizos from South and Central America and continental United States would evolve into today's Hispanics and Latinos. They are connected by their heritage, their history as a mixed-race people, the Spanish language and influence, a common spiritual tradition, and the struggle to free themselves from discrimination. Latino hybrids are the survivors of the conquest and racial conflict, but also represent *resolution and cultural reconciliation*. These traits are evident in Latino leadership today.

Latin Americans and Hispanic Americans today do not celebrate Columbus Day as the date of the "discovery" of America. After all, our indigenous ancestors were already here. Latinos across the hemisphere celebrate the encounter of cultures and the birth of a new race on October 12—*El Día de la Raza*. The term *la Raza* can be best translated as "the new Latino people of the new world." A more inclusive definition of *la Raza* is a new family composed of the original inhabitants of the Americas and all the immigrants from throughout the world who since the time of Columbus have come to the new world in search of a new creation.[23]

But let's not get ahead of ourselves. To move toward this multicultural vision we must first understand and resolve a number of additional historical dynamics. We will circle back to the concept of la Raza in our final section.

*Latinos across the hemisphere celebrate the encounter of cultures and the birth of a new race on October 12.*

—El Día de la Raza.

## *¡Ándale!*—Moving Forward

THIS CHAPTER UNDERSCORED THE cultural fusion that began in Spain and crossed the Atlantic with the conquistadores. These were the precursors of racial integration, the birth of the Mestizos, and the foretelling of la Raza. Now we will take a historical leapfrog to the continental United States, where a different experience was brewing, one that would mold the modern-day US Latino experience. The Spanish penetration into what is now the continental United States encompassed an area that was once half of territorial México. The United States forcibly acquired these lands from México and also began invading Central and South America. These acquisitions were sanctioned by a belief in Manifest Destiny and would seal the fate of US Latinos until the dawn of civil rights in the twentieth century. The next chapter concludes with a discussion of the growing cultural, social, political, and economic influence of Latinos today.

# CHAPTER 2

# The Latino Legacy in the United States

S ITTING IN MY SECOND-GRADE classroom I distinctly remember learning about the "discovery" of America and chorusing with my classmates, "In fourteen hundred and ninety-two Columbus sailed the ocean blue." Next we learned that in 1607 the first British colony was established at Jamestown, Virginia. None of us thought to ask, "What happened in the intervening 115 years? Did the earth stand still?"

In fact, the Spanish conquistadores were trudging the North and South American continents from the tip of Alaska to Argentina and from the Florida Keys to the Hudson River. Saint Augustine, Florida, was founded in 1565, forty-two years before the English colonized Jamestown and fifty-five years before the Pilgrims landed at Plymouth Rock. What an inconvenient truth! Our historical selection process discarded these facts.[1]

European civilization was first introduced to this hemisphere by the Spanish and then advanced by their mixed-race progeny, who are today's Hispanics. They established the bases for agriculture, commerce and trading, mining, and ranching that would eventually drive the engine of the US economy. The Spanish settlers in 1600 introduced the plow and the ox to the native Indians, as well as the first European-bred livestock.

California, Texas, and Florida continue to be among the largest producers of fruit and vegetables in the world today. Hispanics were *los vaqueros*— the original cowboys—and as late as the 1800s were prominent on the open range.

Many institutions that have become identified as "American"—schools, universities, libraries, and state, county, and municipal court systems— were first introduced to North America by the Spanish. The earliest schools in what would become the continental United States were started in 1600 in Florida, Georgia, and New Mexico.[2] The building of the first European-style towns, the first ports for commerce, the initial trade roads, and the original irrigation systems can be traced to the Spanish and their mixed offspring.

Spanish was the first European language spoken in this hemisphere, the primary language in the Hispanic South and Southwest, which is today almost half of the continental United States. The earliest recording of the settlements in Florida was written by Juan Ponce de León in *español*. The written travel diaries of the Spanish expeditions laid the foundation for colonial governance, commercial exploration, and legal precedence and documented the official story of Hispanic life in these lands.

The war with México in 1848 and the annexation of the Southwest territories shaped the second phase of Hispanic history in the United States. Leadership as social activism is grounded in this tale of conquest, land confiscation, and colonization. Many displaced Hispanics became field laborers or immigrated to the cities as factory workers during industrialization. This economic upheaval resulted in Latinos playing a pivotal role in the evolution of the US labor movement.

*Spanish was the first European language spoken in this hemisphere, the primary language in the Hispanic South and Southwest, which is today almost half of the continental United States.*

As early as 1883 Juan Gómez led cowboys in a strike in the Texas Panhandle. Soon to follow were tobacco worker strikes in New York City; Tampa, Florida; and Puerto Rico. In the early twentieth century, Mexican Americans joined with Japanese farm workers to win the first strike against the California agricultural industry.[3] The farm labor movement in the 1960s persisted with the work of César Chávez and Dolores Huerta, who organized the largest union of agricultural workers, creating national boycotts and legislative action in California.

This history paved a tradition of activist-oriented leadership with community organizing at its core. Latino leaders became a voice for people who lived in the margins. This continues today, since 70 percent of Hispanics belong to the working class.[4]

Powerful political and social forces justified the acquisition of the Southwest and set the stage for cultural dominance, exclusion, and a society where racism and discrimination would remain intact for more than four hundred years. Instead of embracing its culturally rich history, territorial United States went from a land that was basically bicultural or multicultural (if we include American Indians, the French territories, and the Louisiana Purchase) to a nation that constructed "American" history to be White, Anglo-Saxon, and Protestant. Accordingly, the first chapter of American history began when the Pilgrims made their long arduous journey to Plymouth Rock. One of the most powerful forces that sanctified this historical whitewashing was the belief in Manifest Destiny.

*This history paved a tradition of activist-oriented leadership with community organizing at its core. Latino leaders became a voice for people who lived in the margins. This continues today, since 70 percent of Hispanics belong to the working class.*

# Manifest Destiny

THE CONCEPT OF MANIFEST DESTINY in the nineteenth century proposed that the United States should extend democracy to coveted parts of the hemisphere. It was based on three rationales: the virtue of the Protestant ethic and the Anglo-Saxon people; the superiority of their institutions; and the God-given mission to redeem the world and remake it in the image of the United States. Manifest Destiny was further supported by the belief that American Indians, Mexicans, and other people of color were incapable of self-rule and would therefore benefit from being under the US mantle.[5] Manifest Destiny rationalized the quest for expansion, land, wealth acquisition, and the domination of other races.

Like a historical rupture Manifest Destiny shaped nineteenth-century history and sanctioned the US acquisition of former Spanish and Mexican lands. The most coveted were the Mexican territories, including Texas, California, Arizona, New Mexico, Wyoming, Nevada, and Utah. In one fell swoop Hispanics became de facto minorities in their own land. Bolstered by this victory, the United States expanded its intervention into Central and South America with the war with Spain in 1898. Cuba, Puerto Rico, Guam, and the Philippines were added to the US cache, consolidating the United States as a world empire and fortifying its belief in Anglo-Saxon cultural superiority.[6]

Manifest Destiny also exported Black slavery into the Southwest. One of the major pushes by the southern states was for the annexation of Texas, then part of México. When settlers from the United States began arriving, they initially accepted Mexican authority. The *problema* was that slavery was illegal in México, and the settlers from the southern states had brought slaves with them. That the goal was to annex Texas to the United States as a slave state was understood from the start. Texas joined the Confederacy at the outbreak of the Civil War. Former Mexican inhabitants would soon join Black slaves in being subjugated by the newly arrived White settlers and ranchers.

The events that led to Texas becoming a state are an interesting machination of Manifest Destiny. Most Americans know the emotional battle cry "Remember the Alamo!" Depending on what side of the Tex-Mex border you were on and your position on the United States' right to occupy foreign land, this was either a Mexican victory or a Texas massacre. In 1893 the Alamo was a mission residing on Mexican land. Several months previously the Americans had driven the Mexican army out of Texas. The battle of the Alamo was the Mexican army returning to defend its land. They reconquered the old Spanish mission in a bloody battle where Davy Crockett and Sam Houston died.[7]

"Remember the Alamo!" became a raison d'être for annexing the Texas territories. Mexican Hispanics became colonized people in their own land, with the Texas Rangers as an arm of domination. Today the Alamo is the most popular tourist site in Texas and was designated an official state shrine by the Texas legislature in the twentieth century.[8] It may be a grievous sin to recognize (or even mention) the irony of this historical Texas two-step, but the fact remains that White colonists invaded Mexican territory and as a result Black slavery was safely secured in Texas.

*Manifest Destiny rationalized the quest for expansion, land, wealth acquisition, and the domination of other races.*

Manifest Destiny had serious consequences for Americans Indians, as well. Continental expansion implicitly meant the occupation and annexation of Indian land. Indians were encouraged to sell their vast tribal lands and become "civilized." This meant abandoning hunting and their nomadic lifestyle, becoming farmers, and reorganizing their society around the family rather than the clan or tribe. Lands were acquired by treaty and sale from Indian nations, usually under questionable circumstances—including a lack of voluntary and knowing consent by the native signers. Advocates of "civilization programs" believed settling native tribes would greatly reduce the amount of land needed by the Indians, making more available for homesteading by White settlers.[9]

One of the most distasteful tenets of Manifest Destiny was the proliferation of the idea of the "white man's burden." Popularized in an 1899 poem by the English poet Rudyard Kipling, colonization or slavery was said to benefit nonwhite ethnic and racial groups. Indeed a noble enterprise! Whites would have to bear the yoke of educating and civilizing these lesser groups until they could evolve enough to adopt Western ways.[10]

Manifest Destiny established the foundation for many of the discriminatory practices that created an unequal society. The history of people of color would be rewritten from a White point of view, and segregation and racism would spread their ugly hand across the United States.

## Latino *Destino*

MANY YOUNG PEOPLE TODAY would be taken aback at a nation touting its superiority and using this as a rationale for expansion, slavery, and the acquisition of land. Understanding how Manifest Destiny shaped our past emphasizes the importance of knowing history. History, it is said, repeats itself—unless we learn from the past. But how is this possible if the past is whitewashed, ignored, rewritten, or erased? Learning from negative historical events—understanding the toil and trouble that resulted—can be the impetus for finding new pathways.

More than a hundred years after Manifest Destiny, a different kind of American future began to emerge as the civil rights movement took hold. Martin Luther King Jr., who gave voice and power to this movement, believed that America had a different kind of destiny—to fulfill its founding values and to unfold a society that established equality and domestic tranquillity for all. King also believed that African Americans who had held on to their spiritual values were destined to "save the soul of our nation."[11] America, at the time a segregated society, would keep its promise: embrace the common good, equality, and justice, and thus fulfill its true destiny.

King's vision and the civil rights movement tore apart the seams of White supremacy inherent in Manifest Destiny. People of color uncovered their history, embraced their identity and power, and realized their immense contributions. The United States took great leaps toward becoming an equitable and inclusive society where all people could realize their potential.

In the twenty-first century another force of destiny is emerging that will further the civil rights movement and transform our country into a mosaic nation. By 2050, Hispanics will make up at least one-quarter of the population.[12] Latino *destino* will encompass a demographic and cultural revolution that will alter America's complexion from white to mocha.

As noted, Latinos are racial and cultural hybrids. In the plant and animal kingdom, hybrids have increased vigor and other exceptional qualities, including improved physical capacity, greater stamina, and higher yield capacity. Hybrid vigor is apparent in the strong Latino workforce, prolific population growth, and physical beauty. Latino destino is to infuse hybrid vigor into the American spirit—to stir salsa into the American melting pot. Latinos are living proof that being a genetic hybrid, embracing diversity, and reveling in a multicultural mélange enriches and enlivens the human experience.

Hispanic historical roots are older than the founding of our nation. Five hundred years have passed since Columbus first docked the *Santa María* in Hispaniola. But now Latinos are ready to be a dominant influence in shaping our multicultural nation. It is time to recognize that the time for Latino destino is now! ¡*Ahora!*

*Latino destino is to infuse hybrid vigor into the American spirit—to stir salsa into the American melting pot.*

# The Latino Explosion

THE LATINIZATION OF AMERICA is changing the way people feel, think, eat, dance, and vote. Latino culture, customs, and values are being adopted by mainstream society.[13] This process is driven by global connections, language, economic viability, purchasing power, small-business expansion, demographic growth, and political clout. Let's examine these more closely.

In this global age, Latinos are a portal to our world village, connected by language, culture, and kinship to twenty-six countries. Latino cultural roots can be found in Europe, throughout Spain, Portugal, Italy, and even Romania. In the East, an incredibly beautiful people in the Philippines mirror their mixed Spanish and Asian heritage. Even on the African continent Spanish remains the official language of Equatorial Guinea (formerly Spanish Guinea).[14]

Latinos are also an integrating cultural force in the Western Hemisphere, the bridge linking North, South, and Central America. This connection should not be underestimated. Our economic future is tied to Latin America. US exports to Central and South America grew 86 percent between 2004 and 2009 and are on track to more than double during the next five years.[15] Latinos are the nexus between countries in the entire Western Hemisphere and the weft upon which our new global culture will be woven.

A recent article in *USA Today* asked: *¿Entiende Ud. español?* If your answer to "Do you understand Spanish?" is no, get ready to be left behind.[16] Call your banks, telephone companies, public service companies, and government institutions, and you will hear "Si quieres hablar español—oprima el número." Many nations understand that speaking multiple languages is a coveted asset in our world community. The futuristic Chileans, for instance, initiated "English Opens Doors" in 2004, a program that was aimed at creating a bilingual country in just a generation.[17]

Fortunately, the United States is quickly becoming a bilingual nation and just passed Spain as the country with the second-highest number of Spanish speakers.[18] Almost 80 percent of US Latinos speak some español at home.[19] Español is the second-most-spoken language in the world. While more people speak Chinese, it is mostly spoken in China.[20] The difference is that español is the primary language in twenty-two countries. It is the *lengua* of the world!

*In this global age Latinos are a portal to our world village, connected by language, culture, and kinship to twenty-six countries.*

And talk about *dinero*! Hispanic purchasing power in the United States is more than $1 trillion annually and growing at a rate three times that of the national average.[21] The World Bank and International Monetary Fund compared the 2010 gross domestic product of nations around the world and found that if Hispanic America were a separate economy, it would rank among the top twelve GDPs.[22] The Latino economy is growing by leaps and bounds. Latinos have the fastest-growing small-businesses sector, which grew 44 percent from 2001 to 2007.[23] Latino-owned businesses are expected to increase their total revenue contribution to the economy by 8 percent annually over the decade from 2005 to 2015.[24]

In the 2012 presidential election, Latinos forged a new political landscape. As the fastest-growing segment of the electorate, Latino voters increased from 8 percent in 2004 to 10 percent.[25] It is not just that more Latinos are voting. It's where they vote. In the oh-so-rich electoral-vote state of California, Latinos cast 67 percent of their vote for President Obama. Three of the battleground states with significant Latino populations—Colorado, Nevada, and New Mexico—reported that the Hispanic percentage of the electorate basically determined the outcome of the election. In the Sunshine State of Florida, President Obama's Hispanic support accounted for 58 percent of the electorate, while he won the state by only 0.6 percent.[26]

Leveraging their growing numbers, Latinos are quickly gaining clout as elected officials and experienced a 53 percent increase from 1996 to 2010. At the highest level of office the gains in federal and state legislatures were 41 percent. Latinas are ahead of the pack and jumped a phenomenal 74 percent in the same period. Geographic influence is also spreading. In 1996 Latinos were elected in only thirty-four states, but by 2010

Latinos held elected office in forty-three states, including Alaska, Georgia, Kentucky, Missouri, New Hampshire, North Dakota, Oklahoma, and South Carolina.[27] These gains indicate that Latino and non-Latino voters understand the rich perspectives and experiences that diverse voices bring to our political system.

*¡Sí, es la hora!* For Latino leaders this is the defining moment. This is our time in history—Latinos are at the crossroads of power. Latino *destino* is calling!

*In the 2012 presidential election, Latinos forged a new political landscape. As the fastest-growing segment of the electorate, Latino voters increased from 8 percent in 2004 to 10 percent.*

## A Latino Cultural Infusion

WHILE THESE FACTS SUPPORT the growing Latino influence in America, the real *caramba* is in the enrichment the Latino way of life offers. Mexican food is now America's chosen ethnic cuisine. Tortillas are better sellers than bread.[28] Tortillas can be wrapped, eaten as burritos, made into tacos, fried for chimichangas or flautas, or broken up for chips. Talk about Latino diversity and versatility!

In the morning Americans wake up and smell the coffee—a favorite Latino tradition. At night they might enjoy America's favorite mixed drink—a margarita—with a little salsa and chips. For almost twenty years, salsa has been our favorite condiment, having passed the more homogenized ketchup in the early nineties.[29] And salsa has almost no calories—what a cultural bonanza! Today people eat more nachos than hot dogs at baseball games, and one-third of players are Hispanic.[30]

Latinos are kinetic people and love to dance! All over America people are joining the salsa dance craze. They are swaying to a rhumba, cumbia, meringue, or cha-cha-cha. For those who like a slower beat, there are the polka-sounding *rancheros* and the country sway of a *bachata*. Latino diversity is evident, even on the dance floor.

Latino music is blasting the air waves. Artists reflect the vast assortment of the international Latino world. Colombian-born Shakira combines her Middle Eastern ancestry with her Hispanic roots. The hot, hot rhythm of Marc Anthony was born in Puerto Rico. Santana's fusion salsa mixes Mexican, African drums, and rock. Celia Cruz, considered the queen of salsa, was as Cuban as the maracas. Singer-songwriter Juan Luis Guerra is from the Dominican Republic, while crooner Julio Iglesias comes from Spain. These singers are transnational, and their music blasts out from Buenos Aires to Barcelona to New York City in español and inglés.

When people turn on the television, they are beginning to see Latino faces. George Lopez has been called the funniest man in America. Even American families are being Latinized. Think of the beautiful and voluptuous Sofía Vergara as Gloria Delgado-Pritchett on *Modern Family*. The international Latino connection is apparent in the film industry, as well. Spanish movie stars like Penélope Cruz and Javier Bardem have won Oscars.

The infusion of Latinos into music, entertainment, and food is the tip of the cultural iceberg—the easiest way for people to enjoy and to integrate *Latinismo* into their life. Rest assured that this blending of US and Latino cuisine has just begun to enrich our country's palate. More good times are ahead as we go full steam ahead into the Latino-flavored multicultural century.

*Mexican food is now America's chosen ethnic cuisine. Tortillas are better sellers than bread.... In the morning Americans wake up and smell the coffee—a favorite Latino tradition.*

## *¡Ándale!*—Moving Forward

UNDERSTANDING THE COMPLEX ANTECEDENTS that shaped the Latino experience prepares us to appreciate its culture and unique leadership forms. The next section looks at the ways Latinos prepare for leadership and overviews three concepts: *personalismo, conciencia,* and *destino.*

Personalismo is the inner work leaders must do to become the kind of person that people will follow; it places high value on the good character, reputation, and contributions of the leader. Conciencia is conscious awareness: the mechanism by which a leader stays consistent and connected to her inner self, personal motivation, and culture. Destino, the third aspect of leadership preparation, speaks to an even deeper understanding of one's unique calling or life's work.

I use these concepts to give substance and structure to how Latinos prepare for leadership. As the Latino culture relies on oral tradition, and is one where knowledge is gained through experience, a methodology for personal leadership development has not yet been framed. I am hopeful that these concepts can serve as guideposts for young Latinos and others who aspire to lead.

# PART II

# Preparing to Lead: A Latino Perspective

M ANY OF TODAY'S LEADERSHIP THEORIES build on the wisdom and experience of earlier times. As far back as the sixth century BC Lao Tzu, the great Chinese sage, counseled people, "Do you want to be a positive influence in the world? First get your own life in order." Lao Tzu divined that the leader's behavior—like a rock that ripples across water—would influence those around him. Thus, he stressed the importance of personal preparation and setting a good example.[1]

A number of leadership concepts today follow Lao Tzu's advice and emphasize that leaders should first be concerned with their own behavior, ethics, and character. In their book *Superleadership* Charles Manz and Henry Sims touted self-leadership: "If a person wants to lead somebody, he must first lead himself." They believed that by demonstrating the behaviors and values they desired in others, leaders would empower people and encourage them to be leaders as well.[2] More recently, Stephen Covey in his work on principle-centered leadership emphasized an "inside out" approach "to start first with the self, . . . your character, and motives."[3]

A similar concept in the Latino community is *personalismo*, which speaks to a leader's character, reputation, and contributions. Personalismo places value on the reliable authentic self and the preparation a leader undertakes to become the kind of person that people will want to follow. For Latinos this also implies having cultural integrity and staying connected to one's community and people.

Second, due to the cultural emphasis on people, personalismo encompasses the belief that every single person has value regardless of status or material wealth and should be treated in a personal and courteous manner. Relating to everyone in this way strengthens relationships—the foundation for community leadership and collective action. Furthermore, by recognizing that everyone has something to contribute, personalismo fosters an inclusive and shared leadership process.

> In *español* there are two verbs that signify "I am." *Soy* is permanent; it means "This is the way I am—it is my essence." *Estoy* is temporary and changeable. *Estoy* means "This how I am feeling, my current circumstances, or what I am doing right now." The saying *Soy como soy* means "I am the way I am." Personalismo is a directive to be yourself. Be authentic and real! Tap into the *soy* of your being!

*Conciencia,* the second aspect of leadership preparation, beckons the leader to know *why* she seeks to be a leader and *what* she wants to accomplish. Conciencia reflects a leader's personal clarity and fosters congruence. For Latinos this entails exploring the effects on one's sense of self and personal power from growing up as a "minority." Leaders must understand how this has affected individuals as well as the Latino community.

In *Leading with Soul,* Lee Bowman and Terrence Deal urge leaders to embark on a journey to explore their inner self, to search for their special contribution, and to tap into their existential core. Leading others, they state, is not possible if a person does not know himself at the deepest level.[4] Inner awareness is conciencia—the firm ground, the nucleus—of the leader.

## Seeking One's *Destino*

LATINOS HAVE AN INTRIGUING concept known as *destino*, which implies that everyone was born for a distinct reason at a precise time in history and has a unique life path. At a deeper level, leadership preparation includes delving into one's destino, or life's purpose. Destino is the existential core or "overarching purpose" that Greenleaf notes in *The Servant as Leader*.[5]

Understanding one's destino is similar to the American Indian tradition of the vision quest, where a person engages in a solitary pursuit to answer questions such as: Who am I? What is my life's work, and what was I born to do? The vision that is unveiled speaks to the true purpose of a person's life and becomes a powerful ally in fulfilling one's life work.

For Latinos the process is not as structured, but rest assured that leaders must have a clear sense of purpose and understand the unique contribution they will make. This is particularly relevant since collective leadership prescribes that every leader has a distinct gift or talent. Unfolding one's destino is an ongoing, organic process that evolves as a person grows and matures. Understanding one's destino requires cultivating conciencia. The more the leader develops this intuitive insight, the more her purpose, or destino, unfolds.

# CHAPTER 3

# *Personalismo:* The Character of the Leader

I WAS A YOUNG LEADER working as the executive director of Mi Casa Women's Center when my mentor Bernie Valdez showed me, through his example and extraordinary life, how *personalismo* was a powerful determinant in leading people. Like many early Latino leaders, Bernie didn't read leadership books. He earned respect because of the kind of person he was and by the way he valued and validated everyone.

The first time I picked up Bernie for our monthly lunch, I expected his home to mirror his stature in the community. Much later, Bernie would have the Colorado Hispanic Heritage Center and a public library named after him. Yet he lived in a little house behind the stadium where the Broncos played football. It was the house where he and Dora had raised their children. He lived simply and modestly, much like the people he led.

Bernie had worked in the sugar beet fields and been a union organizer. By the time we were having lunch together, he had served as president of the Denver Board of Education, headed the Social Services Department, and started numerous community organizations. Bernie had impeccable follow-through, no matter how long it took or how difficult it would be. "You have to work hard and not give up," he would tell me. In the turbulent 1960s, when Latinos were just beginning to forge their identity and to organize as a community, Bernie inspired others to do the same. The decades it took to desegregate the Denver Public Schools are a testament to his endurance and persistence.

Whenever Bernie faced a conflict or challenge, he was gracious and humorous. This "Don't take things so seriously" approach gave people perspective and made working together enjoyable. I later realized that humor and equanimity were smart strategies when strenuous, long-term work was asked of people. (Chapter 11 has more about how making leadership an enjoyable process ensures continuity.)

When I asked Bernie about leadership, he paused and then said, "Well, first, a leader has to be really secure. You have to know who you are and have respect for yourself." He radiated that sense of self, and you could always count on Bernie being Bernie. "To get things done," he cautioned, "you have to be sensitive to what people need and have genuine feelings for them." He demonstrated this by being accessible, listening intently, and having a warm and humble manner.

Bernie and I would eat burritos or egg rolls and "just visit" during our lunches. But our relationship had a profound impact on my leadership. He would counsel, "Be yourself—no one can do that better than you can!" Bernie taught me the essence of personalismo.

1. First and foremost, a leader is an authentic person, which fosters consistency and dependability.

2. Relationships are fashioned in a familial manner like the one I had with Bernie.

3. A leader has genuine feelings for people, listens to them, and treats them with respect and courtesy.

4. A leader is un hombre de palabra (a man of his word). Actions align with words, which fosters congruence and engenders trust, or confianza.

*"Well, first, a leader has to be really secure. You have to know who you are and have respect for yourself. To get things done, you have to be sensitive to what people need and have genuine feelings for them."*

—Bernie Valdez

## The Personalismo of the Leader

W HILE EVERYONE HAS INHERENT worth, respect is given to a leader based on his character, the manner in which he lives, how he treats others, and the contribution he makes to family and community. A leader's credibility depends on having a reputation that he cares about others and treats everyone equally.

To act like one is better than or knows more than someone else, or to practice any kind of elitism, runs contrary to personalismo, where everyone has something to contribute and has inherent worth. Personalismo is the great equalizer driving a shared leadership process.

Leadership is evolving into a collaborative and participatory process in which people, relationships, and cooperation are central—pivotal traits of the Latino culture. Personalismo secures these relational aspects of leadership.

Since personalismo encourages authenticity, spending time with a group of Latino leaders will quickly make it evident that conformity is not a cultural mainstay. The Latino commandment to "be yourself" can be seen in a love of distinctiveness—bright colors, conspicuous jewelry, boisterous conversation, and permission to express your true feelings. This makes for a whole assortment of leaders, a tolerance for different styles, and support for individuality!

I have been the beneficiary of this warm acceptance. My very outgoing, determined, sometimes "pushy" personality could have been rebuffed.

Instead, I have been told it is a gift that allows me to accomplish things others might not attempt (and enables me to enlist others in coming along!). Latinos will say, "That is just Juana," which for everyone means "Just be you. Nobody's perfect, and you can bring your unique talents into play."

*Personalismo is the great equalizer driving a shared leadership process....Personalismo secures the relational aspects of leadership.*

## Personalismo Builds Relationships

IN MORE MATERIALISTIC OR status-conscious societies, a person might be respected for his money, position, and title; the neighborhood he lives in; his car, clothes, and other trappings of "success." But "How much are you worth?" does not reference a person's inner values, morals, or social contribution.

In the Latino culture, people's value stems from who they are unto themselves and from their membership in a family group, rather than from their social status or from their professional accomplishments. Personalismo is the unconditional recognition of the essential value of each individual.[1] The warm, friendly, and personable way Latinos relate to one another and the active interest they take in people's lives reflects personalismo. By emphasizing good manners and congenial interpersonal relationships where people validate and support each other, personalismo reinforces the *We*, or collective. It springs from the culture's humanistic values.

Miguel Corona, a faculty member at the University of Phoenix who speaks on the Latino workforce, explains in his blog *Interns Matter*, how utilizing personalismo gains credibility:

A few weeks ago, I presented to a Latino student organization. Before my presentation, I spent quite a long time talking with many of the students asking them about their backgrounds and experiences, respective majors and classroom work, and plans after graduation. I also shared everything about my background, and how it mirrored many of their experiences.

By the time I was introduced to speak, I had already established an initial relationship with most of the students and could sense that the rapport I developed helped me *generate credibility* before speaking one word. This highlights the special emphasis Hispanics put on relationship-building prior to engaging in business or developing professional relationships. It's based on the cultural idea that individuals are valued more than material belongings and is known as personalismo.[2]

Corona is modeling four qualities of personalismo: (1) respect and regard for the individual; (2) sharing one's own background and personal experiences; (3) building personal relationships; and (4) creating a "cultural bond" with people. These qualities facilitate people's identification with the leader and make it easier to follow and emulate him.

Cultural connectivity is the special tie Latinos have with one another. When establishing a relationship, a person usually shares where she is from, who her *familia* is, and tidbits about her background. Latinos come from intact communities where people feel like they belong; may have similar backgrounds, values, and experiences; and share a collective identity and history. For instance, Latinos might have similar childhood memories (like eating rice and beans, celebrating their first Holy Communion, or having extended familia live with them). They may know a member of someone's large extended family, have a mutual friend, or participate in the same community group or church.

An upward nod of the head and a pursing of lips is the physical signal that Latinos recognize each other as belonging to the same ethnic group. Today, their growing identity and special affinity known as *la Raza* is strengthening the Latino preference for establishing personal relationships and connecting through their culture.

Because leaders come from and derive their authority from their communities, practicing these qualities of personalismo establishes credibility. And it is the foundation for a valued leadership asset—being seen as a person of confianza (trustworthiness).

*Latinos come from intact communities where people feel like they belong; may have similar backgrounds, values, and experiences; and share a collective identity and history.*

## Personalismo Promotes Confianza

BERNIE ALWAYS KEPT HIS word. For Latino leaders this often means never surrendering to the odds and being determined to go the long haul. He modeled dependability and follow-through and stayed active in the community until the day he died. These traits made Bernie a trusted leader and a person *de confianza*. Confianza means the leader has established trust based on his honesty, his personal relationships with people, and his demonstrated reliability.

The saying *hombre de palabra* (a man of his word) emphasizes that a person will do what he says he is going to do. Keeping commitments and following through establishes a leader's track record. Furthermore, since Latinos value cooperation where everyone does his or her part, a person who doesn't is letting down the entire group. The National Community for Latino Leadership (NCLL) found in a survey of over three thousand Latinos that keeping one's word and delivering on one's promises was the most valued quality for Latino leaders.[3] Being de confianza underscores a leader's credibility.[4]

Historical antecedents underlay the significance of confianza. Because Latinos had to succeed in schools, jobs, and other social institutions where rules of the dominant culture were sometimes murky and confusing, they had to rely on one another. Minorities often watched each other's backs and shared information on what was acceptable behavior or what might get them into trouble. Economic survival and advancement required nurturing long-term support and trust. (White privilege and the psychology of oppression are discussed in chapter 4.)

A people-based culture would unravel without confianza, which keeps relationships strong and based on trust, loyalty, and dependability. The extended and elastic familia—which broadly refers to groups that have an affinity and have established mutual trust—reinforces confianza, since relationships are lifelong and reciprocal.

Carlos Orta, president of the Hispanic Association on Corporate Responsibility, observes, "Traditionally, trust (confianza) was the basis for making agreements and conducting business. We don't do business with people we don't know—establishing a personal relationship always precedes any kind of transaction." Shaking hands and relying on the person's word, not lawyers or contractual agreements, was sufficient because neither party would let the other down." When a leader is de confianza, he is trusted as part of the group or accepted as familia.

*"Traditionally, trust (confianza) was the basis for making agreements and conducting business. We don't do business with people we don't know—establishing a personal relationship always precedes any kind of transaction."*

—Carlos Orta

## Personalismo as a Leadership Practice

PERSONALISMO AND CONFIANZA ARE threads weaving together the ongoing sense of community and extended familia that blesses Latino people. By establishing meaningful relationships among people, personalismo strengthens community and establishes a sense of belonging. One generation ago people were not as mobile and lived in intact communities. People knew each other's families and grandparents. Many had the type of relationships personalismo espouses.

In our fragmented world, building a sense of community is a key function of leadership. In fact, Robert Greenleaf in his profound thesis, *The Servant as Leader*, lamented that "building community was the lost knowledge of our times."[5] Personalismo can lay the groundwork for more meaningful and authentic relationships as well as a renewed sense of community. Here are ten practices that help leaders cultivate relationships and gain confianza, all of which enhance personalismo.

1. Bienvenido—Be welcoming! Give a natural, friendly smile and make brief eye contact when meeting someone. Stand up and shake hands both when greeting and when saying good-bye (this indicates respect).

2. Remember the Hispanic hospitality golden rule—*Mi casa es su casa.* Invite people to sit down and make themselves at home. If possible, serve them something to eat or drink.

3. Spend time building rapport before discussing the issue at hand, dealing with problems, or making requests. Meet with people individually or in small groups.[6]

4. Ask people about their family history, where they are from, their values, and traditions. Remember: building confianza takes time!

5. Emphasize personal dignity, honor, and one's "good name"; be sensitive to a person's pride.

6. Take a personal interest in people. Get to know their family makeup and inquire how the family is doing. Ask follow-up questions on other details, such as, "How was your son's birthday party?"

7. Be open! Share your own background, family history, and experiences as a way of making a personal and mutual connection. Include your cultural background.

8. Learn and practice cultural values and tendencies that foster Latino relationships and behavior, such as *respeto* (respect) and being *honesto* (honest) and *simpático* (congenial).

9. Listen carefully when a person is speaking, and take care not to appear distracted or uninterested. Do not do other things like check your email or text messages.

10. Use a few words in *español*. Especially for non-Latinos this conveys the willingness to reach out to people in a way that respects their culture, language, and ways of communication.

Perhaps these are basic courtesies that should be extended to all people. Yet when these hallmarks of personalismo are skipped with non-Latinos, it may not make a big difference in the outcome of the relationship or of future encounters. In fact, there is a common saying, "You don't need to like someone to work with him," implying a more practical and task-oriented process than a relational one.

Failure to connect personally with a Latino, however, can mean a loss of trust and credibility. He may seek a different person (or leader) to work with or go somewhere else to obtain services or make purchases.[7] These ten practices gain trust, nurture confianza, and affirm people's individuality and contributions. They establish the leader as someone who is genuine, caring, and able to make personal connections. With secure relationships, the leader has laid the stepping-stones to a community leadership process based on mutual respect and equality.

## Personalismo—Cult or Credibility?

Unchecked personalismo can become self-centeredness or egocentric. The Latino fascination with individual personality can be magnified and distorted so that the leader is glorified or has a personal following that is not based on accomplishments or concern for other people's welfare. Latin American examples of this include the almost cult-like following of the Peronistas, who supported Juan Perón in Argentina, or the ongoing saga of the Fidelistas that follow Castro. The old caudillo (boss) form of leadership has existed particularly in Latin America, where leadership was an imposed process and part of colonization.

However, Latino leadership in the United States grew out of social-change movements and represented "minority" people. The models presented in this book are based on the incredible gains Latinos have made in the past fifty years because of leaders who surfaced from the community and advanced their people. Personalismo in this context has been a way for leaders to weave the common experiences that connected them to their community and to exhibit the character that inspires people to follow them.

## *¡Ándale!*—Moving Forward

WE CONTINUE EXPLORING CONCEPTS on how Latinos prepare for leadership with our next principle—*conciencia*, which speaks to the inner process that strengthens self-awareness. Knowing oneself is a prerequisite for being an authentic leader and for aligning words with action. It is the foundation for the revered designation as a leader who is de confianza.

# CHAPTER 4

# *Conciencia:* Knowing Oneself and Cultivating Personal Awareness

THE BRILLIANT MEXICAN ARTIST Diego Rivera sketched a powerful black-and-white etching titled "Conciencia." He rendered a young teacher holding beautiful apples in her mantle surrounded by eager children. Rivera, a symbolic artist, included an open book, suggesting the quest for knowledge. The title "Conciencia" implies we must look for deeper meaning. *Conciencia* can be translated as "consciousness," "awareness," and "self-knowledge." Rivera's portrayal suggests the teacher as our inner guide. The children symbolize our pure and receptive self, poised to learn and grow. The apples are pearls of knowledge.

The concepts of confianza and personalismo point to two critical questions for Latino leaders: Who are you? What kind of person are you? Answering these questions requires the practice of conciencia, or in-depth reflection, self-examination, and integration. Conciencia is the connection the leader has with his inner core—the reliable, consistent self that provides direction and guidance. Conciencia is the mechanism for character formation and personal development.

Conciencia entails knowing oneself. This requires tapping into the intuition that allows one to be aware of her motivation, values, intention, and internal dynamics. Greenleaf called attention to this when he stated, "The intuition is the most reliable part of the servant leader."[1] The NCLL survey indicated that the number one trait people wanted in their leaders (58.9 percent) was character, depicted as being honest, demonstrating integrity, and having strong moral values.[2] The word *integrity* comes from the root *integral* and refers to wholeness or being complete. Integration is possible only by cultivating the practice of conciencia—paying close attention to one's intuition, impulses, motives, and inner voice. To cultivate conciencia leaders must also uncover any personality flaws or desires that might get in the way.

Conciencia reflects a leader's personal clarity and fosters congruence. My mentor Bernie Valdez asked questions that helped me define why I wanted to be a leader and what I wanted to accomplish. Because he was my first Latino mentor and teacher, Bernie also helped me incorporate my culture into leadership. This was essential to my personal integration and indispensable for becoming a Latina leader. Bernie believed leadership was helping our people find pride in their cultural roots and tapping into their collective power.

 *Conciencia is the connection the leader has with his inner core—the reliable, consistent self that provides direction and guidance … conciencia is the mechanism for character formation and personal development.*

## Conciencia Rests on Cultural Identity

WHILE SELF-AWARENESS IS AN essential part of leadership preparation for all people, for Latinos it includes integrating one's cultural identity and knowing one's roots and family heritage. Moreover, since US Latinos have grown up as minorities and experienced exclusion, leadership requires healing any scars or insecurities that have resulted.

In 1967, Rodolfo "Corky" Gonzales, a civil rights leader, poet, and boxer, wrote the epic poem "I Am Joaquin," which powerfully depicts the struggles of sorting through negative societal messages, grappling with the pull of assimilation, and seeking a positive Latino identity. The poem laments that Latinos are "lost in a world of confusion" and caught in a whirlwind of a strange society.[3] Gonzales's remedy was to embrace Hispanic history and tap into the greatness of the culture.

Much has changed since the sixties, when Gonzales penned his call for cultural preservation and pride—a time when Latinos did not even have a collective identity. Ensuring the culture is preserved for future generations, however, is still an essential function of leadership. Through national Latino organizations, community-based and leadership programs, leaders support cultural integration and pride and strengthen collective identity.

A crucial aspect of conciencia, then, is being secure in one's cultural identity. By integrating positive cultural aspects, leaders can function effectively in mainstream society without losing their heritage, sense of self, or commitment to their people. They can then teach others how to do likewise.

For many Latinos becoming culturally secure requires resolving the internalized effects of discrimination and exclusion that result from growing up Brown. Latinos have been termed "minorities," a euphemism for people who historically have been in subservient or in oppressed positions. Minorities are on the outskirts of the dominant culture. They are always seen in reference to and measured by dominant norms and values.

In the United States, White culture is presented as the standard, even the ideal, and innately superior. Anglos are the top dogs. The media, school system, and society reinforce this message. White people reap disproportionate economic benefits, have a higher standard of living, and enjoy greater opportunity and certain privileges. In addition, in a materialistic culture the high significance placed on wealth and status is connected to individual value and worth. People who have higher economic status are simply treated as if they are more important, special, smarter, or more talented. White privilege has structured society to favor some groups and to make access more difficult for others.[4] Moreover, there is a general ignorance about the culture and contributions of Latinos, as they along with other minorities were never integrated into US education or history. (Hopefully part I has contributed to a greater understanding of these antecedents.)

 *While self-awareness is an essential part of leadership preparation for all people, for Latinos it includes integrating one's cultural identity and knowing one's roots and family heritage.*

## Resolving the Barriers of Exclusion

BECAUSE OF CULTURAL DOMINATION, success for Latinos meant cloning the behavior and thinking patterns that White society taught in schools and other institutions. This social conditioning can result in Latinos rejecting their culture, becoming "whitewashed," and distancing themselves from their own group. One way that Latinos and other people of color have tried to escape negative cultural images is to *assimilate* into the dominant society. Assimilation erases one's cultural identity and can create feelings of inferiority that function at an unconscious level. The fact is, however, that no matter how hard Latinos and other people of color tried, they could never totally fit in.

When I was seven years old, my family bought a small house in a newly developed section of town. I was uprooted from West Tampa, where the "Spanish" people lived, and walked into second grade to see a whole sea of white faces. Like all other children, I wanted to be accepted and to succeed in school. So little by little, I stopped speaking Spanish, learned to act like the other kids, and even became embarrassed by my immigrant family. Likewise, many Mexican Americans in the Southwest forgot Spanish and even changed the pronunciation of their names.

The psychological pain of rejecting one's own group, together with the confused or splintered identity that can result, was termed the *psychology of oppression* by the perceptive Brazilian thinker and educator Paulo Freire. The psychology of oppression is the process by which Latinos and other "minorities" internalize the negative messages and beliefs about their people and come to believe that they are true. This operates at an unconscious level, so that many are unaware of how this functions in their personal lives or affects their self-esteem. Once this occurs, they are held hostage by their own thinking and begin to collude with the society that keeps them "in their place." They may believe their culture is inferior.[5]

From an individualistic orientation, the feeling that one may not measure up can be confused for a lack of initiative or abilities. However when an entire culture cannot compete equitably and must battle the obstacles of discrimination, this becomes a systemic or social mechanism. Conciencia requires a clear awareness of how exclusion affects Latinos both individually and collectively.

Conciencia entails addressing the subliminal messages about White privilege, resolving the internal barriers of exclusion, and fully integrating one's cultural identity. As a young girl I struggled with this. As an immigrant growing up in a lower-income family, I did not know the social manners associated with White people or the middle class. Children like me who didn't have "the right clothes," know the "right people," or live in the "right neighborhood" often felt inadequate. The language my family used, their table manners, and their jobs put me at a disadvantage. I remember as a young girl feeling inferior. One occasion was especially difficult.

## The Red-Striped Dress

AS A CHILD, I could total up my "social disabilities." I was poor, Brown, small boned, short, and a girl. My mother spoke broken English. I didn't think I was very smart. All in all, this added up to what I later termed *a cultural inferiority complex.*

As a budding teenager, a very sensitive time in my life, I was invited to a special party by a well-to-do Anglo cheerleader. My mother took me to a Lerner Store[6] to buy a dress for the event. Going to Lerner was like a Saks Fifth Avenue expedition! I still can't imagine how my mother got the money to do this. There on the rack was this beautiful red cotton dress with black and brown stripes and a little bowtie at the collar. My mother and I were so happy that I tap danced around the store. Such a treasured moment.

What a trauma to my young soul when I walked into the party and saw the rich girls dressed in fancy taffeta and silk! I was mortified and hid in a bathroom all night, refusing to come out. Years later I saw a TV special on how poverty affects self-image—the story of a little girl who hid in the bathroom during lunch because she didn't have money to eat. When the teacher asked why she did this, she said, "I felt ashamed." This was the same embarrassment I felt that night. Experiences are internalized by minority children, and they think, "I am not good enough," "Something is wrong with me," "They are better than me," or "I won't amount to much."

By the time I entered high school, I decided, "I have to succeed. My parents and *familia* are counting on me and have sacrificed so much." While I was thinking about this, I saw a cartoon that had a wise old owl singing, "It is not what you got. It's what you do with what you got." This became my mantra. "Wow!" I thought, "I may have been born with limitations, but I am going to make it!" I became involved in school activities and sports, wrote for the school paper, and was even elected an officer in several clubs. (Actually if the truth be told, I assimilated, but more about that in part IV.)

I ended up going to college and then, through the transformative experience of the Peace Corps, learned about my great culture. Today I know that as an immigrant growing up in a low-income family, I was resourceful, scrappy, talented, and street smart. In fact, *check it out*: I learned to speak English when I was six years old. I now draw energy, pride, and strength from understanding the obstacles my parents and familia overcame. My mother came here with no money and no education, and yet those obstacles couldn't stop her. If she could do that, think of what I can do!

Latino contributions were never taught in school, portrayed in the media, or acknowledged by people in authority. I had to search for them, talk with others who had similar experiences, and then find these within myself. The decision to be proud of my heritage is one of the integrating factors of my life and work. Conciencia entailed redefining myself by acknowledging my cultural strengths and embracing my Latino identity.

Latinos today must consider their values and upbringing with a new lens—one that portrays the positive attributes of the culture. They need to know their history and unearth the real story of Latino people in the United States. By definition, becoming a Latino leader involves *the integration of one's culture, history, and personal background.*

Leadership preparation in the dominant culture typically does not entail learning about and tapping into one's cultural identity or resolving issues of discrimination or exclusion. Although doing this would certainly expand a person's ability to understand the deep imprint of culture and race, Anglo leaders today are challenged instead to increase their understanding of other cultures and to expand their ability to relate to diverse people.

*"Today I know that as an immigrant growing up in a low-income family, I was resourceful, scrappy, talented, and street smart. In fact, check it out: I learned to speak English when I was six years old."*

—Juana Bordas

## From Conciencia to Action

MANY TIMES OPPRESSED PEOPLE believe they can't change their situation and that circumstances are too great to overcome. To be a leader, a person must heal his own wounds—find out how past circumstances have made him stronger and more capable. Then he can use this awareness to help people transform frustration into a belief that they too can change their lives for the better. This was a hallmark of Raul Yzaguirre's leadership: "The leader has to build his self-confidence. You have to believe in yourself first. You have to convince yourself you can do it before you can convince others."

Personal integration, a secure identity, and self-confidence are not possible if the reference group and ancestry is rejected. Since the gains of the civil rights movement, many younger Latinos have not experienced discrimination personally and can relate to this only by talking to their parents or grandparents. But they can ponder the fact that Hispanics still lag educationally, economically, and in housing and medical benefits, and are scarce at the higher levels of leadership. These are flashing indicators that discrimination and White privilege still persist.

Conciencia must be a collective process because otherwise a person keeps internalizing, believing that he is the only one with the problem or even that these limitations are inherent in Latinos as a whole. As people talk about and release the effects of internalized oppression, cultural pride and a stronger identity emerge. Leaders remind people that historically their salvation came from their culture and community, which sustained and nourished them. Latino leaders are alchemists transforming oppression into energy for positive change and harnessing frustrations into passion. They understand that hardships bring vitality, resilience, and spiritual strength.

Latino leadership programs can facilitate this collective integration by utilizing these practices:

- Teaching US Latino history and advancement.

- Exploring cultural concepts, strengths, and assets.

- Learning about current issues that affect Latinos as well as political and social-change strategies to address these. (Chapter 10 covers this in more depth.)

- Dealing with the aftermath of discrimination and exclusion; learning about White privilege and the psychology of oppression.

- Conveying the concept of leadership as a service to one's community and people. (This is reviewed in chapter 8.)

- Building a support network and integrating people into the Latino community.

- Connecting with and hearing the stories of leaders who demonstrate such traits as personalismo and conciencia.

*Conciencia must be a collective process because otherwise
a person keeps internalizing, believing that he is the only
one with the problem or even that these limitations are
inherent in Latinos as a whole.*

Latino leadership programs must also teach the skills that make people
successful in the dominant culture. For instance, Latinos value modesty
and humility and being part of the group. However, if a person does
not know how to distinguish himself or toot his own horn, he may not
be promoted or seen as a leader. When I was the director of Mi Casa
Women's Center, every participant took an assertiveness training course.
The Young Hispanic Corporate Achievers program has a special "branding
and marketing yourself" segment—an essential skill to move up the
corporate ladder. (The next section on *destino* addresses this concept in
more depth.)

When Latinos master dominant-culture skills and integrate their
cultural identity and assets, they have a competitive advantage. As more
Latinos become educated they have these skills. (Julián Castro attended
Stanford and Harvard law school. Arturo Vargas graduated from Stanford.
Anna Escobedo Cabral attended Harvard.) Latino leadership programs
can assist young leaders to stay connected to their cultural roots and learn
from seasoned leaders.

## Conciencia Is Other Centered

CONCIENCIA IMPLIES THAT A leader has contemplated questions
such as, Why do I do what I do? Many cultures believe that a person's
intention—the *why*, the desired end result—is the nucleus from which
integrity and power flow. In a collective, people-centered culture, leaders
have a natural propensity to serve their communities. Furthermore,
since most traditional leaders have sprung from the public and
nonprofit arena, their leadership is other centered. Cabral notes this

tendency: "There is this basic value that whatever you do, you do for the community and the family. Yes, it is important to do well, but because it will enable others to do well." Dedication to *community stewardship*, overviewed in chapter 8, sets the stage for leaders who uplift people rather than seek power or wealth.

Bernie Valdez encouraged me to tap into my conciencia when he said, "First, a leader has to be really secure. You have to know who you are and have respect for yourself." Knowing oneself engenders consistency and predictability. Then actions are aligned with words.

César Chávez grew up in the migrant camps of California and continued to live humbly throughout his life, never making more than the farm workers he led.[7] Latinos saw him living a simple life, taking personal risks by leading demonstrations, and fasting many days to promote change. A spiritual man, he manifested his inner work in his speeches, behavior, and action. These demonstrations of his personal values led people to believe in him and so they followed and tried to emulate him.

*"There is this basic value that whatever you do, you do for the community and the family. Yes, it is important to do well, but because it will enable others to do well."*

—Anna Escobedo Cabral

## *¡Ándale!*—Moving Forward

THE PRINCIPLE OF DESTINO that follows addresses the unique pattern of a leader's life; it is sometimes referred to as a person's calling or purpose. To tap into one's destino requires conciencia but also implies an outward search. Influences such as recent history, seminal events, and generational perspectives render the landscape in which one's destino is etched. When a leader has conciencia, she understands how her special talents, life events, passion, and interests integrate into her unique calling. Then by embracing her destino, her leadership path unfolds. Destino is the integrating factor of a leader's life.

# CHAPTER 5

# *Destino:* Personal and Collective Purpose

A S A CHILD I didn't believe in *destino* at all. In fact, I thought God had gotten it all wrong. If I had designed my life, it would have been a different movie. Take the first act, for instance.

I was born on a hot, humid clothes-sticking August night, in the middle of the Nicaraguan jungle. Most people in those days didn't even know where Nicaragua was—and if they did, they didn't much care. The mining town of Bonanza spurred the emergence of a small community living in little wooden houses that leaned into the rocky hills. Across from the company's commissary, overlooking a lush green ravine, my mother lay down on that hot summer night to birth her seventh child.

Whose plan was this? What happened to divine providence? Why was I born to a Spanish Indian woman with a fifth-grade education who was as thin as a rail and at forty didn't need another child? My mother was one of those tall coastal women whose strength often allowed them to laugh in the face of the strenuous life they were dealt. But she was buckling under the stress of this untimely pregnancy and the uncertain future that wobbled before her.

My father had brought the *familia* to Bonanza a few years earlier after yet another dervish hurricane had whipped the coast, ripping out trees and homes, turning lush tropical jungle into slithering mud. Cabo Gracias a Dios, which had been our home for generations, was wiped as clean as a chicken bone after our dog Chocho was done. Exasperated, my father came to the Bonanza mine to run the commissary, save money, and take his familia to America—the promised land!

Concerned for my mother's health, the *partera* (midwife) prepared the herbs that would induce contractions. I guess I must have sensed my number was up. The herbs would make me nauseated and drowsy, and then I might never know how to get out of here. A small voice must have whispered, "It will be better if you go of your own volition." Holding my breath, I descended like a locomotive in a tunnel. Bonanza, here I come!

Having been born in the Nicaraguan jungle as a Hispanic girl, the seventh child of a struggling family who had lost their home, was not exactly my idea of "the right stuff" or the ticket to a fulfilling life. *Whose idea was this anyway?* I thought. How would I get from the middle of nowhere to a place where I could get an education, live a halfway comfortable existence, or make a contribution to the world? There was not even a library or a high school. *No way, Jose*, this was not happening.

Today I know that every particle of my life was precisely what was needed for me to become who I am today and to be a leader in my community . . . this was my destino. I would only understand this through *conciencia*—doing a great deal of soul searching, reflecting on my life, and humbly understanding that I know very little about how a life unfolds (or even what is good for me).

## ¿Qué Es Destino Anyway?

STEPHEN COVEY RECOGNIZED THE connection between conciencia and destino when he stated, "You can't become principle-centered without a vision of and a focus on the unique contribution that is yours to make."[1] Consciousness, he said, is the ability to detect our own uniqueness. The essence of conciencia is to know oneself well enough that one's life and actions are in alignment with one's purpose and destino.

Because every person is unique, one's destino is as distinct as her fingerprints or DNA. As a person embraces her life's journey, destino grows, becomes clearer and more encompassing. Like an acorn that becomes a great oak, the seeds of our destino must be nourished and flourish only with patience and persistence.

The search for destino brings a deeper understanding of one's special calling and a clearer sense of direction. When Covey urges leaders to examine their values and principles and to develop a personal mission statement for their lives, he is asking them to explore their destino. This type of reflection provides a firm footing when waters are turbulent or life throws a curveball. Appreciating what makes you unique—your history, life path, and destino—is the true way to know yourself and to understand the special leadership contribution you are called to make.

*Because every person is unique, one's destino is as distinct as her fingerprints or DNA. As a person embraces her life's journey, destino grows, becomes clearer and more encompassing.*

## Why Destino Is Not Fatalism

ANTHROPOLOGISTS WHO STUDY AND categorize cultures deem the tendency to believe that outside circumstances or outside forces control one's life as *fatalism*.[2] Could it be that most anthropologists come from an individualistic perspective and do not understand that destino does not mean that a person cannot mold or change her future? *Fatalism* implies being stuck, unable to choose. Destino is not fatalism, because it does not prescribe or determine. People can still choose how to respond to and utilize life's experiences. Latinos dance with their destino. Like the right-left-right of salsa dancing, it is a back-and-forth interchange.

Destino differs from the Anglo-American belief in individual effort and self-determination. In fact, one of the distinctions between *We*-oriented cultures and those that are more *I*, or individualistic, revolves around the question, How much control do I have or assume in my life? The independent focus says, "To a very great extent, I control my life, chose my experiences, and shape my destiny. I am the captain of my ship." Self-identity, self-determination, and self-interest are keystones in *I* cultures. Individuals believe freedom and personal choice forge one's destiny or future. Rugged individualism dictates that people can become whatever they set their mind to and work hard for.[3]

Ironically, the basis of White privilege is that Anglos have an advantaged position in society just by the nature of their color and race. These social assets remain largely invisible and unconscious partially because Anglos have traditionally not identified as a culture or race. In reality, then, even in the strongly *I*-oriented Anglo society, people's destiny is shaped by outside forces such as social privilege, which gives a head start.

On the other hand, people from collectivist *We* cultures believe some things happen to them and accept that a life power and external influences affect their lives. Latinos know it is impossible to control chance, fate, natural disasters, or unplanned events. *Serendipity*, which means "good fortune, luck, or coincidences," happens to all of us, such as meeting a person "by accident." Latinos see life as an interchange between individual efforts and the experiences, gifts, surprises, and lessons it brings. I may be the captain of my own ship—but the sea of life determines much of my course.

It is important to remember that US Latinos often got the short end of social opportunity and had to make compromises simply because of their heritage, social class, or lack of English fluency (which they had limited control of). Acceptance was a survival mechanism. When people are enslaved, colonized, or marginalized, they can't always change their status. Patience and learning to make the best of your lot might be the best plan.

But doesn't that imply passivity? Isn't this exactly the feared fatalism— the dreaded anthropologist disease that sideswipes Latinos like the wet handkerchief crossing my father's brow in the tropical heat? No! When the hurricane and tidal wave wiped out Cabo Gracias a Dios, a natural disaster that no amount of individual determination could have prevented, my father moved his familia to Bonanza to earn money to bring us to a new land. He defiantly looked destino in the face and followed a new path. There is always choice on how to respond to situations. Latino optimism and the ability to celebrate life under duress are surefire testimonials to steering around life's circumstances and overcoming barriers.

In reality, destino is another reflection of the paradoxical nature of the Latino worldview. Try as one may, it is impossible to control your life, because you were born under certain circumstances, with unique gifts and temperament, into a certain family and at a specific time in history. On the other hand, you can still forge your destiny and chart your life. The great numbers of immigrants who leave their homeland searching for a better life and the scores of leaders who have rallied against social inequities are testimony to this. People must wrestle as well as dance with their destino.

*Destino is not fatalism, because it does not prescribe or determine. People can still choose how to respond to and utilize life's experiences. Latinos dance with their destino.*

## Leaders Seek and Embrace Their Destino

ESTINO IS THE REASON a person was born—the central core, or nucleus—the unique pattern and life path. It is always greater than the individual. Like an unseen current, destino ties the past, present, and future together. While it remains constant, it is not static. As a leader matures, her destino unfolds, becoming richer and more encompassing. Destino is an integrating force, fostering congruency and clarifying choices.

Destino is more than personal vision. *Vision* speaks of imagining and anticipating what will be, while the seed of your destino is already inside you, waiting to reveal itself, and awaits acceptance. Many people can work to fulfill a great vision. However, a person can never adopt another's destino because each one is personal and unique.[4] For instance, César Chávez's dream of fairness and equality was shared by multitudes. His destino, however, was to be the prophetic voice and inspiration for the farm laborers' movement and civil rights for Latinos.

In the American Indian vision quest a person goes into the wilderness to seek his life's purpose. Searching for one's destino is not so direct. Latinos are kinesthetic learners who prefer a practical, hands-on approach and love the oral tradition.[5] Many Latinos don't learn leadership by reading books but by tackling community problems and working with others. When I interviewed former Denver mayor Federico Peña, for instance, he said, "We can talk, but I have really never read a leadership book." Seeking one's destino is an activity entailing retrospection, learning from direct experience, embracing fortuitous situations, and noting when you are most effective.

There are certain markers indicating a leader is on the right path to unfolding her destino. When a leader's talents and skills are uniquely suited for the work she is doing, that means she is on target with her destino. When a leader is passionate about something—well, that's the powerful engine of destino providing energy to do the work. Here are five indicators that help leaders understand and get in tune with their destino.

- Begin with your family history and traditions (the roots of your destino).

- Tap into your heart's desire or passion (the fire and energy to follow your destino).

- Identify your special skills and talents (your destino knapsack).

- Open the door when opportunity knocks (it's your destino calling you).

- Honor your legacy and personal vision (the destino magnet that pulls you forward).

# Begin with Your Family History and Traditions

OUR EARLY LIFE IS the rich soil from which our destino evolves. Our ancestors' lives are footprints pointing us in a certain direction and beckoning us to follow. My parents' lives were dedicated to giving their eight children a better future. No sacrifice was too great. This same passion fuels my life today. I aspire to contribute to young people and to ensure they will have more opportunities—just as my parents did for me.

Examining your ancestry, parents, family history, the circumstances of your birth, early experiences, significant events, talents, and inherent gifts or positive attributes can steer the way to a deeper understanding of your destino. As an immigrant, for instance, I inherited a "can do" attitude, resourcefulness, and determination. Because I am the youngest daughter, I had more opportunities than my older brothers and sisters. Growing up in Florida, I met Hispanics from many countries. That would not have happened if my family had settled in the Southwest, which is predominantly Mexican American. These circumstances etched my destino and the work I do.

The backgrounds of the following national leaders who are pursuing their destino show the influence of family history, traditions, and expectations. Their destino was being shaped before they were born. Likewise, your own history and traditions are a source of personal power and point the way to a deeper understanding of your destino. Latino leadership is based on the tradition that everyone can serve and has special talents. Knowing your own background will assist you in determining the special attributes you bring to leadership and how you can best serve your community.

## A Tradition of Community Leadership

SAN ANTONIO'S JULIÁN CASTRO is the youngest mayor of a top 50 American city. He is the son of Rosie Castro, a '70s firebrand who was among the leaders of La Raza Unida, the political party started by Texas Chicanos in the 1960s. A single mother, Rosie raised Julián and his identical twin, Joaquín, who was elected to the US Congress in 2012, to be leaders with a community spirit.

Julián often accompanied his mother to political and community events, where he met key figures in the Latino political world, learned community organizing, and worked on political campaigns.[6] While he follows the leadership example set by his mother, the times in which he lives are shaping a different type of destino.

Today, Latinos make up 37 percent of Texas and 60 percent of San Antonio; they are on the inside of power.[7] Born in 1974, Mayor Castro is part of a new breed of Latino politicians—intellectual, self-contained, serious, and even-tempered. Much like Barack Obama, he comes out of a broader American experience and was educated at Stanford and Harvard Law School. Castro has been cited as having the potential to become the first Latino president. Yet the essence of his destino is grounded in a tradition of community leadership. "I believe in destino," he says. "I am where I belong. I am in my place. I was born in San Antonio. I grew up here and want to bring opportunity to the people here." As his destino unfolds and political future grows, he will always be rooted in the westside barrio of San Antonio.

*"I believe in destino. I am where I belong. I am in my place. I was born in San Antonio. I grew up here and want to bring opportunity to the people here."*

—Julián Castro

## The Footprints of Our Ancestors

FEDERICO PEÑA'S FAMILY SETTLED in Texas over 250 years ago. His great-great-great-grandfather was a founder of Laredo. His grandfather had a seat on the city council. One ancestor served in the first Texas legislature, another was elected mayor of Laredo, and yet another was president of the school board. Peña has built on this legacy by choosing the path of public service: "I saw my life as one of helping people who were being discriminated against and had no voice."

In 1983, he was elected Denver's first Hispanic mayor and the first mayor of a city in which Hispanics were a minority population. Peña said of his broad appeal, "The way I saw it, I was a servant. I didn't become mayor because I was great but because people voted for me. So I was there to serve them and the Denver community."

After serving as mayor he was appointed secretary of transportation in the Clinton administration. Peña now directs a private equity fund investing in companies that provide clean energy and alternative fuels. Public service is central to his life. He served as the vice chair of the 2008 and 2012 Obama for President campaign and has led efforts to reform the Denver public schools. Peña has spoken out for immigration reform and urges showing compassion and decency to undocumented workers.

## Family Roots Become Great Vision

RAUL SOLIS WAS A union steward in México. Immigrating to California, he met Juana Sequeira from Nicaragua in a citizenship class. They married in 1953 and raised seven children in the barrio of East Los Angeles, a community with 97 percent Hispanic ancestry. Raul worked at the Quemetco battery-recycling plant and organized workers to seek health benefits. Due to the hazards of the work, he contracted lead poisoning. Meanwhile, Juana was an assembly-line worker at Mattel and outspoken about labor issues.

These working-class champions rocked the cradle in which Hilda Solis and her destino was born. In 1979, she was first in her family to finish college. Hilda then ran a statewide program for disadvantaged youth to help them go to college. People urged her to run for office, which would give her a greater ability to change community conditions. In 1992, she was elected to the California Assembly and later became the first Latina in the state Senate. In 2000 she was elected a US congressional representative and served for four terms. Then in 2009 President Obama appointed her the twenty-fifth US secretary of labor. Just like her father and mother, in all her positions, she remains a staunch advocate for workers and fair labor laws.[8]

Staying true to her working-class roots, Hilda Solis lives in a modest home not far from where she grew up. A young woman encouraged to work as a secretary by her counselor in high school ended up as a secretary, all right—the US secretary of labor. *How is this possible?* Many Latinos would answer: She is following her destino. She never forgot her roots, she expanded parents' vision, and said yes to her life's work.

## Tap into Your Heart's Desire

IN THE PAST FEW years, numerous young Latinos have left lucrative corporate jobs to head up nonprofit organizations. Their common themes are finding a greater purpose, wanting to give back, and believing that this is a strategic time for Latinos to make their mark.

A native of Cuba, Carlos Orta was an executive at Anheuser-Busch and Ford Motor Company before taking the helm of the Hispanic Association for Corporate Responsibility in 2006. While in corporate America he saw too few Latinos in high-level positions and wanted to change that. Today his passion is opening corporate avenues for Latinos. A true believer in leadership development, Orta launched the Young Hispanic Corporate Achievers program, through which the brightest Latinos in corporate America stay connected to their culture and work for community advancement.

Orta could have remained on the corporate trajectory. Talk to him today and you will sense an infectious passion and a much broader purpose—ensuring that Latinos have a place at the corporate table! A new creative and challenging chapter in his destino has begun.

### Destino Is Much More than Work

ONE THING IS CERTAIN, following one's destino will ignite the fire that inspires and motivates. Tapping into one's passion requires mulling over questions such as: What do you value and what must you have in your life? What do you love to do? What inspires you? Answering these questions will assist you in identifying your passion and motivation.

As an elder who is still going strong, I am often asked how I have stayed motivated to keep working at such a fast pace for so many years. My answer is that I do not really work. I am pursuing my destino—the source of power, passion, and energy. All of us have had experiences that bring a deep inner contentment. We are doing something that just feels right, a cause we believe in. We are serving—doing a task that needs to be done and just knowing it was ours to do.

Mario Garcia, the director of Chicago's Onward Neighborhood House, has spent the last ten years growing and reenergizing the over-hundred-year-old community-based organization. Mario's work takes many hours. He has to maneuver through countless obstacles and with limited resources. However, his enthusiasm is infectious when you talk to him: "I love what I do! It's not work!" This contagious energy signifies that Mario is in sync with his destino.

Sometimes it takes courage to follow one's passion. Lisa Quiroz was working at Time Warner when she had a brilliant idea. She talked to the CEO and persuaded him to launch a news magazine, *Time for Kids*. The magazine, now widely used in schools, motivates kids to read, learn about real-world topics, and build writing skills. Quiroz, who graduated from Harvard with an MBA, had qualms about working in corporate America because she was passionate about education and thought nonprofit work was a better venue. Today, the award-winning *Time for Kids* has gone digital and spawned a generation of "kid reporters" and a host of educational aids. By being true to her passion, Quiroz found a powerful way to influence education and support reading and literacy for millions of children.[9]

Destino beckons us to consider: What would you love to do even if you weren't getting paid for it? What is in your heart of hearts? What are you passionate about? How are you applying the talents you were born with to make a contribution?

*Destino beckons us to consider: What would you love to do even if you weren't getting paid for it? What are you passionate about? How are you applying the talents you were born with to make a contribution?*

# Identifying Special Skills and Talents

T HE FASCINATING REALIZATION THAT there will never be another person just like you can be a source of great power and determination. Truly each of us is one of a kind. But tapping into our uniqueness requires an honest and thoughtful examination of our talents, gifts, and abilities. I like to call this our "destino backpack" because if destino is "the job you were sent here to do," you will have certain innate skills and talents to help you accomplish this. Yes, you must develop your talents, but first you must know what they are. Then interestingly, life circumstances will provide the perfect training ground to grow these skills.

Uprooted by the Cuban revolution, Carlos Orta had lived in Cuba and Spain by the time he was five, and then the familia settled in Miami, Florida. His father held down three jobs even though he had been a professional in Cuba. His mother worked in a factory and went to school at night. Carlos was raised by his grandmother, who taught him traditional manners. "I was raised to be a *modelo*—a model child." He was taught to be courteous and became self-contained and observant. As an only child, he was used to being with adults. Orta emerged as a poised and collected adult, with a broad perspective and the ability to talk to anyone. Today he converses with a corporate CEO or congressperson as easily as a community volunteer or a young professional. His early childhood was the perfect training ground for the work he does.

Leadership has been described as the ability to stay cool under fire— to perform under pressure and in the face of adversity. In the corporate realm, "executive temperament" signifies a similar trait alluded to in the adage "Don't sweat the small stuff." Orta's natural composure was further developed through experiences in politics and corporate America. As a child, he recalls, "I would 'see things as they could or should be' and had a fascination with building things. Although I did not become an architect, I am builder of sorts. I like growing organizations. I thrive on challenges and developing structure. I enjoy creating a comfortable space and forum for people." Orta has combined his natural abilities with education and experience to embrace a very strategic destino—to lead a coalition of the sixteen largest Latino national organizations that aim to change the way corporate America includes and supports Latinos.

 *'I would 'see things as they could or should be' and had a fascination with building things . . . I like growing organizations. I thrive on challenges and developing structure . . . and creating a comfortable space and forum for people."*

—Carlos Orta

Communicating with people and being able to get ideas across is a cherished leadership trait across the board. As a relationship-oriented culture that values the oral tradition, Latinos also value charisma that allows leaders to connect with and motivate people on an emotional level. Janet Murguía has a fiery charismatic style, which was evident at a very young age. She grew up in a family of nine, where her ability to talk to others was honed at home. Murguía improved her speaking skills when she ran for student body president in high school, became a leader in college, and then went to law school. These experiences sharpened her natural ability to speak in a powerful, passionate, and convincing manner.

A roadblock for Latinos in embracing their special gifts and talents is that they value modesty. Bragging is not a positive trait. However, acknowledging your gifts is only a practice in humility. You were born with these. They were given to you. They were "inherited," so there is no need to boast. (Only by embracing our innate talents can we consciously choose experiences to nurture and enhance these.) And people must know their gifts in order for collective and shared leadership to work. Part of the leader's job is to identify and utilize each person's special skills and talents.

## Open the Door When Opportunity Knocks

O NE SURE WAY TO clarify your destino is to look at opportunities that have been offered out of the blue. We must pay special attention to anything that surprises us or seems like a lucky break. *This is your purpose calling you and opening doors.* Greenleaf advised that when new pathways open, we practice "fresh, open choice" and take the "leap of imagination."[10] Following your destino takes surrender and a little faith in the life process.

We all have had times in our lives when opportunity knocked—a favorable prospect appeared—an offer you could not refuse. Perhaps it was a new job or promotion, a special assignment, the chance to learn a special skill you would need in the future, or "accidentally" meeting a mentor. Orta has an interesting way to look at this: "I have a saying: 'The harder I work, the luckier I get. The luckier I get, the harder I work.' Once you know where you want to go, you will see and act on the opportunities that are presented to you."

Then there are special or unique circumstances like living in another country or learning a new language. Many Latinos of my generation, for instance, grew up in neighborhoods where they were minorities, causing them to adapt at a very early age. This allowed us to be front-runners in learning how to function successfully in the dominant culture. We also changed Anglo perceptions of Latinos as not being able to speak English well or as being poorly educated.

There are also those special moments when things just seem to come together—or what might be called coincidences that converge in a meaningful way. Joe Jaworski, the founder of the American Leadership Forum, termed this *synchronicity* and thought we should pay close attention—this was life guiding us on our path. He believed if we responded to these situations, things would begin falling in place almost effortlessly because we would be allowing our life to unfold.[11]

After returning from the Peace Corps in Chile, I moved to Madison, Wisconsin, with my new husband, who was going to law school. With my papers and commendations in hand I went to the Department of Social Services to apply for a job as a social worker. In Chile I had organized production cooperatives in low-income barrios. (Today these are called microenterprises.) I was fired up! If I could do this kind of work with almost no resources, I could tackle any barrier. The interviewer seemed overwhelmed by my enthusiasm. He stopped me and said, "Look, I can see you are motivated and talented, but we only hire people with a master's in social work."

I was stunned. I was the first really literate person in my family. I had a college degree, and in my world that was *el último*. I gathered my courage, picked up my papers, and empathically put them on his desk: "You don't understand. I *was born to be a social worker*." He looked astonished and then said, "Well, if you can go down to the University of Wisconsin and get into the master's program, we will give you an educational stipend if you will come back and work for us." That was my destino opening the door and preparing me for my life's work. And it wasn't even my idea!

Murguía sees opportunity as "angels in my path along the way." Jerry Rogers, the financial director at the University of Kansas, personally helped her and her twin sister find enough money to go to college. "This angel of a man would sit down with us and made sure our financial aid package worked. He really saw our potential. There wasn't any form of student aid that he didn't help us with. We did work-study, got scholarships and student loans, and kept our grades up. Getting into law school was the same thing. We couldn't afford it. At one point my parents had five children in college. But here was the law school admissions officer who believed in me and helped me. He fought to keep me in that school."

*One sure way to clarify your destino is to look at opportunities that have been offered out of the blue ... or seem like a lucky break. This is your purpose calling you and opening doors.*

# Honor One's Legacy and Personal Vision

I N HIS BRILLIANT EXPLORATION of personal transformation, the renowned scholar Joseph Campbell identified the "hero's journey" as the search for true identity—"to become what we were meant to become—to achieve our 'vital design.'"[12] While the seeds of your destino were present at your birth, understanding your "vital design" requires reflection and integrating the pieces of your life so congruency becomes apparent. Then just as utilizing a muscle will make it stronger, so embracing your destino will make your life plan clearer and more encompassing.

For your destino to expand, continue asking, Where is my life leading me? Or as Greenleaf counseled—How can I best serve?[13] Then again, particularly for Latinos and leaders who are committed to future generations, consider, What do I want my legacy to be? This will begin shaping your choices and life's journey. Covey encouraged people to cultivate the habit of beginning with the end in mind. What are your hopes and dreams for the future? What is the contribution you want to make? Covey urged, "Honor the vision of what you will become."[14]

Murguía believes that she has been guided by the values instilled in her as a child—family, faith, community, hard work, love of country, and sacrifice. These values converge in her desire "to help open the doors of the American dream like they were for my family and for me." This is why she took the helm of the largest Latino advocacy organization in our country—the National Council of La Raza. "I think with my own career and life it has been very mission oriented. I am responding to a calling in some respects, and you know, for us, we're always trying to make sure we're fulfilling that destiny which lies ahead."

Tapping into one's destino requires soul searching and trusting that the inspiration you need will be forthcoming. Just as nature is the great conserver and recycles every leaf, so too every aspect of your life will be integrated into your unique life's purpose day by day.

The first time Arturo Vargas appeared in the *Los Angeles Times* he was ten years old and holding a picket sign. His elementary school had minimal resources and no playground, and because of overcrowding had gone to double sessions where children attended school only half a day. His immigrant parents, who had come to the United States so their children could get an education, joined a group called Padres Unidos. They began picketing the elementary school with the baby in a stroller and Arturo at their side. Padres Unidos changed these conditions, and Arturo learned at a young age the power of activism. Today, he continues fighting for the full participation of Latinos in the political process, including elective office, active citizenship, and public service. His destino surfaced at a very young age and was even documented in the *LA Times*!

 *"I think with my own career and life it has been very mission oriented. I am responding to a calling in some respects, and you know, for us, we're always trying to make sure we're fulfilling that destiny which lies ahead."*

—Janet Murguía

## *¡Ándale!*—Moving Forward

BY DEFINITION LATINO LEADERS are connected to and represent their community and people. Chapter 6 reviews key values that inspire leaders to treat every single person with respect, be generous and kind, have service at their core, and work diligently for people's advancement. Culture is the rich soil from which leadership principles that are rooted in people and community have emerged.

*Latinos are diversity.* They comprise many races from many nations and may have Jewish, Arab, or Muslim antecedents in addition to a historical Catholic tradition. Because Latinos are an ethnic group and not a race, we will learn how this presented a conundrum for the US census. Chapter 7 sets the stage for understanding the emerging Latino identity and how this shapes leadership with a *bienvenido* spirit. The emphasis on intergenerational leadership also reflects the openness and inclusiveness of the culture.

# PART III

# The Cultural Foundations of Leadership

CULTURE DEFINES REALITY. EVEN AS a baby you were swaddled in your cultural loincloth: a tight serape close to your mother's chest, a papoose carrier that kept you strong and upright, a cradle rocking by your parents' bedside, a bold colorful kanga hanging from your mother's back, or a buggy strolling through an urban neighborhood. Sounds, language tones, music, family size, food, home—all were determined by your cultural patterns. Most likely, everything you were taught and believed in was framed by a cultural lens.

Through these lenses, culture provides the focus through which groups of individuals define their world. It has been described as collective programming.[1] Culture is tradition, customs, ethos, philosophy, and a way of life, the cloth that dresses our human experience. Culture is the norms—the dos and don'ts. One of its most significant functions is teaching values—the cultural ideal of how one should live.

Values are enduring beliefs describing ways of acting or being that are preferred by a given group. Cultures organize value systems and reinforce them through symbols, myths, education, role modeling, and oral communication. As noted, *dichos* (adages) are a shorthand way to infuse norms and values.

Two strong cultural streams that integrate Latino values are a humanistic (people) orientation and a love of diversity. These dynamics fashion an accessible, inclusive culture that celebrates people's uniqueness. Most Latinos value people and community before material wealth or individual achievement. *Relationships are the heart of the culture!* Many values, therefore, emphasize the way people should relate to and treat one another. Chapter 6 explores the role that values play in framing leadership. Leaders must model and emulate these values in order to be seen as part of the community and someone people would want to follow.

Chapter 7 weaves the intriguing story of how a conglomerate of races, cultures, and nationalities was given a collective identity as Hispanics. This diversity has infused leadership with a *bienvenido* spirit that embraces an intergenerational approach. Today's youthful demographics and growing influence emphasize the need to bring young Latinos into the leadership circle.

# CHAPTER 6

# *La Cultura:* Culturally Based Leadership

L ATINOS ARE A RICH culture of synthesis and fusion. With such a colorful array of fiesta-loving, family-centered, hard-working, tamale- and salsa-eating Latinos, one might wonder, what could possibly keep this sundry group together? What are the connecting points that give a shared identity to this camaraderie?

Much like the Jewish community, Latinos are an ethnic and cultural group. Latinos are bound together by the Spanish language, a shared history, a spiritual tradition, and common values that stem from both their Spanish and their indigenous roots. Cultural values are fastening points— the nucleus—shaping a collective identity from the many ingredients of the delectable Latino *familia.* As Arturo Vargas, president of the National Association of Latino Appointed and Elected Officials, observes, "I've met Latinos all over the country, and diverse as Latinos are, there's a set of core values we hold. It's about family, and the face of their children, and the face of the future. There's a level of optimism and a sense of community."

This chapter highlights seven key values: familia, a *simpático* (easy to get along with) demeanor, generosity, respect, honesty, hard work, and service to others. The central value of faith is explored in chapter 12.

These deeply intertwined values form the substance of Latino leadership. Former Congresswoman Hilda Solis notes, "My leadership is based on my upbringing, cultural values, ethics, and what I was taught as a young child."

Values, explains Burt Nanus in *Visionary Leadership*, shape our assumptions about the future, provide the context in which issues and goals are identified, and set standards for people's behavior and actions.[1] Values also define the range of people's choices, identify what is good and desirable, and give form to a society's culture. Since Latinos are a cultural and ethnic group and not a race, common values are the fabric that holds them together.

*'I've met Latinos all over the country, and diverse as Latinos are, there's a set of core of values we hold. It's about family, and the face of their children, and the face of the future. There's a level of optimism and a sense of community."*

—Arturo Vargas

## *La Familia*—A *We* Orientation

TRADITIONALLY IN SPAIN, LARGE extended familias lived in the same community for generations and relied on each other for their daily essentials and for special needs. Likewise, in Indian cultures today, as with previous generations, the tribe takes care of its members, land is held in common, and everyone is seen as related. The Aztec civilization was organized into small family groups who governed themselves and worked together as a unit. Thus, the many roots that nourished the Latino tradition had strong family ties and community bonds that provided support and assistance.

These ancestral connections anchor a *We*, or collective, orientation. *We* cultures have been on the earth for a very long time. Tightly woven, stable, and integrated, *We* cultures center on group welfare, interdependency, and cooperation. The family, community, or tribe takes precedence; individual identity flows from the collective. People work for group success before personal gain or credit.[2] It is no wonder that Latinos cherish belonging, mutual benefit, and reciprocity.

*We* cultures revolve around people-centered values. For Latinos, these include generosity, being of service, and respecting others. To keep relationships strong (the fabric of *We* cultures), Latinos strive for unity, harmony, and smooth and pleasant social interactions. They like politeness and good manners.

The *We* orientation is evident in the familia, which is not exclusively bonded by blood or legal relationships, but broadly refers to a group with a special affinity for each other. The familia is e-l-a-s-t-i-c and expands to include *padrinos* or *madrinas* as godparents at baptisms, weddings, confirmations, and other special events. *Tíos* and *tías* are honorary aunts and uncles and close family friends. *Primos*, or cousins, include anyone who is even vaguely (and sometimes mysteriously) connected to your family. Ask who someone is that you don't know at a family reunion, and a common response is *"Es tu primo."* And this is accepted.

Then, again, while you're simply walking down the street with a close friend, another person might suddenly be introduced as a *compadre* or *comadre*, indicating that he or she is part of the family. This goes unquestioned as family connections are elaborate and expansive, reflecting the Latino *bienvenido*, or welcoming spirit, with long-term friends who are considered relatives. I just became a *tía abuela*—a "grandmother aunt" to my goddaughter's baby. I always like to add that these relationships imply responsibility, meaning you are expected to assist when a need arises, which can range from contributing to weddings and special occasions to providing emotional support during stressful times. The tradition of open and inclusive family relations is the foundation for people becoming Latino *by affinity*, which is discussed in our final chapter.

As we shall see, Latino leadership reflects this *We*, or other-centered, orientation.

## Hispanic Value: *Simpático*—Being Congenial

*¡QUE SIMPÁTICO!* IS A prized Latino compliment. It means that people think you are likable, easy to get along with, and charming. Having smooth and pleasant social relationships is of biblical importance to Latinos, who tend to acquiesce to the wishes of others in order to be seen as congenial. Being respectful and courteous, making small talk, and taking a personal interest in people are ways to be simpático—coveted traits in a people-come-first culture.

When Latinos enter a room, for instance, the polite thing for them to do is to say hello to each person, and to inquire how that person is doing, and to ask about his or her *familia*. When leaving, Latinos make the rounds again, this time expressing how good it was to see everyone and requesting "permission" to leave. ("Con permiso"—with your permission—is used to make an exit.) "Relationships take time" could be a Latino mantra. At some events every person in the room has to be recognized and thanked, which means things can go *on and on and on*. This is when the observance of LST, or Latino Standard Time (time that revolves around connecting with people and not just getting things done), tests your good manners.

In surveys Latinos respond that they tend to carry out socially desirable actions and attitudes.[3] A person who is *bien educado*, for instance, acts correctly toward others, is polite and gracious, and takes people's feelings into consideration. The literal translation of *bien educado* would be "well educated." However, for Latinos *bien educado* means a person was *raised right*! How a person treats others is more important in garnering respect than the number of university degrees, amount of money, achievements, or status symbols a person has attained.

People who are simpático are usually good at recognizing and complimenting special traits and contributions.[4] Latinos call this *echando flores*—literally, giving people flowers. Verbal flores express gratitude and celebrate a person's achievements. This tendency will be addressed in more depth in the leadership dynamic *gozar la vida*—leadership that celebrates life. The genuine affection Latinos show toward one another helped sustained them through centuries of living in a society that undervalued their contributions or misunderstood their cultural effusiveness. Acknowledging people's good qualities and accomplishments is an essential ability for Latino leaders.

*¡Que simpático! is a prized Latino compliment.... Being respectful and courteous, making small talk, and taking a personal interest in people are ways to be simpático— coveted traits in a people-come-first culture.*

## Hispanic Value: Generosity and Sharing

MY SISTER MARGARITA WAS raised in Nicaragua and was culturally more traditional (or less assimilated) than I. When I was in my thirties, she was visiting when my next-door neighbor dropped by. He casually admired a poncho hanging on the wall. "Thank you," I smiled remembering its origins. "It's handwoven, and I got it in Chile." When he left, my sister scolded me, "Have you forgotten everything you were taught? You were supposed to give him that poncho!"

This jostled my memory, and I flashed back to a fiesta I attended a few years earlier when Margarita lived in Guatemala. The hostess flung open the door and gave me a big *abrazo* (even though I had never met her and hadn't really been invited). "What beautiful gold earrings," I gasped, somewhat stunned at her generous welcoming. "Here, you must have them—they're yours," she said as she smiled, took them off, and handed me the treasured gift without a moment's hesitation.

The Latino saying *Mi casa es su casa* is the first commandment of generosity. It encapsulates the joy in sharing and implies "What I have is also yours." In collectivist cultures, possessions are more fluid and communal. People take pleasure in giving things away. Generosity, however, is not just a two-way street; it is a busy intersection where everybody meets. A good illustration is the way strangers are always made to feel welcome. One can rest assured that this kindness will come back to you. Even though a particular individual may never be able to reciprocate, someone else will surely return the kindness one day.

Latino fiestas are a testament to collective hospitality. All who attend bring gifts, flowers, food, wine, and special treats to share. Many times when I have a social gathering, it is something akin to the parable of the loaves and fishes in the New Testament. Everyone contributes, and the food keeps coming—there is more to eat and drink at the end of the fiesta than at the beginning. For weddings, graduations, and special celebrations there is the tradition of being a *madrino/a* ("sponsor") and offering to pay for the photographer, *banda* (band), cake, or bar. At Mexican weddings people pin money on the bride's dress or pay to dance with the bride or groom. What fun as one guest after another steps onto the dance floor for a short twirl that contributes to the cost of the celebration!

In traditional families, it can be embarrassing to "have more" or to advance ahead of the group. Having more means a greater responsibility to share more (which is not a burden but a task undertaken with grace and kindness). When my brother John became a successful music executive, he was the go-to person when a family member had a special need, such as money for school or for travel expenses to attend a family reunion. Cooperation, sharing resources, and helping others keep ties solid. Learning to navigate such requests is part of the leader's role.

Generosity is the glue that holds *We* cultures together. Mutuality ensures that people continuously give to each other and everyone is taken care of. Almost unanimously across collective cultures, it is understood that the accumulation of vast wealth and power by a few hinders the well-being of the community as a whole. People taking more than their share and the sharp accumulation of money by some at the expense of others rips apart the community fiber. For this reason *true wealth* is defined as being able to give to others.

Unless one has experienced contagious Latino generosity, people from individualistic cultures may find it difficult to understand or to aspire to this level of sharing. From a *We* perspective, since the self emerges from the collective, generosity toward others is actually giving to oneself.

*The Latino saying* Mi casa es su casa *is the first commandment of generosity. It encapsulates the joy in sharing and implies "What I have is also yours."*

## Latino Value: *Respeto*—Showing Respect

LATINOS BELIEVE EVERYONE SHOULD be treated with dignity and courtesy, regardless of wealth or status. The belief that every person has inherent worth resonates with their people-come-first values and was discussed in the section on *personalismo*. Prolific movie director Moctesuma Esparza, whose credits include *The Milagro Beanfield War*, recalls, "Along with respecting elders, a quality my father had that he passed to me was to treat everyone the same, that is, with respect, no matter what their station in life was, no matter whether they were a president, a rich person, a farm worker, a dishwasher, or anyone else."[5]

While everyone is respected, being looked up to depends on how a person lives, acts, and treats others. Living respectfully means cherishing family, showing gratitude, and honoring cultural traditions. Latinos show respect through their body language, tone of voice, deference, and apologies and explanations (even when not really warranted). Of course all this is interwoven with behaving courteously, offering profuse thanks, and complimenting people. Being respectful also means being open to differing opinions. Mutual respect fosters harmonious relationships, cooperation, and reciprocal support.

Respect is even more important with elders. Since Latinos value real-life learning, hands-on experience, and self-mastery, the wise elder has a wealth of knowledge to share. Latinos also show deference toward people in positions of authority, such as doctors, priests, teachers, and leaders. They respect a person's title, contributions, education, or authority.[6] Paradoxically, people in positions of power must not assume airs or act as though they are better than others, or they will lose this respect.

Plumbers, electricians, bricklayers, gardeners, and people in many trades are respected as well. Someone who is good at a craft or profession is called *maestro*, indicating he or she is eminently skilled at their craft. The beautiful work many Latinos laborers and tradespeople do is indicative of the pride they take in being maestros.

Latinos may communicate indirectly and circuitously if it will spare a person's feelings. Again this is somewhat paradoxical since honesty has such a high value, but in this case courtesy has a higher one. Ask a Latino for directions, and of course he will try to help. You are probably going to get into a conversation even if he doesn't have a clue where you are going. Taking time to be friendly and maintaining congenial relationships is the best way to ensure that Latinos will participate, be committed, and give well-thought-out honest responses. These are building blocks for people-oriented leadership.

## Hispanic Value: *Ser Honesto*—Being Honest

LATINOS HONOR THE ORAL tradition. Agreements made verbally were considered just as binding as legal documents. Traditionally, Latinos did not rely on lawyers or contracts to make agreements or do business—a word and a handshake were sufficient. This worked because people usually knew each other or had mutual acquaintances. As Carlos Orta has observed, even today, "Latinos have to get to know a person and trust them before they can do business with them. Latinos don't do business from a transactional perspective, but from a relational one."

When buying a service or making an agreement to purchase something, Latinos will routinely not ask for the money or talk upfront about how much something costs. This is a compliment that reflects trust in the person's fairness and in the unspoken but binding agreement that they will keep their word. It is also a cultural test—to determine whether this person is honest and someone to befriend. (Of course, in the end, setting a fair price becomes part of the conversation and people strive to make sure everyone feels good about the exchange.)

The phrase *hombre de palabra*—a man of his word—is like the Latino Good Housekeeping Seal. Keeping one's word is a value upheld in many cultures and is certainly an indispensable leadership trait. But in *We*-centered cultures, the threads holding relationships together would unravel if people did not keep their word. People's survival depended on each other, and keeping commitments was essential.

Honesty or being truthful has been identified as the single most important ingredient determining a leader's credibility because it engenders trust.[7] The bankers letting their greed precipitate the housing and banking crises, politicians breaking their promises, corporate executives not accurately disclosing a company's finances, all indicate that many leaders today simply do not tell the truth. Raul Yzaguirre characterizes honesty as aligning words with action: "There are a lot of inconsistencies with leaders today who articulate American values but don't live them. Latinos are living their values every day. As a culture we believe that you do what you say you are going to do."

~~~~~~~~~~~~~~~~~~~~~~~~~~~~~~~~~~~~~~

*"There are a lot of inconsistencies with leaders today who articulate American values but don't live them. Latinos are living their values every day. As a culture we believe that you do what you say you are going to do."*

—Raul Yzaguirre

## Hispanic Value: *Trabajar*—Contributing through Work

EVEN THOUGH A GROWING number of Latinos are now middle class, historically most families, like mine, were working class. Even today 70 percent remain in working-class jobs.[8] This is in part because immigrants often start at the bottom of the economic ladder.

Latinos continue doing all kinds of tedious jobs—putting on a roof in the searing summer sun, cutting lawns, digging ditches, cleaning hotel rooms, cooking, and serving food. Many times, they might be listening to a radio blasting salsa or Mexican ranchera music, having noisy conversations, ribbing each other, or even singing a Spanish tune. What is it about Latinos that enables them to take jobs that people in other cultures might find "beneath" them *and* to be happy and singing while doing these menial and sometimes physically difficult tasks?

In a collective culture, where *We* is more important than *I*, work is not just a person's livelihood; it is a way to take care of the familia. Since familia is the highest value and concern, work has meaning and dignity. A person will do what he has to do. "As long as I can feed my familia, I feel good about myself. I am honorable." Perhaps for this reason Latinos have an impeccable work ethic, which translates into the highest participation of any group in the labor market.[9] Work is not "just a job"; it is a way to contribute to others. Latinos believe in the rewards of hard work. More than eight in ten—including 80 percent of Latino youths and 86 percent of Latinos twenty-six and older—say that most people can get ahead in life if they work hard.[10]

Latinos have traditionally not been part of the elite class: they have not attained benefits, reaped rewards, or assumed privileges they did not earn. They have gotten ahead through their own efforts.

Since sharing and generosity are cultural touchstones, work is also a way to pitch in, making a person a contributor and a valued part of the group. Everyone helps the family and community thrive! At a deeper level, everyone doing their share signifies that we all have something to contribute. This reinforces the Latino sense of equality—no one is better than anyone else and everyone deserves respect. The Leader as Equal discussed in chapter 8 is founded on this belief.

*Latinos believe in the rewards of hard work. More than eight in ten ... say that most people can get ahead in life if they work hard.*

The dicho *Los que no trabajan no comen* (Those who don't work, don't eat) underscores that everyone has the responsibility to work and to give of one's efforts. Taking advantage of others by freeloading or not doing one's share runs contrary to helping others. Doing a good job is also the main way to contribute to one's employer. This connects to Latino generosity—what better way to share than to do one's work with *gusto*— to give it your best shot!

## Hispanic Value: Serving and Helping Others

THE VALUES DESCRIBED ABOVE converge into cultural directives that spell out how people should relate to and treat one another. The essence of *We* cultures is to emphasize the collective well-being—taking care of each other seals this bond.

This is evident when first meeting a Mexican American, who might say, "a sus ordenes" (at your service) when meeting or greeting a person. When a request is made, a Latino might reply, "para servirle" (I am here to serve and help you and do what you request). An even more direct response when someone asks for something is "mande." *Mande* literally means "tell me what you want me to do." The cultural translation is "I will do it if I can." And if the person is simpática, it means, "If this will make you *contento* (happy), I will try my best."

These traditional responses are deeply rooted in the Latino indigenous background and create a collective spirit where people "serve" one another. Consider that the Nahuatl language of the Indians in México had no concept for the word *I*. Their sense of relatedness and helping others was the basis of their worldview. So too, the Golden Rule of the Maya, *In Lak'ech*, signifies "You are in me and I am in you." This saying reflected their belief that human beings are one people and what one does to another affects oneself.[11]

Serving is intricately linked to generosity, group benefit, and reciprocity. People understand that what they give to others will certainly come back to them. While it is not tit for tat, and people do not expect anything in return, they know that the cultural agreement is to help one another. Cyclical reciprocity means what you give will eventually circle back to you and by sharing, everyone will have enough.

In *We* cultures relationships always imply responsibility toward others. This engenders a sense of duty about serving others and is evident in the work ethic described above. *Service* is the nucleus around which Latino leadership revolves. Anna Escobedo Cabral has seen this tendency in her extensive work with Latino leaders: "Our ultimate motivation is a concern for the people we serve."

*"Our ultimate motivation is a concern for the people we serve."*

—Anna Escobedo Cabral

## Leadership Flows from the Culture

TO RECAP THE VALUES discussed above: treating people like *familia*, being generous, having *respeto* for everyone regardless of status or position, always keeping one's word, and being of service are the pillars of Latino leadership. By being simpático, friendly, and accessible, respected leaders become part of the extended family. Keeping positive and congenial relationships is the best approach to ensure that Latinos will work hand in hand with the leader. The bond between leaders and their people has been a motivating force keeping the community together through generations of struggle and challenge.

# *¡Ándale!*—Moving Forward

I HOPE YOU HAVE ENJOYED our foray into the Latino culture, but keep in mind we are a people in evolution. As a fusion people made up of many races and cultures, and one that was included only from the 1980 census on, Latinos are still forging their collective identity. Chapter 7 begins with the designation of Hispanics as an official category in the US census. Interesting, this only added fuel to the ongoing discussion about race and ethnicity both within the Hispanic community and in the nation as well. We will learn how this designation opened the door for greater inclusiveness for both Latinos and non-Latinos.

Latino diversity is also evident in the way they embrace many generations. A Latino event or gathering will have a mélange of *niños* (children), elders, budding teenagers, and adults from every period of life. Likewise, leadership reflects an intergenerational approach. This underscores the broad spectrum of Latino demographics as the youngest group in America, a significant segment of the baby boomers, one-fifth of the Millennial generation (born between 1979 and 2000), and an emerging educated middle class.[12]

# CHAPTER 7

# *De Colores:* Inclusiveness and Diversity

ILLING OUT MY FIRST US Census form in 1970, I searched for a category that would acknowledge my culture and ancestry. I felt a loud thud in my heart as I finally checked the "Caucasian" box. As I filled out the forms, I heard my *abuela*'s sweet voice, "Ay, mi hijita, nunca olvides quien eres y de donde venistes" (Oh, my dearest little daughter, never forget who you are and where you came from). But remembering your history and embracing your identity is a difficult feat when there is no acknowledgment that your people even exist.

We all have a deep need to be accepted for who we are. This is particularly true for Latinos and other people of color, who have been relegated to a minority status and measured by a White ideal. The story of how "the Browns" (Hispanics) became a category in the US census illustrates the unique history of this cultural medley. (Of course, members of other ethnic groups such as South Asians, Pacific Islanders, Middle Easterners, and American Indians may also consider themselves Brown, but in this story *Brown* refers to Hispanics and Latinos.)

The process that changed the census categories made it much more inclusive and offered many more choices of racial and ethnic identities. To make a government and bureaucratic event more interesting, I have taken some creative liberties to spice up the story.

## Latino, Hispanic, Mexicano, Cubano, Mestizo, Puerto Riqueño—Who Are You?

ORE THAN FIFTY YEARS ago a great and articulate Black prophet named King arose from his people and led a movement to assert their rights and forge a strong and powerful identity. This was a time when America saw itself in Black and White. Brown people were trying to figure out, *Who are we?* Yet the civil rights movement planted seeds that blossomed into the many fragrances that make up America today.

From the earliest days of the Constitution, one of the ways the US government distinguished people was by race and color. Every ten years, the census counters scoured the countryside, tallying and identifying the people that made up this great land. It was after the national count in the year nineteen hundred and seventy that the census counters, pulling their hair in frustration, went scurrying to the Great White Father. They asked, "What do we do with this disparate group, 'the Browns,' who are writing down all kinds of concoctions and can't be put into a category?"

The Browns were, in fact, identifying themselves as Mexican, Cuban, and Spanish (in the Southwest many could trace their heritage back eight generations to the Spanish land grants). Others identified themselves by the place they, or even their grandparents, were born—as Puerto Rican, Colombian, Brazilian, Chilean, and Salvadoran. The list was v-e-r-r-y complicated, because the Browns had kinship with twenty-six countries, including Brazil and Portugal. "Ay caramba," lamented the census takers, "we have only four categories: Caucasian, Black, Asian, and Native American. What are we suppose to do with 'the Browns'? They are supposed to check the Caucasian box!"

The chaos intensified when many of the Browns took it upon themselves to embellish *exactly* where they came from. (Well, they were asked, weren't they?) If they were from Texas, they were *Tejanos*. Politically active Mexican descendants wrote *Chicano*. The offspring of Chicanos and Puerto Ricans noted that they were *ChicoRicos* (*chico* meaning "kid" and *rico* meaning "rich, delicious, tasty, and sweet"!) A *CubaNica* was a cross between a Cuban and Nicaraguan—and a great dancer. The red-haired lassies who were Irish and Chicano were *Leprecanas*. And, of course, those of Chinese ancestry got in the game by noting they were *ChinoLatinos*.

The census takers were quickly finding out that the Browns valued something called *personalismo*, which meant everyone was *único*, an individual with a story to tell. Some people proudly noted their entire genetic line on the census forms—French, Spanish, Indian, and Brazilian. These details, the census counter learned, were inherited from the Spanish, one of the links holding the Browns together. Spain for centuries had a history of regionalism and became a nation only through the tenuous marriage of Isabella and Ferdinand right before Columbus set sail on the *Santa María*. Even today the Spanish continue to identify themselves by their states—Basque, Valenciano, or Navarrese, for example. The Basques are still struggling for independence. Since 1841, Navarre has signed five treaties with Spain and has autonomy over most of its governance. Imagine one of the US states having this type of independence![1] This whole thing was un-American. It had to stop. Someone needed to get a handle on *Who are the Browns?*

Then census bureaucrats had a bright idea. Let's ask *them* what they want to be called. A big powwow was called in the Capitol, and leaders from the "Browns" were flown in. One was Leo Estrada of UCLA, a leading demographer.[2] The census counters thought he would know what to call these people, since he was one of them. The leaders deliberated for a very long time. The census counters began to pace. Finally, in the wee hours, a compromise was reached. The government could use the term *Hispanic*, referring to Hispania, the old Roman name for Spain. *Hispanic* was English, not a Spanish word, so the census counters were *muy contentos*!

The head of the Census Bureau hurried to the Office of the Great White Father and urged him to make this official before the Browns changed their minds. And so it came to pass that President Richard Nixon's OMB Statistical Directive 15 came into being.[3] From then on there would be five colors in the American palette. The conglomerate of people spanning five hundred years of the *mestizaje* was baptized Hispanic.

## Just Check the Box

THE DEBATE AMONG HISPANICS, however, continued, reflecting their diversity and the difficulty of finding one communion wafer everyone could swallow. Many prefer the term *Latino*, even though it can be traced to the Roman occupation of Spain many centuries ago. *Latino* is politically and culturally a more useful term because it connects people to Central and Latin America and unites them through culture, kinship, and the Romance languages. And it is a *Spanish* word. (*Latino* was not added as a designation until the 2010 census.[4])

For the census takers, the complex story of the "Naming of Hispanics in America" did not stop with the adoption of Statistical Directive 15. Since Hispanics are an ethnic group and can be Black, White, Yellow, or Red, the census takers took out their racial microscope and surmised that all their categories needed to change to really capture the essence of America's racial genetics. They now began to categorize people—White *non-Hispanic*, Black *non-Hispanic*, American Indian, Eskimo, and Aleut *non-Hispanic*, Asian and Pacific Islander *non-Hispanic*. The whole spectacle of the race-based census was becoming a circus under the multicultural tent. *Hispanic*, which was once a strange mutt that needed a name, now became the standard for all other racial delineations. The Hispanic machinations with the Census Bureau gave new meaning to the biblical phrase "The last shall be first."

Unlike African Americans, Native Americans, or Asian Americans, whose blood content defines them, Latinos are the only group that *self-identifies*. According to F. James Davis in his book, *Who Is Black? One Nation's Definition,* anyone with any known Black African ancestry is considered Black.[5] In the racist South this was the basis for the one-drop rule, which came to mean that anyone with any Black blood was considered Negro. Native Americans have blood quantism, imposed by the treaties, which means a person must have legal proof of their bloodline to be enrolled in a tribe.[6] *Asian* refers to a person having origins in any of the original peoples of the Far East, Southeast Asia, or the Indian subcontinent.[7]

On the other hand according to the US census, "An individual's responses to the race question and to the Hispanic origin question are based on self-identification."[8] It could be said then, that to identify as a Latino, you simply *check the box* on the census. Regarding this distinction Raul Yzaguirre surmises, "America needs a different paradigm of what it means to be Latino. The prototype of the Native or African Americans, where your blood content defines who you are, doesn't work. Latinos are a culture, not a race. Culture, it must be remembered, is learned and not inherited. My definition of *Latino* is anybody who wants to be a Latino, *bienvenido*—welcome to the family."

*"America needs a different paradigm of what it means to be Latino....Latinos are a culture, not a race. Culture, it must be remembered, is learned and not inherited. My definition of Latino is anybody who wants to be a Latino, bienvenido—welcome to the family."*

—Raul Yzaguirre

Latinos hold the promise of a new America with inclusiveness and diversity at its core. They invite people to look beyond race to the cultural, spiritual, and historical bonds that hold us together. Yes! For those hankering to truly experience another culture, *come on in.* The door to partake in the Latino culture is a revolving one and remains wide open! Chapter 13 invites non-Latinos to incorporate Latino values and way of life and to use this as a launching pad to experience other cultures. But, if you really want make a stand and be part of the Latino *familia*, in the next census, *just check the box!* This would start a cultural revolution and end centuries of race-based identity in the United States that commenced with the Constitution. As Yzaguirre concludes, "This concept would revolutionize America's race consciousness."

*Latinos hold the promise of a new America with inclusiveness and diversity at its core. They invite people to look beyond race to the cultural, spiritual, and historical bonds that hold us together.*

## Leading with a *Bienvenido* Spirit

MANY TIMES, SUCH AS in the history of North America, colonization or conquest did not result in a blending or fusion of cultures, particularly not on a mass scale. Perhaps the many connecting points between the Spanish and Indian cultures fostered this integration. Or possibly, the indigenous hope, as represented by Our Lady of Guadalupe, engendered faith that eventually the mestizaje would herald a better future. In spite of the historical trauma of the conquest, a positive result was that the Mestizo, or blended, culture had permeability and an ability to incorporate differences. Bienvenido, or inclusiveness, is part of the Latino DNA.

*Bienvenido* means "to receive or accept with pleasure; to approve or appreciate; and even to embrace."[9] The bienvenido spirit is evident in Latino hospitality, generosity, and receptivity to differences. The large extended family, sense of community, and inclusive leadership approaches also reflect a genuine openness. Bienvenido can be found in the acceptance and integration of immigrants into the Latino community. (More on this in chapter 9.)

Of course, the vast diversity presents an ongoing challenge: leaders must forge a common identity, vision, and purpose from a conglomerate of people who are blended together like a delicious *pico de gallo* (chopped-up salsa ingredients that retain their separate flavors). Forging a collective identity from expansive diversity has been the ongoing work of leaders. By infusing leadership with an inclusive and celebratory nature, and by reinforcing the values that hold people together, leaders build cohesiveness and identity.

Inclusiveness is reflected in many organizations that were initially begun by a specific Latino subgroup, but in step with the culture's bienvenido nature, they have extended their reach. The Mexican American Women's Association, the largest Hispanic women's organization in the United States, for example, changed its name in the 1990s to MANA—a National Latina Organization. This enabled it to reach out to Latinas from every subgroup. The Cuban American Council (CAC) began in 1972 and initially served the needs of Cuban Americans. Shortly after its founding, CAC expanded to serve all individuals in need with a focus on Hispanic Americans. Today the council sees its mission as providing human services to persons in need from all racial and ethnic groups. CAC assists individuals in becoming self-reliant and builds bridges among America's diverse communities.[10]

In assessing Latino inclusiveness it is important to remember that historically and even today more than 60 percent are of Mexican American descent. Before the 2010 census, over 50 percent of Latinos reported living in Texas and California.[11] Thus geographic boundaries and national ancestry could have splintered the Latino identity. Instead, organizations such as the National Council of La Raza (NCLR), originally founded as a civil rights organization to assist Mexican Americans, has made great strides in bringing subgroups together around a unified Hispanic agenda. In 1968, when NCLR began, there was no national voice for Latinos equivalent to that of the NAACP or the National Urban League. Today NCLR makes concerted efforts to have diverse representation on the board, staff, programs offered, and even geographically. Another inclusiveness indicator is that in 1973 the bylaws were amended to require equal representation of men and women.[12] (Chapter 10 will expand on this inclusive collaborative trait.)

*Forging a collective identity from expansive diversity has been the ongoing work of Latino leaders. By infusing leadership with an inclusive and celebratory nature, and by reinforcing the values that hold people together, leaders build cohesiveness and identity.*

## Inclusivity across Generations

LATINO INCLUSIVENESS IS EVIDENT in the way the culture embraces all ages and stages of life. The leaders in this book, for instance, span decades: Mayor Julián Castro is thirty-seven years old, while Raul Yzaguirre is seventy-three. Latinos respect the circle of life—from the promise of youth to the wisdom that comes with age.

Unlike societies where people retire, the Latino culture honors its elders, who remain in leadership roles and continue contributing. Since it was understood that it would take many generations for Latinos to advance, the mentoring and preparation of subsequent generations has been an age-old practice. Hilda Solis, the US secretary of labor, notes its importance: "We have to motivate our young people to build upon our legacies. We have to encourage them to reach out and include other people. We need to make sure there is a pathway to follow and that leadership is passed down generation to generation."

This approach is even more pertinent today because an immense generational shift is occurring. The Millennials are the largest and most diverse generation in history. Latinos are at the headwaters of this change and compose 20 percent of the Millennials.[13] Moreover, one in five school children today is Hispanic, as is one in four newborns. Never before has an ethnic group made up so large a share of the youngest Americans.[14] By force of numbers alone, young Latinos will shape the twenty-first century.

Simultaneously, because of the graying of White America, baby boomers are retiring at a rate of ten thousand per day.[15] Due to the urgency of these changes, the intergenerational practices described below have been tailored to apply to the Millennial generation. Since one of this book's purposes is to inspire young Latinos to stay connected to their culture and to learn the practice of established leaders, this section provides insights for working with younger generations.

*"We have to motivate our young people to build upon our legacies. We have to encourage them to reach out and include other people. We need to make sure there is a pathway to follow and that leadership is passed down generation to generation."*

—Hilda Solis

## Intergenerational Leadership

IN MANY TRADITIONAL CULTURES, mentoring was a way to prepare young people for leadership. This implied a hierarchy and a one-on-one approach where established, usually older, leaders handed down knowledge and bestowed influence. Mentoring was integral to succession planning so power could be retained and passed on to select groups.

In contrast, Latino mentoring implies an intergenerational approach that reflects the family structure. Leaders groom the younger generation in order to strengthen community capacity, ensure continuity, and build the critical mass needed for social change. Intergenerational leadership is sharing responsibility with people of all ages. Mayor Castro speaks to this: "People from different generations need to work together. This way we can preserve our history, keep the integrity of those who came before, and young people will understand the sacrifices made in the past. Otherwise young people may compromise and lose their culture. Only by staying connected across generations can we keep moving forward together."

The civil rights movement produced a formidable group of Latino leaders who created organizations that laid the foundation for current progress. To continue this progress, young people need to lead, starting at an early age. Arturo Vargas was a leader in high school. "I was on student council, and then student body president. I was involved in church and became president of the altar boys' club and coordinated a full guitar group. When I got to college I was ready to get involved on campus."

In 2000, recognizing the need to groom young Latinas, I invited a group of seasoned Latina leaders to talk about the need for additional reinforcements to keep up the progress we had made. We realized that our hands-on, long-term experience had made us effective leaders. Our success was due to mutual support, networking, and having been groomed by more established leaders. Quite frankly, we weren't getting any younger and were passionate about passing on the leadership legacy in our community.

Thus was born the Circle of Latina Leadership, a year-long intergenerational program for emerging leaders in their twenties and thirties that would guide the Denver Hispanic community's future. We didn't realize it, but we were paving a path for Latinas of many ages to learn and lead together. One founder was Lena Archuleta, the first Hispanic principal in the Denver Public Schools, who continued mentoring and working with Circle women until she passed away at ninety. Along with other founders she was part of the Leadership Council who acted as *madrinas* (godmothers) and shared their wisdom and experience.

The young women participants were mentored by established leaders in their forties and fifties that helped them chart their careers, connect to their culture, and contribute to the community. Participants in turn were asked to mentor junior high school girls, helping them to succeed in school and embrace their cultural roots. Each woman completed a Community Action Project in which they practiced and strengthened their skills. To date, over 165 emerging leaders have completed the program and are already becoming the next generation of leaders.

In a similar fashion, the National Hispana Leadership Institute (NHLI), which prepares Latinas for national leadership, requires graduates to mentor two young women. In 2001 NHLI also developed Learning to Lead—a training, mentoring, and networking program for college-age Latinas. NHLI programs require participants to create a community-impact project. Assisting the community and mentoring the younger generation are trademarks of Latino leadership programs.

Organizations such as the US Hispanic Leadership Institute based in Chicago focus on youth development and have structured internship programs for college students to promote grassroots community organizing and leadership.[16] Perhaps the best example of intergenerational leadership is ASPIRA, which has now trained six generations of Puerto Rican youth. The four intergenerational leadership practices that follow build on these traditions and suggest strategies to engage youth.

*"People from different generations need to work together. This way we can preserve our history, keep the integrity of those who came before, and young people will understand the sacrifices made in the past. Otherwise young people may compromise and lose their culture."*

—Julian Castro

## 1. Change mentors to allies

WE NEED A NEW concept for "mentor," one in which all ages contribute and share responsibility. This concept would reposition the one-up, one-down of traditional and hierarchical mentoring, which usually implies an older leader teaching and guiding a younger one. Perhaps when change happened more slowly and young people were not as educated, technologically savvy, or as experienced, this passing on of knowledge on a one-way street might have been appropriate.

Today, each generation has unique perspectives and skills to contribute, which requires a more *lateral and equal relationship* in which information and knowledge is exchanged. Sharing experiences, distributing work, and offering mutual respect are integral to Latino leadership. These values are embraced by the Millennial culture as well. They thrive on collaboration. (Wikipedia, Yelp, and Facebook reflect this trend.)

While fully 94 percent of Millennials have said they have great respect for the older generation,[17] they also want to be respected as equal contributors. Searching for a new word for *mentor*, I asked the 2012 class of NHLI to think of a more term suitable term, and they brilliantly suggested *aliados*—allies. An ally infers a connection—mutual help and support—with someone who watches your back and stands hand in hand with you.[18]

## 2. Cultivate circular relationships

SINCE OVER 40 PERCENT of Millennials come from communities of color and were raised in traditional *We* cultures, they value connectivity and value group welfare over individual reward. In fact, they have been termed the *We* generation.[19] Latino leaders can capitalize on these preferences by supporting circular relationships that foster participation, support, and mutual learning.

Mutual learning requires listening across generations and being open to new ways of communication and self-expression. For instance, a historical perspective that helps young people understand and integrate past experiences is a great gift that a more mature person can offer. More traditional ways of communication can bring increased depth and commitment. Younger people can transform this knowledge into innovative practices that are in sync with the needs of today. They can use their social networking and technological skills to expand and disseminate these practices.

Cooperation between generations requires older leaders to shake off a belief that they always know best or should be in charge. Young people must develop patience and learn from and respect the achievements of those who have come before them. Antonia Pantoja, who started ASPIRA to train Puerto Rican youth, had a knack for building circular relationships and encouraging young people to share responsibility: "What do you do about the future?" she asked. "I make the future. You make the future. We make the future together."

*"What do you do about the future? I make the future. You make the future. We make the future together."*

—Antonia Pantoja

### 3. Promote meaningful participation

LATINO LEADERS UNDERSTAND THAT developing youths' capacity necessitates hands-on participation, which increases skills, ownership, and commitment. For intergenerational leadership to be "real," responsibility and power have to be distributed among all ages. Young people must share in the decision-making power and be equal players. To be ongoing, this commitment should be integral to the organizational structure and culture.

NHLI is celebrating twenty-five years of operations, and today the majority of board members are alumnae. Although they have matured, they still represent the younger participants who will eventually become board members. As board members, they learn strategic leadership and shape the future of organization. Likewise, after ten years of operation, 50 percent of the Circle of Latina Leadership's 2012 board of directors was made up of alumnae. And they now compose the majority on the executive committee.

Because state laws required board members to be twenty-one, ASPIRA leaders went to the New York state legislature to get an exemption. They changed the bylaws, lowering the age to eighteen. Student representatives are full-voting board members. According to Ron Moreno Blackburn, the longtime national president, this promotes leadership development, strengthens youth empowerment, and ensures a strong youth voice in the organization. Through intergenerational leadership, ASPIRA is ensuring the progress and sustainability of the Puerto Rican community.[20]

### 4. Foster social action

SINCE THE LEADERSHIP OF a minority without substantial power or influence requires a long-term social activist approach, leaders must pass on this activist spirit to subsequent generations. Fortunately, this is in line with the beliefs of Millennials, who show a deep concern for social inequity. Nine out of ten feel a responsibility to make a difference in the world. Seventy-eight percent are willing to make significant sacrifices, such as earning less money, to address the major environmental, economic, and security challenges facing our country.[21] This is not surprising—diverse and multicultural, they are the children of the progressive boomers and stand on the legacy of civil rights.

This generation has good reason to pursue a social activist agenda. The national debt stands at $10 trillion, or $30,000 for each of them; one out of two is predicted to get cancer; the rivers, air, and land are polluted; and they will not live as long as their parents.[22] In 2009, 67 percent of college graduates had debt averaging $24,000, up 6 percent from the previous year.[23]

Millennials, and the growing Latino youth population, will become the political and social activists of this century. In these pressing times, leaders are compelled to pass on their knowledge, perspectives, and experiences on how to promote social change to the younger generation so they have the tools to address the critical issues they will face.

## *De Colores*—of Many Colors

IN THE 1960S, WHEN humble farm workers marched with César Chávez they sang "De Colores." A traditional and beloved song, thought to have been brought over from Spain in the sixteenth century, "De Colores" literally means "of many colors."[24] The song celebrates the incredible beauty of diversity—the multicolored birds, the radiant garden flowers, the luminescent rainbow. The chorus of "De Colores" says that because life by its nature appears in so many colors, so too great love also comes in a multitude of colors.

The love of diversity reflected in this song is deep within the Latino soul because Latinos are de colores. The many colors of humanity are right across the family dinner table. While the US census took over two hundred years to recognize the Latino identity, the song "De Colores" clearly defines it.[25] We are a diverse people that represent the beautiful colors of humanity.

Interestingly, in 2000 for the first time the Census Bureau gave people the option to identify as de colores by choosing more than one race. In 2010, 3 percent used this option. However, the multiracial population younger than eighteen has grown almost 50 percent since 2000, making it the fastest-growing US youth group.[26] Young people today are increasingly de colores.

This moment in history when the Latino community is coming of age is also the time when leaders must ensure that people of different races, sexual orientation, ages, nations, religions, and cultures work and live peacefully together. We have surmised that Latino destino is shaping the diverse and inclusive society. De colores offers a pathway to accomplish this—to integrate our kaleidoscope society and to embrace the gifts of all people, including every generation. For this reason, I believe "De Colores" should be the Hispanic national anthem.[27]

*While the US census took over two hundred years to recognize the Latino identity, the song "De Colores" clearly defines it. We are a diverse people that represent the beautiful colors of humanity.*

## *¡Ándale!*—Moving Forward

PART IV OFFERS FIVE principles that describe the ways Latinos lead their communities. These principles offer valuable insights and knowledge for leading from a Latino perspective and structures leadership to contain a higher sense of community, a deep social responsibility, and a strong sense of service. Leadership is a collective process that can be seen in the internal and external coalitions leaders build and in the global vision they uphold.

Leadership is renewed through celebration that replenishes people's resolve to work for long-term change. The deep well of *fe* and *esperanza* (faith and hope), described in chapter 12 sustained Latinos through their tumultuous past, continues to inspire them today, and provides esperanza for a better future.

# PART IV

# Putting Leadership into Action

OUR FIRST THREE SECTIONS LOOKED at history and culture, the unique way Latinos prepare to lead, and the inclusive and diverse aspects of their leadership. We are now ready to learn about the actions that leaders have taken to propel their communities forward. Because of these tireless efforts, Latinos are the vibrant, hopeful, and contributing community they are today. Looking at how mainstream leadership is changing is a good starting point because we will find synchronicity between this and how Latinos have traditionally led.

For generations, the centerpiece of mainstream American leadership was the individual leader. This fashioned a hierarchical form, which was very effective in an assembly-line economy where people followed orders and looked to a boss for direction. Today, our economy centers on service, technology, communications, and industries such as health care, where people skills, joint problem-solving abilities, and on-the-spot decision making are required. To address this, leadership has become collaborative and team oriented.

Latinos are in sync with this change because they are natural collaborators, having learned to work with others at an early age. As discussed, the *familia* and *comunidad* cooperate for the common welfare. Values such as reciprocity, sharing, and generosity encourage collaboration. Collectivity, in fact, has been a survival tactic.

Leadership is also changing due to the external environment. The United States is becoming a diverse nation, and in most of our major urban areas it already is! Civil rights, changing demographics, democratic values, higher educational levels, and political awareness have transformed leadership into a more inclusive and participatory form. The diverse, better educated, tech-savvy and increasingly young workforce expects to participate and even functions more autonomously.

As explored, *bienvenido* is a cherished value—diversity and inclusiveness are rooted in Latino history, culture, and leadership. Many generations have traditionally worked together and contributed to mutual advancement. Managing diversity is a Latino leader's competitive edge.

We should also consider that in our rapidly changing, supercomplex world, even the smartest and most experienced leader will simply not have all the answers. Leaders must be skilled in creating an environment that supports people in working together to generate viable solutions and achieve desired results. They must hand over the reins and shift the locus of control from *I* as the leader to *We*—the people served by the leader. Pivotal is defining the leader's role as serving and developing people. Perhaps we can say then that leadership by the few is being replaced with leadership by the many—a revered Latino leadership principle.

Latino leadership aligns with today's collaborative orientation. Latino leaders serve people, share responsibility, and build community—a rich foundation for creating inclusive and empowering environments.

Latinos know that the journey to social justice and economic equality has been a long and winding one. Leadership has entailed ardent community organizing and social action. We have advanced as a people only because of the struggle and dedication of our leaders. Latinos find examples of this right in their familias. Just as I honor the sacrifices of my mother, María, and know that all that I accomplish is due to her vision and determination, so too Latinos can look back and learn from the leadership of their *antepasados*. The National Council of La Raza's Janet Murguía follows such *consejo* (counsel). "I think my parents in their own humble ways taught me a lot of the great skills of leadership," she says. "They were honest and hardworking, sacrificed for their children, helped their community, and taught me responsibility for others. These are actually valuable cultural assets. If we embrace these, they will serve us well."

The leadership principles that follow offer young Latinos and others who desire to create a more just and inclusive world proven ways to educate, inspire, and mobilize people. Latino leadership has passed the test of time. It has a centuries-old track record for collaborative, collective, and activist leadership. *The Power of Latino Leadership* honors this tradition and lays the foundation for the evolution and expansion of this dynamic form of leadership.

# CHAPTER 8

# *Juntos*: Collective Community Stewardship

A S NOTED, THE ANCESTRAL groups that melded into the Latino culture had strong family ties, community bonds, and centered on *We*, or the collective. Leadership flows from this orientation and is based on a communal process where people work together to serve their communities. This spirit is captured in the word *juntos*, which means "union, being close, joining, being together"—and expresses the principle of collective community stewardship.

Whether *I* or *We* is central to a society contours the shape of its leadership. In an *I*, or individualistic, culture, *I* become a leader because of my initiative and competence as well as my winning personality. *I* am a can-do, take-action person. By calling attention to myself—my accomplishments and skills—people believe *I* am competent and follow me. Unanimity or group consensus *follows* the leader's decisions. The leader strives for self-mastery—as *I* become empowered, *I* can empower others. Leaders maintain status by remaining youthful, vigorous, attractive, and able. Seniority is secondary to performance.

In contrast, the status of a collectivist leader increases as he or she becomes older and acquires seniority and experience.[1] A *We* identity prompts a collective view of leadership. *We* cultures acknowledge that the community has nurtured them. In individualistic cultures, there is a belief that *I made it on my own.* Collective cultures understand that success is due to the *familia* and the community. Antonia Pantoja, who started ASPIRA, understood this: "I am interdependent. I was nurtured to be who I am and am responsible and accountable to a community of others." Pantoja urged an aspiring leader to answer this question, "Am I a leader that is going to be accountable to my people, to the community from whence I came? If you decide to be that kind of leader, then your skills, energy, and endurance are for the well-being of your community."

The heart of leadership, therefore, is sustaining, educating, and advancing the community. Anna Cabral describes this commitment: "What motivates people in our community who are doing great work and leading efforts is that they are looking out for the collective. *The collective good drives them.*"

*"What motivates people in our community who are doing great work and leading efforts is that they are looking out for the collective. The collective good drives them."*

—Anna Escobedo Cabral

# From Servant Leadership to Community Stewardship

**B**ECAUSE LATINO LEADERSHIP IS rooted in serving the community, it resonates with the work of Robert Greenleaf, who wrote *The Servant as Leader* in 1970. Greenleaf set the stage for a collaborative process in which the leader serves people. A philosophical and reflective man, he surmised that the hierarchical approach he had witnessed in his career at AT&T did not nurture people's leadership skills and, in fact, did not develop the leader's higher capacities, either.

Greenleaf began reflecting on why a person aspired to lead. Thus, he tapped into the practice of *conciencia*, where a person's intention— the *why*—is the central core from which other actions flow. In an individualistically oriented society, people are taught that personal motivation, the *why*, is generated by self-interest. Leadership brings privilege, status, position, and financial rewards. Greenleaf concluded that these types of leaders did not have a lasting influence on society or the people they led. In fact, leaders who have made the greatest contributions to humankind sought to *serve first* and then became leaders in order to expand their capacity to serve.

In looking at the leaders profiled in this book, and the thousands of community collaborators who are working to advance Latinos, we can agree with Greenleaf. Having a lasting impact means serving people, communities, and the ideals a leader seeks to further. Greenleaf called people with these intentions *servant leaders*. Carlos Orta describes this commitment: "My drive and motivation comes from a place of service and righting wrongs. I truly believe that I have been given many opportunities and have the responsibility to give back."

Greenleaf also believed that the litmus test of whether someone was a servant leader was his or her effect on people: *do they become freer, more autonomous, and more capable of serving others?* In other words, were people empowered? Greenleaf added another caveat, which was a revolutionary departure from the hierarchical leadership of previous times. What was the leader's effect on the less fortunate members of society?[2]

This connection to the social good and to people's needs repositioned leadership, bringing it back to the beliefs of indigenous people and to a model closely aligned with the Latino community. In *We* cultures, leaders function as stewards of their communities. Latinos are therefore expanding the focus and scope of servant leadership to *community stewardship*. This echoes with the NCLL survey: Latinos want community-centered and community-serving leaders.[3] *Community stewardship* involves many people, develops their capacities, and uses power for the public good.

*"My drive and motivation comes from a place of service and righting wrongs. I truly believe that I have been given many opportunities and have the responsibility to give back."*

—Carlos Orta

## The Leader as Equal

CREATING A COMMUNITY OF leaders is essential when a group's advancement depends on people power and collective resources. Social action requires a critical mass of skilled and motivated people. Ironically, one way leaders develop people is by staying a part of the group and never thinking they are above or better than others. Being humble, not taking oneself so seriously, and not getting snarled in the web of power or money ensure that leaders remain part of the community. This facilitates people's identification with the leader as "being one of us" and reflects the Latino value of *igualdad* (equality, fairness, and justice). *The leader is one among equals.*

Such leaders must roll up their sleeves, stuff envelopes, clean up, serve food, attend community functions, and pick people up for meetings. Any type of elitism or projection that one is above a certain task lessens credibility and reestablishes hierarchy. For Latinos who struggled with exclusion and discrimination, this would reinforce the psychology of oppression and their "minority" status. Standing out too far from others or calling too much attention to oneself can damage the group cohesion so central to collectivist cultures. Leaders are expected to accomplish extraordinary things but remain ordinary and humble.

In the hierarchical system a leader might take big bonuses, fancy perks, or fat salaries. The *leader as equal*, however, cannot take more than his share. When leaders become wealthy, an economic and social chasm can open up that disconnects them from people. Many leaders and politicians today are disengaged from real people because of this.

There also seems to be an unwritten agreement that leaders can make their own rules or even break the law. (The bankers responsible for the housing crisis of the late 2000s and politicians who continue to get wealthy at the public trough are examples.) If through legal measures or by nature of their position people can become rich, then this is an entitlement. A leader as equal on the other hand adheres to the same rules as everyone else. Raul Yzaguirre reflects, "You've got to be fair. You've got to say, 'These are the rules. I will abide by them.' You need to be willing to sacrifice if you want others to sacrifice."

*Personalismo*, the quality of leaders who are respected because of their character and the way they live, prescribes treating every person equally, fairly, and with respect. San Antonio Mayor Julián Castro lives by this code: "My values include family, service to others, and a deep respect for other individuals. I need to be respectful and even deferential to others." This attitude boosters people's self-esteem and elevates their belief of what they can contribute.

When the leader assumes no special status and works side by side with people, this levels the playing field, so others believe they too can become leaders. The result is authentic collaboration where people work as equals to attain mutual goals. Since everyone can contribute, leadership is rotated depending on the task or function and is much more distributed. Thus, a community of leaders emerges and the critical mass needed to purse social change is cultivated. In a truly equitable environment the *We* identity is strengthened and the spirit of mutuality flourishes. Leadership is an *inside-out* process where people feel connected—they reinforce each other's motivation and commitments.

*"My values include family, service to others, and a deep respect for other individuals. I need to be respectful and even deferential to others."*

—Julian Castro

## Leadership Is Conferred

A LATINO CAN BE a leader in a group or organization, *but not necessarily a Latino leader*. A Latino leader's authority and designation comes from the people she serves and to whom she is accountable. While there is no formal ceremony or ritual, there are standards for conferring leadership. As noted, personalismo implies that leaders are chosen because of their character—they must be the type of person people want to emulate and follow.

Second, leaders must play by the rules and be seen as one among equals. This facilitates people's *identification* with the leader. Third, the leader has to have a record of demonstrated results. Leadership does not refer to a position; instead it is a lifelong commitment. When people see this dedication, they sanction a person as a leader and trusted role model.

Fourth, people must believe that the leader is serving something greater—a cause, an issue, a higher calling—and is addressing people's needs. In other words, he is following the path of servant leadership and not seeking power for his own aggrandizement. Such was the path of Federico Peña: "I saw my life as one of helping people who were being discriminated against and had no voice."

Anna Cabal speaks to this focal point: "César Chávez was working in the fields and saw people who were being badly mistreated and needed someone to advocate for them. He rose to the occasion, and it was very difficult. He wasn't educated in leadership techniques; he learned these afterwards. But that wasn't his goal—to name himself as leader of the farm workers and assume a position of power. He was really addressing a tremendous unmet need in a specific population."

Sometimes leaders are enlisted through the pleas of their followers or drawn to leadership to address the injustices of their times. Consider Mayor Castro: "I did not want to run for office," he recalled, "but then saw the potential to make a real difference in people's lives. Now I see politics as a way to construct and create a better community. For instance, I believe we need to preserve the Latino culture. As a policymaker I can work to create mixed income neighborhoods—make it attractive so Latinos move back to the neighborhoods they grew up in." Yzaguirre tells a humorous tale of becoming president of the newly formed National Council of La Raza. Paul Mateo and another board member met with him. The other board member said, "You know, Paul is a union guy. Rumor is he has ways to help people say yes when they don't do what he asks." And then Paul said, "You *will* do this. The movement needs you and you will do this." Yzaguirre had already turned him down three times, but he said, "No, You WILL do it."

When people see a leader rising to the occasion—making the *conscious choice* Greenleaf designates as answering the call to serve—then he is designated a leader. In my work with Latino leaders for the past five decades, an overwhelming majority have kept their promise to serve. Evidence of the fruits of their labor is the vast number of community leaders they have nourished and the incredible progress Latinos have made while holding on to their values and vision for a better future.

*"I saw my life as one of helping people who were being discriminated against and had no voice."*

—Federico Peña

## Creating a Community of Leaders

J UNTOS EVOKES COOPERATION, SHARING, and teamwork. Since leaders identify with, arise from, and depend on their community for power and authority, leadership is group driven. Yzaguirre notes, "A Latino leader's effectiveness depends almost entirely on their ability to work with people and engage them in community issues." People power and combined resources are how Latinos get something done, whether it's planning a family reunion, putting together a community celebration, building an organization, or electing more Latinos to office. Latino unity and empowerment today is not dependent on a single leader or a small cadre of influentials, but on a community of leaders.

And how do these diverse leaders work together and get things done? Latinos utilize a collaborative process. As Hilda Solis describes, "Leaders have to educate our community about issues and do this in a way that is not top down, but connects people and brings them together." Then the work is distributed based on skills and abilities, interests, and resources. Collaboration promotes ownership, shared responsibility, and accountability.

Four practices anchor the collaborative process: (1) the power of *shared vision*; (2) the power of *history and cultural traditions*; (3) *compartir*, the power of participation and shared responsibility; and (4) *paso a paso*, the power of a step-by-step approach.

"*Leaders have to educate our community about issues and do this in a way that is not top down, but connects people and brings them together.*"

—Hilda Solis

## The Power of Shared Vision

GREENLEAF'S BELIEF THAT SERVANT leaders are guided by an overarching, prophetic, and transforming vision[4] resonates with destino and purpose. Collective leadership speaks to a broader vision that springs from the community, fosters involvement, and targets people's well-being. Values such as inclusiveness, cooperation, and mutuality facilitate the shared-vision process.

When the Latino Policy Forum in Chicago strove to develop "an American agenda from a Latino perspective," they brought together eleven organizations and six hundred civic leaders, religious organizations, businesses, elected officials, and community activists for a series of meetings. By listening to different points of view, communicating in an open, give-and-take fashion, and welcoming new ideas, the forum was able to weave common threads and integrate people's contributions into a collective vision and a comprehensive agenda.[5]

In San Antonio, Mayor Castro invites citizen participation. "You have to ask people what they want to accomplish. That's what gives the vision life. People also define the terms and mechanics of how things get done. And then leadership entails motivating people and supporting collaboration toward realizing that common vision."

A shared vision also links the past, present, and future. It integrates history, addresses today's compelling needs, and points to future advancement. Understanding one's roots nurtures a feeling of family and unity, and a sense of continuity and wholeness emerges. Anna Cabral observes, "Leaders in our community have a really good sense of the past and how it relates to the present. However, they know that in the end, they have to address the challenges the community is facing today and be concerned with the future. Our past guides us. It is important to know the struggles our community faced, but we cannot live in the past. The challenge is to make sure our community is evolving and creating a better future."

Grounded in people's collective experience, a shared vision articulates possibilities, opportunities, and spurs people into action. The Latino Policy Forum's vision, for instance, casts a wide net: "Advancing Latinos advances a shared future." It envisions "societal prosperity, unity, and equity in our nation and in the global community." And how will it accomplish this? By building "the power, influence, and leadership of the Latino community through collective action to transform public policies that ensure the well-being of our community and society as a whole."[6] The power of this inclusive vision galvanized a busload of people to travel to the Illinois state capitol in Springfield to successfully advocate for funding for early education—a critical issue given the large youthful Latino population.

A shared vision is the substance of juntos—a magnet fostering unity and consensus—a focal point channeling individual skills, talents, and resources. With a compelling vision, people are willing to assume higher risk, work harder, make sacrifices, and believe they will succeed! Leaders are then spokespersons communicating the vision with passion and conviction and inspiring people to get on board. They are trustees of their community's future and guardians of tomorrow's children.

## The Power of History and Cultural Traditions

TO BRING THEIR CULTURAL assets into the mainstream, Latinos must have a strong identity, be proud of their heritage, and be rooted in their history. Knowing the struggles of the past, they will understand what needs to be done to keep advancing. Julián Castro emphasizes this: "Many young Latinos don't know who César Chávez is—I feel blessed that I grew up with a mother who was an activist, who understood what it took to get to where we are. I attended Chicano rallies as a child, and I learned about the sacrifices made by previous generations."

Hispanic history is very complex. Since it is not taught in schools or integrated into American history, Latinos are at a disadvantage. Often they do not know the leaders who advanced their people or the seminal events that shaped the Latino experience. Unlike the dominant-culture leadership, which emphasizes *acting in the present*, understanding one's past is key to Latino leadership. The diverse backgrounds make this historical connection a necessary prelude to action. I begin all Latino leadership programs with a historical timeline of Latinos in the United States. While it would be impossible to describe this lengthy process, the following summaries offer a snapshot of the historical footprints of Latino subgroups:

- The first US Latino organization—the League of United Latin American Citizens—was formed in Texas in 1929 to advocate for civil rights. It was a coalition of three early organizations, thus setting the stage for coalition-centered leadership.[7]

- At this time, Mexican American children could not attend school with Anglos, and the Texas landscape was peppered with signs saying No Mexicans, No Dogs.

- In 1954 *Hernandez v. Texas* challenged the common belief that Hispanics were *not* being discriminated against, because they were considered White. The US Supreme Court ruled Hispanics were "a class apart" and could indeed suffer discrimination.[8]

- Puerto Rico became a commonwealth in 1952 after years of war, colonization, and uprisings. This special status means Puerto Ricans are US citizens. They frequently return to their beloved island reinforcing a strong cultural identity and keeping their Spanish fluency.[9]

- The influx of Cubans seeking political asylum in the 1960s shaped Miami into a bilingual international city and the heartbeat of a vibrant Cuban community. Cubans have the highest Latino educational and economic level and tend to vote more conservatively.[10]

- The unstable economies and political unrest in Latin America continue to fuel immigration and diversify the Latino familia. The 2010 census lists two new groups: Salvadoran (3.4 percent ) and Dominican (2.8 percent). Central and South Americans grew to 15 percent. Puerto Ricans were 9 percent, and Cubans 3.4 percent. Mexican Americans remained at 66 percent due to the close proximity of México and the fact that over one-third of continental United States was historically México.[11]

Promoting an understanding of Latino history is the first step in identifying commonalities and honoring differences. Leaders assist people in identifying points of cohesion such as shared values, traditions, and language. Unlike Black Americans and American Indians, whose identity is defined by blood and biological heritage, Latinos as a conglomerate culture must *choose* to embrace a common identity. (They check the box!) Leaders bring people together to share common experiences as minorities, as immigrants, and as a fusion people from many races, faces, and places. *Forging Latino identity is a critical function of leadership today, and this begins with tapping into the power of history and cultural traditions.*

## *Compartir*—The Power of Shared Responsibility and Participation

COMPARTIR MEANS "TO SHARE" and reflects a collaborative approach where people are encouraged to take responsibility. Arturo Vargas notes, "When I am asked to make a decision, I've got to check with the people who are going to do the work. For people to follow your leadership, they also need to be an integral part of it so that they're leading as well."

Compartir encompasses Latino values such as cooperation, generosity, and service. As Mayor Castro observes, "Latinos are simply more communal and more inclusive. If everyone chips in and does his or her part, things get done quicker, relationships become stronger, and we can have a good time."

Compartir also extends to sharing and distributing rewards. While many espouse collaborative leadership today, there is still great income disparity and privilege. When one succeeds in a collectivist culture, however, the good fortune is shared. Since the purpose of leadership is to benefit the community, the rewards must benefit everyone as well.

Latinos love to work and especially relish working with others. There is also the desire to *hágalo con orgullo* (do it with pride), to add a little passion and energy, to give it your best shot. This not only drives excellence but also urges people to enjoy what they are doing! For Latinos, compartir—sharing responsibility—strengthens relationships and allows everyone to contribute and have a good time. Latinos add the spice and salsa to collaborative and collective leadership. (More about this in chapter 11.)

Mayor Federico Peña's campaign slogan way back in the 1980s was "Imagine a Great City!" What a pipe dream! Denver was then a cow town with a faltering economy. But Peña got people involved. "When I was mayor, I always invited people to participate and to be part of the solution. There was a great deal of community involvement. People would say, 'Why is the mayor putting together another task force?' Well, I understood that you get things done by involving people and working as a community. Now people reflect back and say, 'By having that task force, you saved fifteen years.' When people become part of the effort, they want to support the effort, and then they are helping to shape their destiny."

During his tenure Denver passed more bond issues than any previous city in the United States and achieved great feats: it built a new airport, a convention center, and a performing arts center; drew a Major League Baseball team; expanded the library; and revitalized downtown.[12]

*"Latinos are simply more communal and more inclusive. If everyone chips in and does his or her part, things get done quicker, relationships become stronger, and we can have a good time."*

—Julian Castro

## *Paso a Paso*—The Power of a Step-by-Step Approach

LIKE SLOWLY SIMMERING A pot of green chili so the spicy ingredients meld into a flavorful dish, keeping people involved and motivated takes a great deal of patience and perseverance. In a community that grapples with historical disparities, countless needs, many interests, great diversity, and bourgeoning growth, cultivating a sustained commitment is an ongoing process. Raul Yzaguirre, who basically wrote the handbook for Latino advancement, advises: "We have to have a strategy of little victories. We can change things but in bite-size pieces. Leaders need to think big, but it is the little success that builds people's self-confidence. Having both a long-term vision and building sequential steps, paso a paso, keeps people moving and motivated. As people succeed, their vision of what is possible to accomplish becomes wider and more expansive."

Paso a paso—taking it step-by-step—recognizes that it took generations for Latinos to be where we are today. By remembering the struggles of their parents and grandparents, people find the resilience and courage to continue working for Hispanic progress. The past has made Latinos stronger, wiser, more resourceful, and determined. Hilda Solis captures this spirit. "We are persistent and continue to move along even in the hardest and worst times," she says. "We move forward and we're relentless. We don't give up."

*"We have to have a strategy of little victories.... Leaders need to think big, but it is the little success that builds people's self-confidence... paso a paso, keeps people moving and motivated. As people succeed, their vision of what is possible to accomplish becomes wider and more expansive."*
—Raul Yzaguirre

As an intact community, Latinos have a sense of destino, being part of a greater force. When Maria Antonietta Berriozábal served on San Antonio's city council from 1981 to 1991, she used the metaphor that she was in the middle of a stream of change. It began with her ancestors, flowed through the many leaders who had gone before her, and continued through the community leaders she worked with. As the stream continued to flow into the future, it would gather strength and momentum. It would be there when she was gone. "I do my part, and others do theirs. Eventually we will make the current so strong that it will sweep away the old and make things ready for a new world." The belief that they are part of a historical movement is the power of Latino leaders. It keeps leaders moving paso a paso and sustains their lifelong commitment.

Paso a paso is a strategic leadership tool that requires planning, analytical thought, careful execution, and incrementally building on progress. It reminds people that by staying on track and remaining focused, small contributions add up and collective efforts pay off. Collective community stewardship is sustainable only when people persevere step-by-step and day after day. Then they are ready to become advocates for change. Janet Murguía connects collective community stewardship with social activism: "Leadership is having a sense of responsibility but also having a shared vision for the change that you want to see in society. Then being able to actually create that change and execute ideas into action. This means building a sense of unity with people." (Chapter 10 discusses this aspect of Latino leadership.)

*"Leadership is having a sense of responsibility but also having a shared vision for the change that you want to see in society. Then being able to actually create that change and execute ideas into action. This means building a sense of unity with people."*

Janet Murguía

## *¡Ándale!*—Moving Forward

LATINO INCLUSIVENESS AND A penchant for diversity is evident in our next principle: *¡Adelante!* Global Vision and Immigrant Spirit. Historical connections across the world give the Latino culture an international flair that is being revitalized by immigration, technology, travel, communication, and globalization. Second, Latino growth has been fueled by immigration. America is a nation of immigrants whose ancestors came seeking freedom and prosperity. This same desire persists in Latino immigrants who come seeking a better life and who bring their optimism, hard work, and enduring contributions to our nation.

# CHAPTER 9

# *¡Adelante!* Global Vision and Immigrant Spirit

**M**Y FIRST MEMORY IS being in the hull of a banana boat as we rocked and swayed across El Golfo de México. My mother, four brothers, my sister, and I hunkered down in bunk beds as we left our beloved Nicaragua. Scared, excited, and hopeful, we were on the way to the land of opportunity! This immigrant dream has been the promise of America and the wellspring of its greatness. No one knows this better today than the millions of Central and South Americans who have made the long trek across deserts, oceans, rivers, and mountains to share in the bounty of this great country.

Anna Cabral remembers her grandparents' stories about their perilous crossing of the Rio Grande and then walking all the way from Texas to California with no money. They took jobs in the fields to care for the family. Julián Castro's grandmother was five when she came from México. She worked as a maid, cook, and babysitter so his mother could go to Catholic school and eventually get a college education. Hilda Solis's mother fled the turmoil of the wars in Nicaragua to work in factories in East LA. Leaving their possessions behind to escape Fidel Castro's regime, Carlos Orta's father worked three jobs to support his family.

Arturo Vargas's parents met on a bus they took to work in Chihuahua, México. They married and moved to El Paso seeking a better *vida* (life) for their children.

For these leaders, as for many other Latinos, immigration is a recent experience, molding their worldview and influencing how they approach leadership. Immigration roots run deep and strong—they shape the Hispanic psyche. Consider that until the last few years about 40 percent of all Hispanics were foreign born. Unlike US Latinos, who have been minorities and are still forging their identity, immigrants were raised in countries where their identity, language, and cultural are primary and integral.[1] Because of this, immigrants keep the Latino cultural memory alive, reinforce core values, and instill an indomitable spirit. At the same time, immigration presents daunting leadership challenges.

 *Immigrants keep the Latino cultural memory alive, reinforce core values, and instill an indomitable spirit. At the same time, immigration presents daunting leadership challenges.*

# The Immigrant Spirit

IMMIGRANTS THROUGHOUT HISTORY HAVE been willing to pay extraordinary costs and take enormous risks. Just over a century ago most immigrants arrived via a hazardous sea journey. Today's immigrants often cross the desert, not the ocean—but the risks are the same and the costs just as high. And why do they take these risks? Immigrants seek economic prosperity, education, opportunity, and freedom. They are pioneers, front-runners, dreamers, and achievers. Most of all they have a vision for a better future.

The United States is a nation of immigrants. No other country has ever absorbed so many people from so many different places and melded one country from their energy and spirit. *E pluribus unum*—to make one out of many—was the crucible of the American experiment. Immigrants gave us the values we hold most dear—initiative, hard work, tolerance, freedom, optimism, and faith. The immigrant spirit endowed us with the belief in endless possibilities and people's ingenuity.

The early waves of immigrants in colonial times came mainly from northwestern Europe—England, Ireland, Scotland, Germany, France, the Netherlands, Scandinavia, and Poland. They had a common heritage of being White Anglo-Saxon Protestants.[2] Immigrants today look more like my family, and yet my parents made the same sacrifices and pursued the same dream that brought the early pioneers and colonists. Latino immigrants today follow a great American legacy and are breathing new life into our economy, culture, and democracy.

*The United States is a nation of immigrants ... Immigrants gave us the values we hold most dear—initiative, hard work, tolerance, freedom, optimism, and faith.*

## The "New" Hispanic Immigrant

THE YOUNG HISPANIC CORPORATE Achievers is a dynamite well-educated, community-minded group that is bringing Latino assets to corporate America. I have worked with the group since its inception six years ago and see an interesting shift occurring. Although 63 percent of the US Hispanic population is of Mexican descent,[3] the majority of the most recent class in the Corporate Achievers program was born in Central and South America. The thirty participants came from Bolivia, Chile, Colombia, Cuba, Ecuador, Honduras, México, Puerto Rico, and Venezuela. About 70 percent of South American Hispanics in the United States are foreign born.[4]

There are myriad reasons why a steady stream of educated young Latinos is leaving their countries of origin to seek opportunities in the United States. Immigration from South America has increased significantly due to the introduction of new technologies, education, and economic development, many sponsored by the United States. This began in the 1960s, when John F. Kennedy launched the Alliance for Progress with the aspiration of creating a strong, highly educated, and technically skilled middle-class sector that would help modernize oligarchic societies, stabilize economies, and spur democracy.[5]

But unfortunately, there were limited professional opportunities in South and Central American countries for the growing educated class. A brain drain started in the 1970s and continues today. Educated Cubans, Chileans, and Venezuelans have also left their homelands due to political repression.[6] These immigrants are known as the new economic exiles and are arriving at a time when organizations and businesses are eager to tap the assets of educated, bilingual, and globally oriented Latinos. This wave of educated South and Central American immigrants is enhancing the global identity of US Latinos and engendering a stronger, more diverse leadership cadre.

At the same time, working-class and rural immigrants from Latin America continue to make up the majority of the newly arrived. Measured in raw numbers, the modern Latin American–dominated immigration wave is by far the largest in US history. Nearly forty million immigrants have come to the United States since 1965. About half are from Central and South America.[7] When asked why they came to this country, 55 percent say for economic reasons, while 24 percent for family reasons.[8] While Central and South American immigration has greatly diminished due to the United States' adverse political climate, the US Latino community continues to embody the optimistic and enduring immigrant spirit.

## Why Don't Latinos Assimilate like Other Groups?

WHEN WHITE IMMIGRANTS LANDED on Ellis Island, they were urged to shed their cultural skin, change their names, lose their language, and merge into the melting pot. The message was "Assimilate—don't look back!" Because they had common racial, cultural, and religious roots, they were able to do this. Most disconnected from their countries of origin and lost their language and culture. Perhaps, this was a small price to pay to partake in the American dream and may have been necessary when our young country was forging its identity.

As noted previously, because of exclusion, discrimination, and racism, Latinos historically did not assimilate. They *acculturated*. (The assimilation-acculturation process will be reviewed in more depth in part V.) Latinos kept their communities intact and remained connected to their culture, language, and countries of origin. When Latin American immigrants arrive, therefore, they have a cultural oasis waiting. They can be part of the US Latino culture whose inclusive values say *bienvenido*. Furthermore, the newly immigrated are a critical mass—numbering almost twenty million. Thus, because of their sheer numbers Hispanic immigrants are able keep their identity and acculturate.[9]

The Spanish conquistadores imprinted not only our country but also Latin America, resulting in strong cultural affinities that other US immigrants did not have. The proximity of Hispanic homelands and the relative ease of modern communication and travel have also reduced the need to assimilate. Our growing realization of the benefits of cultural diversity may encourage modern immigrants to keep their ethnic identity when this was previously seen as a handicap. Finally, the Latinos' demographic growth and rising influence offer many advantages to immigrants who wish to become bicultural rather than assimilate.

## Immigrants Are Building Our Future

BEFORE EXPLORING HOW IMMIGRATION impacts Latino leadership, let's look at the critical role Latin American and other immigrants play in the viability of the United States.

A recent study by the Small Business Administration found that immigrants are 30 percent more likely than native-born Americans to start a business. Mexican immigrants constitute the largest share of these. New businesses create jobs and boost our economy. The economist Robert W. Fairlie, author of the study, notes: "Anyone who invests the time and effort to move to a second country obviously has an entrepreneurial spirit."[10] The Hispanic belief in the efficacy of hard work also plays a role.

Three in four Hispanics say most people can get ahead if they work hard. By contrast, just 58 percent of the general public says the same.[11]

Most critical is that immigration is projected to be the key driver of population growth in the coming half century. New immigrants and their descendants will account for 82 percent of this growth, so that by 2050 nearly *one in five Americans will be foreign born.*[12] But is this cause for alarm? Will this dilute the United States' distinctive characteristics? Will it lose its economic prominence?

Quite the contrary. Demographers are predicting that without immigration, the declining US birthrate and the graying of the White population will result in a dearth of workers and a faltering economy. In 2005, there were fifty-nine elderly people and children for every hundred Americans of working age. The dependency ratio—the number of elderly people and children relative to the number of people of working age— will rise sharply, mainly because the elderly population will grow more rapidly than the working-age population. In 2050, assuming current trends continue, the ratio will rise to seventy-two dependents for every hundred Americans of working age.[13] Japan, Eastern Europe, Italy, and the former Soviet republics are already grappling with the depopulation of their countries.

Immigration and the growing number of Latinos will sustain the US economy, take care of the elderly, and educate our youth. Consider that between 2000 and 2050 new immigrants and their children will account for 83 percent of the growth in the working-age population.[14] Latinos will triple in number and will account for 60 percent of the population growth from 2005 to 2050.[15] Janet Murgía, who heads the National Council of La Raza, connects this to our economic future: "The growing Latino population ensures the steady supply of future workers and taxpayers needed to maintain the social contract between generations."

As far as preserving our distinct characteristics, we have already seen that in our global and diverse world, the old patterns of ethnocentricity and cultural conformity are antiquated responses. Instead, leaders need to know how to effectively deal with people from many cultures and many parts of the world. Immigrants can be prototypes for this cultural adaptation, because to succeed they must become bicultural, learn the "American way of life," and fit into mainstream society. They bring new perspectives, a global mindset, and cultural gifts that can enrich our society and prepare us to navigate successfully in our global village.

*"The growing Latino population ensures the steady supply of future workers and taxpayers needed to maintain the social contract between generations."*

—Janet Murguía

## Global Leadership Begins at Home!

ONE WAY WHITE PRIVILEGE and ethnocentricity surface is when Anglo intellectuals talk about leadership as if it includes everyone when really they are mostly talking about the dominant-culture White, male, Eurocentric leadership. Thus the knowledge and contributions of other communities and cultures are not validated or utilized.

I say this because the 2011 book *What Is Global Leadership? 10 Key Behaviors That Define Great Global Leaders*, by Ernest Gundling and others, puts forth the intercultural capacities that leaders will need to be effective across the world. However, the outstanding abilities and experiences that people of color in the United States, particularly Hispanics, already have in this arena are not even mentioned. Yet most of the ten capacities proposed are integral to Latino leadership today. We will look at five key behaviors as a way to understand what Latinos can contribute as global leaders.

Let's start with cultural self-awareness, which the book notes is the *first step* in being able to discern differences among people. Cultural self-awareness is defined as the realization that our leadership practices are shaped by the environment around us, and that there are different and perhaps equally or even more viable ways of getting things done. A person's leadership orientation is a product of a particular cultural context, but to have a global mindset, leaders must place their experiences in perspective. Leaders must adapt to new environments.[16]

For people of color, cultural self-awareness has been a survival tactic—to succeed they have had to adjust to, and function in, mainstream society. Latinos developed cultural awareness when they walked into their elementary school and the teacher, other children, the language, and learning methodology were foreign. And if they or their parents had immigrated to the United States as did Orta, Vargas, Murguía, Solis, Pantoja, and my family—cultural awareness and adaptation were an integral part of their lives. For Latinos cultural self-awareness and adaptation are called *crossing over* and imply that a person is able to go back and forth from one culture to another, to straddle two worlds. She is at home in her own culture *and* has the ability to succeed in the Anglo-European one. Latino leaders must master this capability.

Moreover, Latino families and history reflect a multitude of races and nationalities. As we have noted, Latinos are the offspring of cultural synthesis and come from twenty-six countries. Thus Latinos, so culturally self-aware and adept, are familiar with the second capacity noted in the book—the ability to discern *cultures within cultures.* The authors describe this as being able to take a flexible approach to leadership that accommodates the behaviors of people from the same country who identify with a different cultural spectrum.[17]

Cultures within cultures is described *as internal diversity.* Vargas, whose parents were from Chihuahua, México, recalls growing up in south Los Angeles in a mixed white and black neighborhood that was becoming more Mexican. Later it became a migration point for Salvadorans who were war refugees. By the time he was eighteen, Vargas attended Stanford University and was adept at maneuvering within cultures—internally in the diverse Latino community and externally in the dominant culture. Today, as president of the National Association of Latino Elected and Appointed Officials, he uses these skills to bring the complex Latinos subgroups together and to build coalitions with other groups to work on political empowerment and citizen participation. (The next chapter describes the requirements of coalition building as including not just understanding cultures within cultures, but also being able to discern differences, build on commonalities, and then focus people on concerted action.)

One intercultural capacity noted in *What Is Global Leadership?* has already been defined as a Latino cultural and leadership commandment—*relationships first*. The authors note that in foreign environments leaders must rely on strong, trusting relationships more than they would in more familiar territory. Putting relationships before tasks is a "practice that is considered common sense in many parts of the world." The leader must be willing to join in and become part of the group.[18] To be authentic, the authors note, this needs to be done at a personal level and away from work. Latino leadership practices such as personalismo, developing *confianza*, and being *simpático* all resonate with this global competency. Putting relationships first and staying a part of the group—the leader as equal—are mainstays of Latino leadership.

The authors continue by describing global leadership as the ability to *frame-shift*—to modify perspectives and leadership methods to better fit different circumstances and people. Leaders must be able to understand indirect communication; be comfortable with emotionally expressive styles; develop personal loyalty and interdependency; change the pace of work or *slow down*; and deal with great complexity.[19] These abilities are all integral to all *We* cultures. Frame-shifting could be defined as learning to cross over from an *I*, or individualistic, orientation to a *We*, or collective, one.

Another competency of successful global leaders is having a multilevel, open approach to developing others. Global leaders are committed to rapid empowerment and to cultivating leaders at all levels, especially the young and emerging. This ability was noted in the discussion about collective community stewardship in chapter 8: Latinos are growing a nation of leaders at every level and have a strong commitment to developing the next generation.

Finally, personal example (or, for Latinos, *personalismo*) is described by the authors as the most effective way for leaders to inspire people from different countries. The authors note that the many challenges of global leadership require leaders to rely on others to assist them, especially as cultural guides. Perhaps we should do a little frame-shifting here. We do not need to cross national boundaries to find cultural guides or to learn global leadership skills—Latino leaders can serve as prototypes, as they are already utilizing the majority of intercultural capacities described in *What Is Global Leadership?* In fact, we might say that Latinos have a global advantage.

Another source, the book *Leadership Is Global,* contains essays from twenty-five writers from across the world. The editors contend that because of complexity of thought and cultural diversity, a unified framework for global leadership is not readily attainable. In perusing the deep thought of the many contributors, however, one can see that they ascertained "a powerful common essence."

The authors believe that global leaders bridge cultures, disciplines, and sectors and advocate a worldview that focuses on the "whole." Second, leaders explore the relationships between the global and the local and then seek pragmatic yet inspired solutions, leaving behind ideological dogma. Third, global leaders choose collective intelligence and collaborative action over individualism. And finally, they acknowledge the integrity of heart and mind, body and soul.[20]

*Leadership Is Global* has an expansive view but explores global leadership competencies from an external (other countries) frame of reference. This excludes the practical homegrown experiences and global connections that Latinos and other communities of color have in the world. American Indians, for instance, are related to indigenous people across the planet. A review of the proposed competencies of global leadership shows that Latinos bring these capacities to their work every day. They use them to form partnerships with the many immigrants, nationalities, and expanding diversity that make up the global Latino community in the United States and across national boundaries. As Julián Castro surmises, "My vision is that Latinos can be America's greatest asset to compete in a global context."

*"My vision is that Latinos can be America's greatest asset to compete in a global context."*

—Julián Castro

# The Latino Global Advantage

EVEN THOUGH MY FAMILY emigrated when I was a child, I still consider myself a Nicaraguan with Mexican antecedents (as well as a Latina and an American). The Latino propensity to refer to a country of origin is similar to that of American Indians, whose identity is based on tribal affinity. Indians introduce themselves by their tribe: "I am a Cherokee" or "Apache" or "Lakota."

A recent study by the Pew Research Center found that 51 percent of US Latinos identify with their family's country of origin, using such terms as *Mexican, Cuban,* or *Dominican*.[21] This trend is continuing with Latinos between sixteen and twenty-five. When asked about the terms they have ever used to describe themselves, 94 percent say they have used their family's country of origin, 87 percent say *Hispanic* or *Latino*, and 67 percent say *American*.[22] Acculturation allows Latinos to have multiple identities and to value each one. These identities function as bridges or crossroads that allow a person to bring forth the best from each culture. In our global village this is a great asset—particularly with our neighbors in the Southern Hemisphere.

We noted that the history of the United States with Central and South America has been laden with colonization and occupation. In 1916, for instance, the Dominican Republic was occupied by the United States when President Theodore Roosevelt (as part of Manifest Destiny) sought to protect the construction of the Panama Canal. A more recent invasion of the Dominican Republic occurred in 1965 in response to political instability and a military coup. President Lyndon Johnson feared "another Cuba" and the proliferation of communism in the hemisphere.[23]

Fortunately times have changed. President Barack Obama has called for a "new era of partnership," lauding Latin America's economic growth and increased democracy. US Latinos—with their cultural, historic, and linguistic ties—are playing a greater role in building these alliances. In 2009 Raul Yzaguirre became the ambassador to the Dominican Republic. His approach echoes the partnership model he promoted among US Latinos. Yzaguirre crafted a shared vision for the embassy: "Whatever the history, there can be no question that as we move forward today we are united in our vision . . . working together for the continued development of a democratic, equitable, and prosperous Dominican Republic."[24]

After her appointment as US treasurer, Anna Cabral became the unit chief for Strategic Communications in the External Relations Division of the Inter-American Development Bank. Established in 1959, the bank is composed of forty-eight member countries who have a majority ownership. It is the largest source of development financing for Latin America and the Caribbean. Programs aim to assist the most vulnerable and support such areas as health, agriculture, education, and infrastructure like roads and electricity. Cabral is using the skills and talents she acquired on the home front to connect with and support Latinos internationally.

Secretary Hilda Solis, who travels globally representing the United States on labor issues, immigration, bilateral agreements, and human trafficking, believes Latinos have an advantage in the international arena. She has signed workers' rights agreements with ten countries. "There is a tremendous asset having parents born in other countries. People show me more acceptance, respect, and courtesy. I can enter into conversations much more easily because of my Spanish. There's even a sense of pride. They say, 'The president actually has someone who understands us, who is one of us, whose family comes from our roots.' We share that commonality even in the way I look, and that gives me more entrées to work on issues."

*"There is a tremendous asset having parents born in other countries. People show me more acceptance, respect, and courtesy. I can enter into conversations much more easily because of my Spanish … and that gives me more entrées to work on issues."*

—Hilda Solis

## Cultural Revitalization: The Young Latino Immigrants

WE HAVE NOTED THE many reasons why Latino immigrants are acculturating and enhancing the global perspective of US Latinos. Predictions are that this trend will continue well into this century. Consider that in 1995, nearly half of all Latinos aged sixteen to twenty-five were immigrants. By 2009, this number was 33 percent; another 37 percent were born in the United States to immigrant parents. New immigrants and their descendants will account for 74 percent of the projected Latino growth in the United States until 2050.[25]

According to the 2009 Pew Hispanic Center Report *Between Two Worlds: How Young Latinos Come of Age in America,* even second-generation Latinos (41 percent) identify themselves first by the country where their parents were born. Immigration is birthing a Hispanic revival: consider that young Latinos are more likely than older Latinos to say their parents raised them with a more Hispanic focus than an American one. More say their parents have often spoken of their pride in their family's country of origin. Sixty percent report their parents encouraged them to speak Spanish and not just English.[26] (Young children will learn English and become acculturated because of schools and other dominant culture institutions. Preserving the Latino culture and identity must be nourished at home and by Latino organizations.)

Young Hispanics are growing up in family settings that place a strong emphasis on their Latin American roots and nurture their intercultural identity. The global mindset that young Latinos are forming will strengthen connections with people from many countries. Solis notes this important role: "As more Latinos become educated and are able to serve in leadership positions, the more we're going to be able to start dealing on a much broader, global level around the Western Hemisphere, Europe, and other places where we have similarities—whether it's España, or the Portuguese, or Alemania [Germany]—because Latinos have a little speck of everybody, don't we?" (German influence is evident in countries such as Argentina, Brazil, Chile, and México.)

*"As more Latinos become educated and are able to serve in leadership positions, the more we're going to be able to start dealing on a much broader, global level around the Western Hemisphere, Europe, and other places where we have similarities."*

—Hilda Solis

## Immigration: Connecting to Latino Advocacy

IT WOULD BE EASY for US Latinos to walk away from the immigration debate and to stop advocating for compassionate and fair ways to deal with people who have crossed the border. After all, 60 percent of Americans were in favor of Arizona's Support Our Law Enforcement and Safe Neighborhoods Act, which allowed police to "stop and verify the immigration status of anyone they suspect of being an illegal immigrant."[27] Furthermore, leaders are already addressing the litany of issues that face other underrepresented groups: the lack of education, inadequate housing, economic disparity, and political exclusion.

It is also more challenging to unify the community because interests and perceptions can be so different between US Latinos and newly arrived immigrants. US Latinos have suffered discrimination and been deemed "minorities," while Central and South Americans grew up with their identity intact and know their history. Many times immigrants don't understand the economic, social, and psychological struggle of US Latinos. On the other hand, US-born Latinos may feel that Central and South Americans are benefiting from their centuries of struggle. Leaders have to do a great deal of mending and weaving to foster understanding between these two groups.

Yet Murguía believes immigration is a pressing issue that Latinos won't abandon. "Nearly half of our affiliates [a total of 150 community-based organizations] are working every day to support and integrate immigrants fully into American society. The National Council of La Raza, its partners, and affiliates teach new immigrants English and have helped more than 1.5 million people apply for citizenship."

Latinos were part of the civil rights movement and fought to be treated fairly and equitably. In the contentious immigration climate, civil liberties have been denied. Murguía comments, "Every day, parents are being torn from their children and families are ripped apart, leaving those behind emotionally scarred and often financially destitute. Swept up with this aggressive focus on deportation are thousands of US citizens and legal residents that have been forced to prove they have a right to be here, simply because they are Latino." According the Federal Bureau of Investigation, crimes against Latinos increased 11 percent in 2010, and over 66 percent of victims of ethnically motivated crimes were targeted because of anti-Hispanic bias.[28] The activist nature of Latino leadership mandates that this situation be addressed.

Advocating for just immigration policies reflects the Latino values of community, inclusiveness, and social justice. Immigrants are part of the *familia* (both literally and metaphorically) and Latinos assume responsibility for their "relatives." In fact, immigration reform was a major driver of Latino voters' political choice in the 2012 presidential election.[29] Arturo Vargas believes, "We see each other as extended family. I see older Latinos as if they are my parents who were immigrants. I want to give them the same respect I give my mother and father." Immigration has actually become a unifying factor for Latinos. Leaders recognize that immigration is one of the pressing civil rights issues of our times.

*"We see each other as extended family. I see older Latinos as if they are my parents who were immigrants. I want to give them the same respect I give my mother and father"*

—Arturo Varas

## *¡Ándale!*—Moving Forward

OUR NEXT PRINCIPLE, *Sí Se Puede*: Social Activism and Coalition Leadership, explores how immigration and other critical issues converge into a social and political action agenda. A strategic way this has been accomplished is through coalition building. According to Solis, the first Latina to serve in the California Senate, Latinos are adept at working with different groups and networks around a concerted goal. "I learned early on that bringing people together meant more strength. When I wanted to pass the first environmental legislation in California, I had to involve Blacks, Latinos, labor, women's organizations, and environmental groups and help them understand why this was beneficial to them. I learned from my father that a good organizer reaches out, persists, and serves people's needs."

~~~

# CHAPTER 10

# *Sí Se Puede*: Social Activism and Coalition Leadership*

**B**RINGING PEOPLE TOGETHER, REINFORCING a strong sense of culture and community, and articulating a vision that inspires people are the preludes to the real work of Latino leaders—*concerted and collective community action*. As "minorities," Latinos have experienced discrimination and exclusion. Pressing needs drive a form of leadership that challenges the status quo and aims to change the social and economic conditions that perpetuate inequality. This necessitates a coalition and activist leadership form that cultivates a critical mass of people with the capacity to take action.

Leaders become activists because of the economic discrepancies and inequities that exist in their own families and communities. When Arturo Vargas joined his parents in picketing his overcrowded barrio school, which had only half-day classes, this affected his life's work. "Leadership, for me, is about clarity of purpose and courage. I think we need to be very clear that the purpose of leadership is for the progress and improvement of the collective and the community. Courage, because true leadership needs to be bold, to sometimes make unpopular

* In the 1980's, Dolores Huerta coined the phrase *Sí Se Puede*, which is now a cherished Latino call to action.

decisions, and to battle infrastructure and institutions that keep our communities from progressing."

*"Leadership, for me, is about clarity of purpose and courage. I think we need to be very clear that the purpose of leadership is for the progress and improvement of the collective and the community."*

—Arturo Vargas

Hilda Solis learned advocacy from her father, a union steward. "My father took a leadership role—he was a fighter. There were three hundred workers, most of whom were Mexican immigrants who really couldn't speak a word of English. He helped to organize and mobilize them and won some great concessions. He did not get there by sitting in the back of the room quietly. He was outspoken. He knew he could make a change and a difference, and he did it."

Raul Yzaguirre became determined to organize Latinos because he grew up in the poor areas of the Rio Grande Valley in south Texas. He remembers those signs that said No Mexicans, No Dogs in restaurant windows. His grandmother talked about the "race wars" in which the Texas Rangers systemically beat up and killed Mexican Americans. His grandfather was almost lynched for being on the streets after dark.

Janet Murguía recounts how her father showed his children how to be "strong, hard-working and to stand up for ourselves. . . . My dad was a very tough man, and he wouldn't let people push him around. He worked very hard at a steel plant for thirty-seven years. In those days he was denied access to the bathroom where most of the workers went because he was Mexican. I remember my dad facing down some of those guys. They never stopped him from going to the bathroom again."

# Advocating for *We*

T HE SHAPING OF LEADERSHIP as social activism was a natural evolution for collective cultures, in which protecting and sustaining the *We* is the heart of a leader's responsibility. This emphasis is one of the sharp distinctions from mainstream American leadership, where there is a strong focus on developing the individual, managing organizations, and running businesses. Addressing the public welfare, social institutions, or community involvement is not integral to this approach. In fact, public service usually pertains only to government, public office, or the nonprofit sector.

In contrast, *sí se puede* is a roll-up-your-sleeves kind of leadership— good old-fashioned *community organizing, coalition-building, and advocacy.* Yzaguirre reflects on this challenge: "Oppressed people have been taught they can't get things done. 'It's impossible and going to end in failure.' They have to be convinced they will succeed and *can* do it! So the first step—the ultimate, all-important step—is to *build their faith in themselves.*"

Murguía, who was groomed by Yzaguirre to take the helm of the National Council of La Raza, is a master at motivating people and reinforcing the *We* identity, "For too long we have counted on others to be our champions. *We* need to be our own champions. *We* need to empower ourselves. *We* are a community of fifty million people. . . . *We* need to start acting like it. If *we* organize, if *we* engage, if *we* mobilize, if *we* vote, *we* won't need to hope our issues get addressed. *We* will *guarantee* it."

*"We are a community of fifty million people. . . . We need to start acting like it. If we organize, if we engage, if we mobilize, if we vote, we won't need to hope our issues get addressed. We will guarantee it."*

—Janet Murguía

Antonia Pantoja, an early pioneer with Puerto Rican immigrants in New York City, reflected on this form of leadership in her autobiography, *Memoir of a Visionary*. "I had to find a way to become an agent of change working in partnership with the community," she wrote. "I learned that we could work collectively to find solutions to our own problems."[1] Leaders as advocates require determination, commitment, and utter reliability. This is contained in the Latino concept of *consistencia*—fierce determination. Consistencia is the promise that a leader will never give up or abandon the community or people. "I had to find a way to become an agent of change working in partnership with the community," she wrote. "I learned that we could work collectively to find solutions to our own problems."

*'I had to find a way to become an agent of change working in partnership with the community. I learned that we could work collectively to find solutions to our own problems'*

—Antonia Pantoja

## *Consistencia*

WHILE PERSONALISMO AND CONCIENCIA are the *inner* preparation for leadership, the goal is *external and action-oriented*. Leaders must demonstrate through their behavior essential traits such as consistency, follow-through, and honesty. *Consistencia is the public dimension of the character issue.* Consistencia is perseverance and commitment—regardless of obstacles or personal sacrifices, the leader will do whatever it takes to deliver. A leader's reputation as being reliable, dependable, and accountable is anchored in consistencia.

In their groundbreaking book, *The Leadership Challenge*, James M. Kouzes and Barry Z. Posner surveyed thousands of business and government executives to determine the characteristics people looked for in a leader. The survey, which has been conducted since 1987, remains constant over time. It is not surprising that the most valued trait chosen by 89 percent of respondents is honesty—being truthful and reliable and aligning words with action. According to the survey, honesty engenders trust so that people believe in and, therefore, follow a leader.[2] Honesty and keeping one's word fosters the coveted trait of credibility, establishes a track record, and reflects the leader's *consistencia*.

Since leadership is not a position or a passing stage, *consistencia* reflects lifelong relationships. Trusted Latino leaders are regarded as part of the family. Relationships are permanent. This bond assures people that they can count on their leaders. Endurance is validated by the many elders who continue playing a prominent role. Bernie Valdez kept fighting for Hispanic progress until he passed on at eighty-five. His *consistencia* was reflected in over sixty years of activism. The absolute assurance that he would be there for the long haul encouraged people to follow him—from street demonstrations to the boardrooms of high-level organizations. Likewise, Dr. Pantoja continued leading into her eighties.

At its heart, *consistencia* is a commitment to keep the values you were raised with and to always remember where you came from. For leaders who work to keep the culture alive, *consistencia* means nourishing people's identity, pride, and connections to the past. They weave an intergenerational force where leadership lessons are passed from one generation to the other.

*Consistencia is the public dimension of the character issue. Consistencia is perseverance and commitment— regardless of obstacles or personal sacrifices, the leader will do whatever it takes to deliver.*

## Consistencia Is Collective Action

TENACITY USUALLY CONNOTES RESOLVE of an individual leader.[3] Because they lead from a collective perspective, Latinos instill *consistencia* into the community and their organizations. Long-term commitment is sustained by having a strategy for sequential success and building a community of leaders, as discussed in the previous chapter. By practicing *paso a paso*, leaders divide the work into small pieces, strategically choosing issues where successful is probable. Then people will say, "Well, if I can do this, I can do twice as much and then be four times as good."

Consistencia engenders loyalty to the leader, but by working side by side and experiencing success, people also develop confidence in each other. Consistencia has fostered long-term incremental progress, continuity, and stability in the community and in Latino organizations.

Luz Sarmina is barely five feet tall—but don't let her size fool you: she is small but mighty. As president and CEO of Valle del Sol for over sixteen years, she grew the organization into one of the largest nonprofits in Arizona. Her ability to build partnerships across communities and sectors was essential, as was transforming the agency's vision to serve individuals from diverse backgrounds. Today, Valle del Sol's mission is helping people achieve a better life while emphasizing culturally sensitive services.

As a strategic leader, Luz understood that long-term security for the organization meant acquiring a large facility in which to provide its behavioral health and human services. But how would she secure those kinds of funds in an economically tight era? Working with community partners, she positioned the organization as a needed resource and built political alliances to support its work. Then when Phoenix passed its 2006 Citizen Bond to invest in our community, she was at the forefront—$4 million was allocated to help Valle del Sol acquire a three-story service center. Relentless consistencia, cultivating a community of supporters, and having the political clout from years of hard work paid off for her organization.

Consistencia follows the dicho wisdom *Con gotas se llena el valde* (the barrel fills up drop by drop). This illustrates that every small contribution, every little victory, every success, adds up. Then one day the barrel will be full. *Con gotas* refers to a collective process where people work patiently one day at a time. If they try to do too much or get spread too thin, they might fail. The barrel represents the container, the community reserve, where everyone's contributions and collective endeavors add up. Through consistencia and a collaborative community process Latinos will continue to advance.

## Leadership by the Many

JAMES MCGREGOR BURNS IN his 1978 Pulitzer Prize winning book, *Leadership*, believed we are living in a time of "postheroic leadership."[4] The "great man" theory of leadership was finally over! This resonates with Latinos who are striving to build a community of leaders. But more than that, Latinos have a different model—*leadership by the many*.

While some people might lament that there is not one leader—a Martin Luther King Jr. or a César Chávez—others believe that an individual, one-person leadership model is not effective for such a diverse and growing community. Activist leadership requires the *fuerza*, or strength, of many hands and many voices. As Arturo Vargas observes, "We're not going to have this one charismatic leader who's going to bring everybody together. It's thousands of leaders. It's thousands of movements in thousands of communities across the country, whether it's the immigrants who are organizing at a local level or the head of a nonprofit organization that is mobilizing his community or the young politician that gets elected to office. It's a different kind of leadership."

*"We're not going to have this one charismatic leader who's going to bring everybody together. It's thousands of leaders. It's thousands of movements in thousands of communities across the country."*

—Arturo Vargas

Vargas continues, "The challenge for Latinos is not to find a single spokesperson to unite the many disparate communities and causes found among a people fifty million strong. The challenge is to coordinate these efforts, to build on successes, and to support communities that are most in need—and it can be done! Such was the case in 2006 when the national Latino community rose up to support immigrants, particularly in Arizona." Estimates are that the first May 1, 2006, protests against immigration laws brought over two million people to the streets and occurred simultaneously in cities across the United States.[5] These marches have continued every May 1 and have helped establish immigration as a key Latino political issue.[6]

Leadership scholar and activist John Gardner believed that our highly volatile times require "a whole army of leaders." He predicted a very different model of leadership. "I can't emphasize strongly enough that we are at a historical moment. The next America is going to be forged at the grass roots. It is going to emerge from the communities of our great nation."[7]

Sylvia Puente, who heads up Chicago's Latino Policy Forum, understands the power of "an army of leaders," declaring, "Our strength lies in our numbers, in our collaborative work with hundreds and hundreds of community members. Every day we're working to train community members—more than five hundred this year—in parent education, fair housing, and to understand the complexities of immigration reform. Then they become community leaders in these areas."

Murguía predicts, "I think that we are going to see a rising tide of Latino leaders in the next generation that is not only going to serve our community, but serve our country as well." Vargas concurs. "If people are waiting for the great Brown hope, give it up. It ain't gonna happen!" he says. "Instead we have thousands and thousands of leaders working collectively everyday throughout our communities. That's the new model of Latino of leadership." Latino leadership is *of*, *by*, and *for* the many.

## An Inclusive Latino Agenda

EVEN THE DOCUMENT'S TITLE, *An American Agenda from a Latino Perspective*, speaks to the inclusive vision of the Latino Policy Forum: "Parallel to a political agenda our society must articulate a moral agenda to fulfill its obligations to the public good and to transcend the racial and ethnic tensions that prevent us from taking responsibility for one another and our collective future."

Likewise, San Antonio Mayor Julián Castro connects Latino progress with American progress. "I believe if we recommit ourselves to doing the hard work that it takes to mobilize our communities, if we work at that harder than ever, then we can ensure that this twenty-first century is a time of prominence, global superiority, excellence, and economic prosperity for our entire nation."

In the chapter on *"De Colores,"* we used the phrase *leading with a bienvenido spirit* to capture Latino inclusiveness. Vargas is adamant that this is the correct course: "I have heard people talk about how we are now the largest minority group, so let's start pushing our weight around. I'm like, 'No, no, no!' We need to express and *develop a new style of leadership that is much more inclusive.* We need to be prepared to provide leadership not just for Latinos but for everybody—that is the new frontier."

"We need to express and develop a new style of leadership that is much more inclusive. We need to be prepared to provide leadership not just for Latinos but for everybody— that is the new frontier."

—Arturo Vargas

By crafting inclusive agendas that speak to the welfare of all Americans, leaders ensure that people from other groups understand how their interests and those of Latinos intersect. Vargas speaks to this: "We are the future workers of America, and we are not going to succeed if we're not educating our children today. We need to convince people to begin investing in this generation, to understand that the Hispanic dropout rate is not a Hispanic problem; it's an *American* crisis."

Leadership with a bienvenido spirit is evident in the way Latinos reach out to other groups and build coalitions. This was a trademark of Solis's terms as a congresswoman: "I learned to engage with people in other communities and include them in helping me address issues and develop policies. Leaders have to build networks, to always be inclusive, to show people that good things can come out of working together, that there is more strength in numbers."

Solis established a track record in coalition building: "I was able to get legislation passed because I had previous experience working with many different people on issues. They knew me and trusted me. I brought people together that had never really talked to each other before—Latinos, women, African Americans, labor, environmentalists. As a leader I knew we had to break down barriers and find the common ground."

*"Leaders have to build networks, to always be inclusive, to show people that good things can come out of working together, that there is more strength in numbers."*

—Hilda Solis

## Building Partnerships and Coalitions

Latino leaders reach out and cultivate the critical mass to propel social change by building coalitions *internally* with Latino subgroups and *externally* with other groups. Coalitions increase the power of collective action by bringing people and organizations together to impact specific issues or causes. Let's look at how internal and external coalition building complement each other to build the Latino community's capacity.

The National Council of La Raza (NCLR) is the largest civil rights and advocacy organization in the country, representing a coalition of over three hundred community-based organizations from every Latino subgroup. These organizations have joined forces in order to have a national impact on issues such as education, jobs, employment, health, and homeownership. NCLR is a political watchdog and strong advocacy arm that speaks for Latinos on Capitol Hill and in the mainstream media. It has organized action alerts to mobilize people to push for humane immigration policies, educational equity, and equal opportunity for Hispanics. Murguía, who has led NCLR since 2005, aims to grow Latino political strength through advocacy and voter mobilization and use this to change public policy.

While NCLR mobilizes people at the grassroots level, working with community-based organizations, the Hispanic Association on Corporate Responsibility (HACR) brings national organizations together with a very specific focus. Realizing that one organization trying to influence corporate America would be a voice crying in the wilderness, a group of leaders, including Yzaguirre, started HACR in 1986. HACR builds internal coalitions within the Hispanic community and external partnerships with corporate America. As a coalition of sixteen large and influential national Latino organizations, HACR represents such diverse constituencies as Hispanic businesses, youth-serving organizations, veterans, publishers, women's leadership, and Hispanic-serving colleges and universities.

HACR's mission is to advance Hispanics' inclusion in corporate America at a level commensurate with their economic contributions in four areas: the board level, employment, philanthropic practices, and procurement. Over twenty-five years later, HACR has established partnerships with forty of the largest corporations and has made a strong business case for Hispanic inclusion.[8]

Building external coalitions requires leaders to assume the role of cultural brokers who can identify resources and organizational supporters. Brokers are able to maneuver in multiple cultures and articulate the benefits of forming partnerships and coalitions with Latinos. Partnerships indicate relationships with mutual benefits. Carlos Orta, who has served as HACR'S president since 2006, previously worked for three Fortune 500 companies. He is an adept cultural broker, helping businesses to understand the need to tap into the growing workforce, the lucrative market, and the talents of Latinos. At the same time, he assists corporations who want to strengthen their social responsibility efforts.

Over twenty-five years ago, when I was designing the National Hispana Leadership Institute (NHLI) curriculum, I knew Latinas needed to learn the best aspects of mainstream leadership. After surveying programs across the country, I forged partnerships with the Center for Creative Leadership (CCL) and the John F. Kennedy School of Public Policy at Harvard University.

These partnerships continue today. Harvard has substantially expanded the number of Latinas obtaining master's degrees in public administration. A more diverse student body adds richness and enhances learning. CCL has had almost six hundred Latinas attend programs; this has diversified their classes and connected the organization with a new and growing market. More than ten thousand corporate executives have interacted with these high-level Latinas during these classes, thus learning in a more inclusive and culturally dynamic environment. NHLI women expanded their knowledge of how to work and build partnerships with corporate leaders.

## The Latino Agenda

WHILE LATINOS OWE A great debt to African Americans and the civil rights movement, there are indications that the Black community has not remained as united or focused on its own activist agenda. Eugene Robinson's influential book, *Disintegration: The Splintering of Black America*, proposes that Black America has separated into four groups: the mainstream middle class; the large abandoned poor; a small, wealthy transcendent elite; and the emergent, who are mixed race and recent immigrants. "These four groups," he writes, "are increasingly distinct, separated by demography, geography, and psychology." Robinson laments that there is no longer a common Black agenda—these groups come together only when there is a threat or boldface discrimination. And yet he believes that "solidarity has been one of black Americans' most powerful weapons in the struggle for freedom, justice, and opportunity" and urges a return to a united Black social and political agenda.[9]

The growing gap between the rich and the poor, the concentration of wealth in the 1 percent, the need for investment in education and health care, the housing and banking crises—all indicate that economic and social disparity is not being actively addressed by many established Anglo leaders, who are still the majority and the most influential. In the last century the women's movement had an agenda to structure a society that supported equality, health, education, childcare, and family issues. This momentum has certainly dimmed as individual women assumed leadership roles and did not keep the activist agenda of the early feminists.[10]

The Latino social-change agenda, on the other hand, is gaining momentum. It has been fueled by immigration, growing numbers, and a stronger Latino identity. In the national exit poll in the 2012 presidential election, for instance, 77 percent of Hispanic voters said unauthorized immigrants working in the U.S should be offered a chance to apply for legal status.[11]

Latino organizations are maturing (many were founded in the 1980s) and now have the capacity to promote a broader social agenda. Murguía notes that strong coalitions increase organizational clout: "Our numbers alone don't equate strength or power unless we leverage them. Those numbers will just be numbers unless we take actions to empower our communities. That's the strength in NCLR and other organizations that they take specific action and grow our voice as a community."

The emerging leaders and the youthful promise of the Latino population are infusing the community with new energy and drive. But all of these dynamics would not converge into a social agenda if they did not rest on a foundation of activism—a dedication to change social and economic conditions that limit people's potential.

Antonia Pantoja described this approach: "The role of the leader is the role of advocate. The purpose of leadership is to exercise one's power, knowledge, and access to change the oppressive and destructive situations in society." This commitment to advocacy is based on the humanistic Latino worldview, which has people's welfare at its heart. Solis makes this connection: "There were a lot of kids who were brighter than me. I know they could have been great leaders, but they just didn't have the right opportunity or didn't meet the right person who could have helped them. But I believe there has to be justice. There has to be equal opportunity, fairness, and protection under our laws."

## Keeping Activism Alive— Thoughts for Young Latinos

THOSE OF US WHO remember the Chicano movement, the Brown Berets, and La Raza Unida Party are becoming relics, like an old pair of Mexican huaraches (sandals) from the 1960s whose soles were made of tire treads. Today, young activists might be wearing a suit and have a law degree from Harvard, like Julián Castro, or may have worked as successful executives in corporate America, like Carlos Orta. They might be leading powerful national organizations like Janet Murguía and Arturo Vargas.

Young Latinos are heeding the call to the activist tradition—to work for an equal and just society. In 2006, 25 percent said that they had participated in a protest, more than twice the proportion of any other racial or ethnic group. Since 2000, Latino youth have showed a steady increase in voter turnout. Latino youths (aged eighteen to twenty-four) have increased their voter turnout by 13 percent.[12] And as noted in our section on intergenerational leadership, the Millennials—of which Latinos make up 20 percent—believe in social responsibility. Nine out of ten Millennials feel it is their responsibility to make a difference in the world.[13]

Young Latinos recognize today's opportunities are due to the tireless efforts of the past. They also know that Latinos are still dealing with gross inequities. The Hispanic dropout rate hovers at 50 percent. Only 12 percent of Latinos complete college, while 30.5 percent of non-Latinos do. Homeownership lags 22 percent behind the general population. Unemployment looms at 12 percent.[14]

Young leaders of tomorrow, I hope this book helps you to understand the leadership practices that have advanced our community and to stay connected to your culture. Murguía urges you to hold the course: "I have every confidence that with hard work and perseverance, we will succeed. We are America. And it's time. Our voice will be heard."

## *¡Ándale!*—Moving Forward

OUR NEXT CHAPTER ANSWERS the questions: How have Latinos stayed the course? Why are Latinos on the forefront of leading a social-change agenda? Why is it that despite the tribulations of being minorities and immigrants, and on the short end of economic equity, Latinos are still the most optimistic people in America?[15]

# CHAPTER 11

# *Gozar la Vida*: Leadership That Celebrates Life!

I TELL FRIENDS THAT I sometimes get on my knees and just thank God I was born Latina because it is so exciting and so much fun. Latinos introduced the word *fiesta* into our society! In a "we love people" culture where resources have been scarce, it's easy to gather folks together; everyone brings something (we have to eat anyway); the music starts playing and . . . *¡Orale!* Everyone is having a good time!

My working-class family didn't have money for vacations, eating out, or entertainment. My parents didn't have hobbies or leisure time. Their good times centered on their children, outings to parks, church events, and family celebrations. Like many other Latino mothers, however, my mom had a knack for making everyday things fun.

Although my mother worked five days a week in the school lunchroom and Sundays at the church nursery, on Saturday, her day off, she would organize a "housecleaning party." With salsa music blaring, my brothers, my sister, and I would find ourselves washing walls, sweeping the sidewalk, vacuuming, and making everything spick-and-span. Housework was a family affair. My sister Margarita called us the "busy beaver club." My mother loved *música*, dancing, and singing. She was a fantastic cook who could s-t-r-e-t-c-h a single chicken to feed a whole tribe. She stayed positive and happy during hard times because her deep-rooted philosophy of *gozar la vida*—to enjoy life—was grounded in her spiritual beliefs.

My mother taught me a valuable leadership lesson, which I found again in Rich Castro, a civil rights activist who began his political career as fiery campus radical and at twenty-five was elected to the Colorado state legislature. During the 1970s, when Hispanic political power was just budding, he became one of Colorado's most significant leaders.[1] Today an elementary school and a city building bear his name. A bust of him sits in the state capitol, and the University of Denver awards the Richard T. Castro Fellowship each year. Yet he was only forty-five when he died of an aneurism. How could he touch so many people in such a short time?

Yes, Rich served ten years in the legislature, was a key ally of Denver Mayor Federico Peña, ran a city agency, and contributed to the emergence of countless organizations, but that still doesn't explain the special place he held in people's hearts. Rich was intelligent and always willing to help people, and he lived for his community. He also had a hilarious sense of humor, *corazón* (heart), and *pasión*. He truly loved people and made the hard work of civil rights exciting and fun. The *personalismo* that encourages self-expression was certainly evident in the life of Rich Castro.

Rich often dressed up in a dark suit with sunglasses and a black fedora hat. He and his coworker Michael Simmons, who headed up Denver's Youth Commission, would entertain *gente* with rocking renditions of songs by the Blues Brothers. Rich also talked a group of high-level leaders into forming the Latino Temptations to sing hits like "Get Ready" and "My Girl." When I asked Rich why he did this, he said, "People have to have a good time if you want them to keep doing the hard work. And they must be able to laugh at you, to see you are not taking yourself too seriously. This way they know you are one of them."

Today when I teach leadership, one of my adages is "Nobody wants to follow an uptight leader or one who stresses people out!" Making work fun is a key dynamic of Latino leadership and one that was first taught to me by my mother and was truly lived by my friend Rich Castro.

*"People have to have a good time if you want them to keep doing the hard work. And they must be able to laugh at you, to see you are not taking yourself too seriously. This way they know you are one of them."*

—Richard Castro

## A Cultural Tradition

THE CULTURAL TRADITION OF gozar la vida can be found in the oh-so-good-for-you salsa, the spicy, hot condiment giving food flavor and bringing zing to the palate. Since each batch of salsa is different, it is a good metaphor for Latino diversity. And yes, salsa is also a dance. But remember, salsa is also a way of life—the spice, the energy, vitality, and *gusto*! Salsa is a communal celebration to be shared with *familia* and *amigos*. One bowl with everyone dipping their chips puts a little gusto into life. Salsa reflects the culture's festive nature so beautifully contained in gozar la vida—to enjoy life, relationships, work, and community.

Life can be difficult and, like a roller coaster, it has ups and downs. For minorities who have struggled economically and have not always been validated for their contributions—life can be even more trying! For immigrants separated from their families, for migrant workers, or for children starting school not knowing English, life can be difficult indeed. The feeling of not belonging can be disorienting and defeating. Latinos have faced all of these obstacles, but they are still dancing, singing, celebrating, enjoying their families, and having more fiestas than any other group in America.

The *banda is* blaring, people are conversing at full throttle, waving their hands and making expressive gestures. Everyone is talking at the same time. The noise level is decimals above a nice Anglo cocktail party where people are chatting. Latinos are loud! Bright colors, spicy food, and having fun are mainstays. Latinos commemorate many occasions by entertaining family and friends. Supporting this tendency are consumer studies: Latinos spend more money on food, entertainment, restaurant meals, and music than other market segments.[2] Gozar la vida fashions a celebratory leadership process.

Gozar la vida reaches back to the indigenous people of the Americas, who had many community celebrations and festivals that honored the changes in seasons, rites of passage, and people's special feats and accomplishments. Community celebrations strengthen bonds, bolster collective identity, and create communal memories.

Similarly, the highly sociable Spanish are devoted to their *días de fiestas*—a one-week community celebration where everyone eats, drinks, and dances together. Main streets close as people promenade dressed in red and white, which adds to their sense of camaraderie. Días de fiestas are a community vacation. Everyone is off at the same time and public funds are set aside to pay for bands, parades, fireworks, and entertainment. Bread, sausages, wine, sardines, and coffee are free on special days. Since each town has its días de fiestas, some of the folks attending come from other places. *No importa*—if you are there, you are welcome to share in the food and festivities. (Another antecedent of Latino inclusiveness and *bienvenido*.)

Like their indigenous and Spanish ancestors, Latinos will find any excuse for a fiesta: hosting visitors; celebrating births, baptisms, birthdays, anniversaries, Holy Communion days, or *quinceañeras* (when a girl reaches fifteen); or getting a new job, moving to a new place, getting a promotion, or retiring. Although Anglos celebrate similar life events, the Latinos' large extended family, which is more like a tribe, makes fiestas into community celebrations. For hundreds of years, it was the propensity to gozar la vida that shaped the optimistic, hopeful, and festive nature of the culture and its leaders.

## Leadership as Celebración

IN CELIA CRUZ'S LAST recording, the venerated salsa diva sang, "Ay, no hay que llorar, porque la vida es un carnival." No need to cry, because life is a carnival. *La vida* can be difficult, but it is still an amazing, interesting, and festive journey. Just imagine how this good counsel uplifts people when they are having a crisis, don't have enough money, or are dealing with social inequities.

In a *cultura* that regenerates through fiestas and celebrations, gozar la vida flavors the leadership process to be congenial, to include good times and laughter. Before and after any gathering or meeting, a social window must be open to allow people to connect and communicate. Like good cooks, Latinos are stirring the gusto into leadership. Leaders make tasks exciting, meaningful, and a chance to work with friends and make new ones. Commemorating group achievements and individual contributions, recognizing anniversaries and birthdays are ways to celebrate people. A hard and fast rule is to celebrate small and large wins, *and always serve food.*

*In a* cultura *that regenerates through fiestas and celebrations, gozar la vida flavors the leadership process to be congenial, to include good times and laughter.*

Remember the old business adage, "You don't need to like someone to work for him"? Well, my answer has always been, "Yeah, but wouldn't it be a lot better to like or even love and admire him?" Great Latino leaders care about their people, and in turn, they are loved by their communities. Dora Valdez was once asked about her husband's close relationships with people. "It was very simple," she sighed, "Bernie loved his people. And his people loved him."

The love of socializing, dancing, and sharing food is even evident in many national Latino conferences, which are always headlined by several popular singers or music groups. Lunches might feature a jazz *conjunto* or mariachi group. Conferences close with a big fiesta. Many Latinos dances are with partners so people get up close and personal even at business events. Yes! People dance with their leaders. Intergenerational aspects are also evident, since young and old dance together. Conferences still have information, learning opportunities, and workshops, but just as important (and maybe more) are venues for sharing good times, seeing friends, and strengthening relationships.

## Communicating with *Carisma* and *Cariño*

INDIGENOUS PEOPLE PASS ON values and history through storytelling. The Spanish are loquacious and expressive. Rooted in both cultures, Latinos cherish the oral tradition. Integral to gozar la vida is the ability to *charlar* (converse)—as a way to express feelings, share appreciation, and get close to people. Latinos are a talk, talk, talking group that loves chatting about ideas, interests, dreams, plans, possibilities, and people. Being able to converse is part of being *simpático*, a great leadership asset. Communication is quintessential in a community that centers on getting things done through people. Leaders assume many communication roles: as translators, storytellers, community scholars, dream makers, consensus builders, and the voice of the people. Let's take a look how leaders leverage their ability to converse in a heartwarming, inspiring, and convincing manner.

Being able to charlar—make small talk and friendly conversation—is the prelude to any leadership action! A leader must understand the Latino experience, culture, and speak the people's language and not use fancy or technical terms. A leader can't swagger, brag, or act important. (That would go against the grain of being humble and modest—a valued trait.) Raul Yzaguirre says, "When I speak to Latinos, if I say a *dicho*, it resonates. Or if I speak a few words in Spanish, and it's genuine and relevant, it establishes a bond. People know I understand where they come from because of my background. I have lived with many of the same issues they have, so I can connect and use this as a springboard. I know the levers that attract Latinos and can get a response from them." Connecting with people in this manner can be a highly effective tool not just for Latinos but for other leaders across a wide spectrum.

*Being able to converse is part of being simpático, a great leadership asset. Communication is quintessential in a community that centers on getting things done through people.*

On a collective level, since the community is still in the identity-formation stage, leaders must traverse the diversity of Latinos, communicating with recent immigrants, grassroots people, youth, and elders, as well as educated professionals, and speaking to their common elements. They must be able to talk with diverse Latino groups, help them identify commonalities, find consensus, and agree on collective action.

Leaders are storytellers who share the lessons about the courageous deeds that have kept Latinos moving forward and who integrate history into the present. Thus young people connect to their roots and take pride in their community's accomplishments. Building on the successes of yesterday, leaders help people believe in the possibilities of tomorrow. Latino leaders are thus *dream makers*, sharing a vision of what could be and pointing the way for collective advancement. culture.

Leaders function as community voices speaking in a strategic, convincing, and culturally appealing manner. They are *translators*, ensuring that the interests and concerns of the Latino community are represented in mainstream culture and that partnerships are built with mainstream groups. Finally, they serve as "community scholars," reaching out and bringing information and knowledge to people in a way they can understand and utilize.

As discussed, leadership has a community organizing and social-change orientation. Because of limited resources, leaders can't compensate people with money, special perks, or pork-barrel rewards. Community leaders must find other ways to inspire and unify people. Two revered ways they do this is through *carisma* and *cariño* (charisma and affection).

## Con Carisma

LATINOS VALUE EMOTION, SELF-EXPRESSION, and spontaneity. They admire charismatic leaders who speak with passion and conviction. Carisma is the ability to convey ideas with influence and persuasion so people are moved to action and overcome doubts and difficulties. "Carisma," reflects Carlos Orta, "is the ability to use your charm, your wits, and personality to get people to do what you need them to do. Charismatic leaders are positive and likable."

*"Carisma is the ability to use your charm, your wits, and personality to get people to do what you need them to do. Charismatic leaders are positive and likable."*

—Carlos Orta

Yzaguirre frames carisma as inspired leadership: "When people are asked to take something on, there is no concrete reward. They have to be motivated, not ordered around. It just won't happen without inspired leadership: being able to encourage folks to take on perhaps an impossible task, against what might seem like insurmountable odds, is the ultimate leadership task."

The fiery and powerful Janet Murguía has a special knack for stirring a crowd. She often starts in the oral tradition with the story of her parents: "They were two people with very few means, from a small town in México, who worked very hard, sacrificed much, and dedicated themselves to the education of their family and service to their community." Then she speaks to the obstacles they overcame. "In Kansas City in the fifties, when my parents went to the movie theater, they had to sit in a separate section. My father, other Latinos, and persons of color had to use a separate bathroom at the steel plant where he worked." She has touched people's *corazones*.

Since carisma can move a crowd to action, people must be assured that the leader is motivated by service to her community and their well-being. By developing *conciencia* and preparing themselves, leaders temper this special talent and ensure their carisma is not serving their own agenda. Speaking to young Latinos at their college commencement, Murguía reminds them of their responsibility to serve others: "The American dream is now officially within your reach. As you go forward on your life's journey, my hope is that you will help to open the door to that American dream a little wider so that others can see that their own dreams are also possible."

## Con Cariño

BY EXPRESSING AFFECTION, OR cariño, leaders establish personal relationships. Latinos surveyed by National Community of Latino Leadership indicated they wanted loving and kind leaders who could be considered part of the family.[3] Cariño is the emotional current connecting people with their leader. In a world where many feel isolated and alienated, expressing cariño is a special contribution Latinos make. Leaders demonstrate how truly caring for people and seeing them as *familia* holds people together during difficult times and makes the journey more enjoyable.

*Cariño is the emotional current connecting people with their leader. In a world where many feel isolated and alienated, expressing cariño is a special contribution Latinos make.*

As a contact culture, Latinos are comfortable with physical closeness, touching, and self-expression. Leaders are expected to relate in this manner and have close interactions. Many Latinos, for instance, don't shake hands; they give each other *abrazos*—warm hugs. Leaders routinely hug and kiss people and give them warm abrazos. Traditionally, Latinos kissed each other on both cheeks when greeting each other!

The warmth and affection Bernie Valdez showed toward people aligns with the concepts put forth by the Spanish Association on Personalismo, which emphasize the dimensions of feelings and affection. The association promotes the belief that the heart rather than the intellect is the key element in human relationships.[4] They stress the relevance of love. Love? Now there is a concept that would transform communities and leadership theory! A congenial, charming, charismatic leader that is *muy simpático* and makes followers feel loved is the Latino ideal!

## Expressing Feeling— Living with *Corazón* and *Pasión*

A GREAT WAY TO EXPRESS cariño is sharing *sentimientos*, or feelings. Emotions and feelings are the joy of life—a way to show love to family and friends. Feelings join people together. The prominence of feelings and passion is one of the distinctions between the Latino culture and the Anglo-Saxon one. Sentimientos influence the way Latino leaders relate to their people and actually reflect a different philosophy of life.

Suppressing one's feelings would stifle the flair, gusto, and passion that bring color, vibrancy, and amiability to the culture. Since feelings and emotions are so cherished, I distinctly remember sitting in my college philosophy class when suddenly my mind shattered like falling glass as we studied René Descartes—one of the fathers of modern philosophy (European, that is).[5] I instinctively knew that his renowned quote, "I think, therefore I am," was not on point! But how does a nineteen-year-old immigrant from the back hills of Nicaragua validate her belief that *I feel, therefore I am*, when she is up against seventeenth-century rationalism?

Many years later, I went to España. On the very first *noche* (night) at a fiesta, I was approached by a dashing Spaniard. After the customary niceties I asked, "What do you think is the main distinction between US culture and the Spanish?" "Yo siento, ergo soy," he replied, as if he had been waiting all his life for someone to ask this question. The shattered glass became a mirror in which I could see myself clearly. *I feel, therefore I am.*

Descartes saw the mind and body as separate. As an integral culture, Latinos tend not to compartmentalize but rather to embrace mind, body, and heart (feelings) as well as spirit as glorious aspects of life. Sentimientos are charged energy and light life's fire—the source of *ganas*, or desire!

Feelings spring from the ever-powerful subjective, or right, brain, the source of vision and inspiration. And feelings allow people to gozar la vida and to nurture close relationships!

Cultures that are more intellectually oriented and self-contained may be uncomfortable or think that Latinos are "hot blooded," volatile, or overreacting when they express their feelings. Ideas and opinions may appear emotionally charged. Several studies seem to confirm this tendency: Latinos who respond to surveys are more likely to choose the extreme response categories (strongly agree, strongly disagree) than the middle categories, to a greater degree than Euro-Americans.[6]

## Sentimientos Are Good for You

LATINOS ARE A "HUGGY-FEELY" culture and convey this by drawing physically closer and being more likely to touch during a conversation. Something to consider is that expressing sentimientos is actually good for you. Keeping emotions bottled up negatively impacts health, well-being, relationships, and longevity. Emotions are tied to the autonomic nervous system, which controls the heart rate, blood pressure, digestion, respiration, and perspiration.[7] Feelings signal that something is happening that we should attend to. We know our hearts beat faster when we are excited. The challenge for leaders is focusing this energy and using it to nurture relationships as well as to get results.

Living *la vida latina* means tapping into the wellspring of our emotions, so we can enjoy better health and lead a more fulfilling life. Expressing positive sentimientos can bring happiness and joy to our lives and to people around us. Daniel Goleman in his revolutionary book *Emotional Intelligence* relates that learning to express feelings can have a larger impact on living successfully than our intelligence quotient.[8] People from backgrounds where expressing emotions is not encouraged might find that learning to share feelings is one of the advantages to becoming a Latino by *corazón*, or affinity. (This process is described in more detail in chapter 13.)

Passion has been described as a powerful and compelling feeling. Antonia Pantoja, a charming, courageous, and charismatic leader, urged people to tap into this energy: "One cannot live a lukewarm life. You have to live with passion!" Leadership experts James M. Kouzes and Barry Z. Posner have espoused leaders to "encourage the heart" because this will provide the emotional fuel to inspire and motivate.[9] Latino leaders bring this passion to their work—a fire ignited by their love of people, commitment to social justice, and desire to improve life for future generations.

 *"One cannot live a lukewarm life. You have to live with passion!"*

—Antonia Pantoja

## Achieving a Cultural Balance

STRATEGIC THINKING, PROBLEM SOLVING, and the ability to analyze and synthesize information are key leadership functions that require objectivity. These actions often necessitate a mental separation from a problem or group. This can sometimes be difficult for Latinos because the culture is feeling and process oriented and centers on *We*, or the collective, and not the *I*. Closer connections and identification with people can make separating oneself and being objective more challenging.

Another consideration is that many leaders have traveled the path of social activism. Their sense of urgency can be unfamiliar to people who come from the majority or from an affluent group. The many needs and challenges in the Latino community drive its leaders to want action *now*—not at a more comfortable timeline. The stakes are high! This may lead to the perception that they are too emotional or too pushy, and perhaps do not have good manners or know protocol. Latino leaders must learn to step outside of their emotionally centered culture, channel their feelings, and moderate their expressiveness and tone of voice when dealing with the majority culture. They must step out of their *collective cultural field*.

The leaders interviewed for this *libro* all have advanced degrees from prestigious universities. Julián Castro, Anna Cabral, and Janet Murguía have law degrees where they learned to integrate the analytical, strategic, and problem-solving abilities of mainstream leadership with the passion, feeling, and celebratory tendencies of Latino leadership.

## *¡Ándale!*—Moving Forward

UNLIKE THOSE IN THE Anglo-American culture, which tends to focus on production and "getting things done," Latinos accomplish many things but strive to balance *doing* with *being*. This means taking time for people, sharing feelings, telling stories, and enjoying good food. Gozar la vida generates Latino optimism, cultivates relationships, encourages self-expression, and puts salsa into leadership.

The next chapter explores the spiritual roots of leadership. Concepts such as personalismo (good character), community stewardship, a respect for differences, valuing every person, and social responsibility all flow from the deep well of faith.

# CHAPTER 12

# *Fe y Esperanza*: Sustained by Faith and Hope

I N MY FAMILY "ESTÁ en las manos de Dios" (It's in God's hands) was never far from my mother's lips. My brother Chris needed a baseball outfit; a stray dog wandered in, and David couldn't bear to part with him; my class needed costumes for the school play. And where were the cookies for the church social? "What are kookees?" my mother would ask. No matter what the need or challenge, somehow she always managed to get what was needed for her eight children and to help others in the community as well.

God looked after her. How else could Celia María Bordas have ended up in the three-bedroom house at 3713 West Platt Street in Tampa, Florida—not far from the same ocean waters that lapped up onto the Caribbean shores where she was born—if God hadn't put her there?

Generations of Latinos simply believed in God's providence and guidance. In fact, my Tía Anita summed up her *fe* in six words. When asked about what was going to happen or something that was planned, she always prefaced it with "si Dios quiere" (if God wants this to happen). After the event happened, her response was "gracias a Dios" (thanks be to God). So coming or going, she had it covered.

The waters of Hispanic spirituality run deep. Fe is a deeply seated thread that permeates everyday life and prescribes how people should treat one another. Building on the generosity, mutuality, and service orientation of their *We* cultural roots, Latino spirituality is a mandate for *social responsibility*—to do good for others and help others in need. Arturo Vargas recounts, "Even to this day, my mother is packing up a bag of nonperishables to take the church because it's the first Sunday of the month. We're supposed to take food for the hungry, and I'm thinking, 'Mama, you don't have that much yourself.'"

Fe has been the sustainer—the integrating force holding Latinos together from the time of the conquest to colonization, being deemed a minority, and suffering discrimination. Faith engenders hope, humility, courage, gratitude, and celebration—all spiritual qualities that enrich leadership.

## *Esperanza*—Hope, Gratitude, and Celebration

A S A CHILD I remember *mis padres* singing a favorite lullaby, "Ay, ay, ay, ay, canta y no llores" (Sing, don't cry). They taught me that when you're facing hard times, singing will change your attitude and get you through them. How amazing that given their hard work and meager resources, my parents were telling me to sing and be happy. *Canta y no llores* also nurtures a "can do" attitude, fosters perseverance, and counsels people to stick together—all valuable leadership traits.

In his book *Emotional Intelligence*, Daniel Goleman defines optimism as the greatest motivator, because it expresses a strong expectation that things will turn out all right, despite setbacks and frustrations. He cites research that optimistic people tend to be more successful.[1]

Optimism is *esperanza* (hope)—an essential Latino quality. This was validated by a New York Times/CBS News poll noting that 75 percent of Latinos believed their opportunity to succeed was better than that of their parents. Only 56 percent of non-Hispanics thought this was true. Additionally, 64 percent of Latinos thought life would be better for their children. This jumped to 83 percent for Hispanic immigrants, but was only 39 percent for non-Latinos.[2] Optimism is Hispanic immigrants coming to a strange land, struggling to learn English, and working difficult jobs while never faltering from their belief that things will get better.

The Hispanic Alliance for Career Enhancement study "Latino Professional Pulse" found that 72 percent of Latino professionals were positive about the future.[3] This is a no-brainer for Latinos. My house is the nicest I have ever lived in. I have more disposable income and nicer things than my parents. From the low-income situation many Latinos grew up in, of course their future is brighter—we are moving on up.

In the early eighties, as a young leader, I designed Mi Carrera (My Career), a nontraditional jobs program for high-risk teenage Latinas funded through the US Department of Labor. The program was chosen as a national project to be replicated across the country. That year, however, President Ronald Reagan was elected. All federal funds were frozen. Mi Carrera was kaput. But what a valuable program—we had to do something! We gathered supporters, threw a big community fiesta to celebrate our accomplishments, and announced Mi Carrera's continuation. Like a magnet, this optimism drew supporters and funders. (We operated on 36 percent of the previous year's budget—a testimony to Hispanic do-more-with-less and resourcefulness.)

And *milagros* (miracles) happened! I was sitting in my office pondering how to pay a counselor to monitor summer jobs. In walked Lisa Quiroz, a student at Harvard University, who wanted to work for the program that summer. "*¡Dios mío!* You would be perfect, but we don't have money to pay you," I exclaimed. Her mind started clicking, "If you can pay me a stipend, I can get another job and make it work." Lisa was the perfect role model. When she graduated, she worked for Time Warner and established *Time for Kids* magazine, which melded her concern for youth and education. Latinos believe that doing good comes back to you.

*Canta y no llores* reminds Latinos that by staying positive, by singing and dancing together, we can overcome difficult situations. Leaders tap into this optimism to inspire and motive people to work together even when the odds are stacked against them.

## *Gracias*—Gratitude and Thanksgiving

GRATITUDE WAS DEEPLY INGRAINED in early Mestizo-Hispanic culture, in which just surviving was a blessing indeed. From before the European conquest of this hemisphere, the seeds of gratitude were nourished by indigenous people. The two meanings of *gracias* ("grace" as well as "thank you") imply that to be happy and to live in what Christians refer to as "a state of grace," one must be *grateful*. *Gracias a Dios*, a cherished philosophy of life (and my Tía Anita's mantra) was traditionally a common refrain in conversation. Gratitude encompasses an appreciation for parents, *familia*, the community, the *antepasados*, and the blessing of children.

"Gracias a la Vida" (Thanks to Life), a treasured song by Chilean artist Violeta Parra, is steeped in this spirit of thankfulness. The song thanks life for our ability to see and to hear, and to have feet to walk with; for cities, puddles, beaches, deserts, mountains, plains, the stars in the heavens; for the alphabet and words so we can communicate; and for our mothers, friends, brothers, and sisters. We are grateful for both smiles and weeping because they allow us to distinguish happiness from sorrow. The ending confirms that this is your song and everyone else's: "Thanks to life that has given me so much."

Expressing gracias is a great gift that Latinos bring to America—an antidote to the raging materialism that is dividing our nation into a land of haves and have-nots. It is the opposite of taking more than one's share. Gratitude allowed people to be generous and give back. Like a spiritual salve, gracias can soothe the cultural angst that comes from always wanting more "stuff" than one has. By focusing on thankfulness, Latinos have been able to maintain a deep-seated optimism among people who sometimes had little economic means or resources. Gracias anchors the Latino "we can do it" (*sí se puede*) spirit.

*Expressing gracias is a great gift that Latinos bring to America—an antidote to the raging materialism that is dividing our nation into a land of haves and have-nots... Gratitude allowed people to be generous and give back.*

## Spirituality as Celebration

GOZAR LA VIDA ENCOMPASSES leadership as celebration—this tendency springs from Latino spirituality. Unlike the subdued Protestant or Baptist orientations, Latino spirituality has many community celebrations. In the Catholic tradition, for instance, Latinos are named for saints, and each saint has a special day on the calendar. Your saint's day is akin to your birthday—and another reason to celebrate! Every Latin American country also has a patron saint, and people get a day off to commemorate their *santo.*

Puerto Rico is a small island with only 311 miles of coastline, but it may have more patron saints per capita than any other place on earth. Each town has a *Festival Patronal* (Patron Saint Festival). Add up the number of towns on the island, and you're talking about a festival every week. Throw in the fact that the party tends to go on for days, and you will understand the lively tropical spirituality of Puerto Rico.

Processions and rituals such as *el Día de los Muertos* (the Day of the Dead) include elaborate altars, special foods, and marigold flowers, multitudes of candles, music, and remembrances of people's ancestors. On the night of October 31, people pray, eat, and ask for guidance from their ancestors. The next day, there is a community celebration where people dress up in costumes and dance all night, traveling from house to house with a *banda* in tow. These festivals weave together history, culture, and community into a spiritual celebration that strengthens people's ability to collaborate and do the hard work of community organizing.

Celebration was also evident in the farm workers' strikes of the 1960s. Their long marches were spiritual processions with a statue of Our Lady of Guadalupe leading them as they sang "De Colores." Chávez encouraged them, "Let us bring forth song and celebration so the spirit will be alive among us!"[4] Hope, gratitude, and celebration transformed oppression and need into an enduring faith in life's goodness.

# Spirituality as Responsibility toward Others

THE HUMANISTIC PEOPLE ORIENTATION of Latinos, their values of service, compassion, responsibility toward others, and profuse generosity are all grounded in their spiritual beliefs. Janet Murguía reflects, "Early on my parents helped me develop a sense of responsibility in caring for others. They really instilled in me and my brothers and sisters a sense of caring not only for the family but also for our neighborhood and community." Chávez made the connection between individual contributions and community service. "Being of service is not enough. You must become a servant of the people."[5] This was part of my upbringing as well. If I was unhappy, my mother in her simple but wise way would say, "Get busy and do something for somebody else."

*"Early on my parents helped me develop a sense of responsibility in caring for others. They really instilled in me and my brothers and sisters a sense of caring not only for the family but also for our neighborhood and community."*

—Janet Murguía

Latino spirituality centers on *relationships and responsibility for others*. In fact, the truest sentiments of the Christian faith follow in this vein. People are described as brothers and sisters and are urged to feed the hungry, give shelter to those in need, and to take care of the sick. Spirituality is a moral obligation to ensure others' well-being and the collective good. For Latinos and other communities who have dealt with inequities, *spiritual responsibility* implies removing the roadblocks that limit opportunity. Social and political action are intertwined with spiritual responsibility.

Federico Peña describes this commitment: "I saw my life as one of helping people who were being discriminated against and had no voice." On May 1, 2006—designated a nationwide "day without immigrants"—Peña asked the organizers of the Denver march if he could address the group. He urged people to speak out for what is right: "For those of us who attended religious worship this past weekend, we should conduct a full moral gut check as we watch immigrant workers wither in our deserts, drown in our rivers, and die on our highways. . . . I believe that a great people live by their moral and ethical principles every day. I believe that a nation earns respect when it shows compassion and decency."[6]

*"I believe that a great people live by their moral and ethical principles every day. I believe that a nation earns respect when it shows compassion and decency."*

—Federico Peña

Archbishop Óscar Romero of El Salvador was part of the liberation theology movement that interlaced social justice and responsibility, particularly for the poor in Latin American countries. César Chávez uplifted the farm workers' strikes with such traditional religious practices as pilgrimages, fasting, retreats, public prayers, and worship services. Perhaps Chávez explained the integration of faith and social action most succinctly. During the *huelga* (farm workers' strike), when asked how they would achieve their goals, he said, "We're going to pray a lot and picket a lot."[7] The leader as community stewardship and social activist is rooted in spiritual responsibility.

## Three Spiritual Virtues: Humility, Courage, and Forgiveness

THE INTEGRATION OF FAITH, social responsibility, activism, and celebration is the spirit of Latino leadership. Now let's consider three virtues that flow from this orientation: courage, humility, and compassion.

## Faith Inspires Courage

LATINO ADVANCEMENT HAS REQUIRED hard work, determination, and the courage to do what is right. Vargas reflects on this: "We must be bold—make unpopular decisions and battle infrastructures that keep our community from progressing." Social activism requires courage, which gives people the strength to face dangers and difficulties. Courage is required every time we try something new, battle the odds, or stand up for injustice. Immigrants, for instance, show tremendous courage by coming to a foreign land and not being able to speak the language.

Courage also comes from having strong convictions: "Right makes might." Moral courage is developed through right action and by making choices and decisions that align with our values and beliefs.[8] This underscores the importance of leadership preparation and *conciencia*. Like the roots of the great ponderosa, your core values, your history, and the trials and tribulations of those who came before can ground you and give you courage when you have difficult decisions to make or must go against the tide.

Murgía finds courage in her faith: "*Con Dios por adelante, todo es possible* [with God's help, all things are possible]. And so for me it was a sense that we shouldn't believe people anytime they say, 'You can't do that,' or 'No,' but to know all things are possible with God's help." Murgía went from a humble barrio in Kansas City to working in the White House—all the while keeping faith and service central in her life.

Hilda Solis concurs, "We are a very spiritual people. I look to my faith to guide me in many decisions. I'm able to rely on that when I am in difficult conversations, when I'm being challenged, or when I may have to set myself apart from other people because I'm going to say something or do something that may not sit well with a lot of people. My faith gives me courage." (Solis was the first woman to receive the Profile in Courage Award from the John F. Kennedy Foundation.)

*"I look to my faith to guide me in many decisions … when I am in difficult conversations, when I'm being challenged … I'm going to say something or do something that may not sit well with a lot of people. My faith gives me courage."*

—Hilda Solis

Without the gift of hope, Latinos would not have had the courage to stand up against the inequalities of the past. Leaders have to dispense hope because if people are not hopeful, they won't act to change things. Hope and courage are the keystones for the social activist nature of leadership.

## Humility

I ASKED RAUL YZAGUIRRE, if he were speaking to a group of Latinos about our special contribution and what we should "hold on to," what would he say? His answer surprised me: "A sense of humility, modesty, and courtesy." And then he went on to say, "A truly complete human being is one who treats the maid with the same kind of respect and dignity that he affords the president or CEO." Yzaguirre was defining the leader as equal. To embody this perspective, leaders must be humble, accept their own shortcomings, and appreciate the inherent worth of others.

Arturo Vargas also recognizes humility as essential. "Leadership—for me it's about clarity of purpose, courage, and being humble. Without humility there is the risk of leadership becoming a cult of personality." US Representative Lucille Roybal-Allard could certainly have taken that path—many people in power do. She was groomed by her father, Edward Roybal, the first Hispanic elected to Congress in California. He served thirty years, during which time he was a staunch advocate for civil rights and people's issues. Her father would remind her, "Never forget where you came from." Today Royal-Allard remains true to her father's advice: "I can see where it would be very easy to get caught up in the glory of Washington. It's really important to remember who are, who you represent, and why you are there."[9]

Leaders who are clear on their purpose, who put an issue or a cause first, and who actually serve something greater, lessen their self-importance. Anna Cabral observes, "Latino leaders think about the broader good and are not so focused on individual success, but rather, How do we achieve success for the larger community?" This shifts the focus from the individual leader to the people he or she serves. Humility is the essence of servant leadership, where the people's needs come first.[10]

Many Latino leaders come from or have family members from a lower economic status and humble background. Their *padres* or *abuelos* overcame Herculean obstacles to provide the opportunities they have today. Latinos, therefore, value humility and look for that quality in their leaders. In collective cultures, humility allows the leader to connect with people and to be seen as one of them. If a leader focuses on *I* rather than *We*, this damages the collective identity and group empowerment. Orta says, "Good leaders have empathy. They've put themselves in other people's shoes. It goes beyond caring. You have to understand where people are coming from and how your decisions are going to impact them."

*"Good leaders have empathy. They've put themselves in other people's shoes. It goes beyond caring. You have to understand where people are coming from and how your decisions are going to impact them."*

—Carlos Orta

Humility does not imply a leader does not know her worth. It is an understanding that the gifts one was given should be placed at the service of others and that in the last analysis everything a person accomplishes is because of the support and help she has received. Murguía clearly understands this: "In the Latino community, we have this sense that we never do this alone. We rely on family, we rely on community, but in the end we rely on that higher being to help get us through the darkest times and to illuminate our path, and for me that's always been true."

## Forgiveness and Healing

IN PART I, WE explored the history of the conquest and the colonization of Hispanic ancestors. These antecedents provided the backdrop for leadership aimed at changing these conditions. This chapter surmises that it was the spiritual roots of Latino people that gave them the hope and strength to overcome adversity. Now we will consider forgiveness, which entails the healing of historical traumas and has birthed an inclusive, caring, and giving spirit. Forgiveness has strengthened and nourished the spiritual roots of Latino people.

The story of Our Lady of Guadalupe brought together Catholic and indigenous beliefs and laid the foundation for the unique brand of Latino spirituality that emerged in this hemisphere. Guadalupe's message was one of perseverance, hope, compassion, and racial and cultural integration. Her lowered eyes and supplicating hands invoked humility. She spoke to a peasant and not a Spanish high official. These qualities are intrinsic to Latino faith today and are reflected in their leadership practices.

As a Mestiza, Guadalupe represented the vision and promise of the future—a healing force that planted seeds of forgiveness and compassion. Today Latinos recognize that the blood of the Spanish conquistadores runs through our veins—they are our ancestors. Their influence is present in the language we speak and in many positive aspects of our culture. Rejecting this heritage would be denying an integral part of ourselves. Bringing the Spanish into our cultural *familia*, however, required the forgiveness of historical transgressions (including the trauma of my grandmother and so many other Indian women).

Our Lady of Guadalupe is the face and image of the *mestizaje*, of the forced cultural integration and fusion that took place. Yet her message was of compassion, hope, and inclusion. She is perhaps the reason that Latinos are the only people of color in the Americas who have made peace with their oppressors, embraced their multiple racial backgrounds, and courageously look their history straight in the eye.

Forgiveness allows people to begin anew, to birth new understandings and new pathways. Forgiveness releases and heals the past. The vibrancy, resilience, productivity, and energy of the Latino culture is the result of the complex, historically painful, and yet genetically powerful mestizaje. Forgiveness has allowed Latinos to reconcile the past, have gratitude for what we have today, and be optimistic for the future. Forgiveness is also a wise and magnanimous leadership trait.

*Latinos are the only people of color in the Americas who have made peace with their oppressors, embraced their multiple racial backgrounds, and courageously look their history straight in the eye.*

## *¡Ándale!*—Moving Forward

WE KNOW THAT LATINO values revolve around relationships. People-centered leadership reflects this by taking responsibility for the welfare of others. Additionally, the multicultural global age beckons us to create authentic diversity. Due to their history as a Mestizo people, and their inherent diversity, Latinos leaders are prepared to guide this transformation. The last chapter proposes that Latino *destino* (our unique contribution) is to build a diverse and humanistic society.

To accomplish this, leaders must empower the Latino community to reach its potential and invite others to work with us in creating a caring and inclusive society. Ten strategies will be suggested that can further this work. In keeping with our *bienvenido* spirit, non-Latinos are invited to join in and be part of this transformation by becoming Latino by *corazón*. We will look at the acculturation process that allows people to become cultural adaptives and to fully partake in our increasingly diverse world.

# PART V

## Latino *Destino*

**O**UR MULTICULTURAL NATION IS RAPIDLY emerging, and Latinos will be at the headwaters of this transformation. But a new vision of inclusiveness is needed if we are to build a truly diverse society.

When the Constitution was written, only White male property owners were allowed to vote in most states. Black men, as slaves, were counted as only three-fifths of a person, and women could not vote until the passage of the Nineteenth Amendment in 1920.[1] Although Hispanics could vote, we did not have an official US designation until 1980, and Latinos weren't "official" until the 2000 census.[2] Our multicultural society requires us to change this race-based view of our country and embrace a more encompassing vision of our humanity. Because of their inherent diversity and inclusive culture, Latinos can guide this change.

A strategic way to do this is to expand the Latino concept of the extended community and *familia* by welcoming people who connect to our culture and values as Latinos by *corazón,* or affinity. Not exclusion, but *inclusion.* This would turn America's race-based consciousness upside down! Becoming a Latino by corazón—embracing and adopting key cultural aspects such as being generous and simpático—is possible because we are a culture. And, oh yes, one more time: *culture is learned.* Furthermore, Latinos are the only group that self-identifies—that speaks to our ability to welcome different people into the culture.

In reality, most Latinos already have familia who are not Latino by birth, and our *comadre-compadre, madrina-madrino, tía-tío* custom has traditionally included people who are not blood related. Our extended familias are elastic and stretch to embrace others.

One more caveat: once a person becomes a Latino by corazón—then by definition he or she is a *cultural adaptive*—a person who adopts beneficial behaviors, values, and reference points from a variety of cultures. And why is this so important? In our multicultural global village leaders will need to be culturally adaptive and culturally competent. Frances Hesselbein, former CEO of Girl Scouts of the USA, speaks to this: "Perhaps the biggest question in today's world is, 'How do we help people deal with their deepest differences?' Governance among diversity is the world's greatest challenge."[3]

Second, Latino humanistic values emphasize social responsibility, a needed attribute in fashioning a society that not only embraces diversity but also truly cares for (and takes care of) its people—a society that incorporates values such as being generous, being helpful to others, respecting people as equals, and cooperating with others.

Fostering an inclusive and caring society will require a critical mass of people who are *culturally adaptive* and *socially responsible.* Part V summarizes ten strategies that leaders can use to strengthen the Latino community and foster partnerships and coalitions with different groups in order to achieve this good work.

One roadblock is the history of assimilation, by which immigrants were urged to conform and erase the traditions and languages of their grandparents. To shed a little light on this, I will share my own assimilation experience. Hopefully, people who have done likewise can choose to "retro-assimilate" as I did and become cultural adaptives.

Our journey ends with an intriguing vision put forth by the Mexican philosopher José Vasconcelos: *la Raza Cósmica*—the Cosmic Race. His vision foresaw the mixing of the four major groups of humanity into a new familia that combined the best characteristics of all the races. This time is coming! The fastest-growing youth demographic comprises people who identify as multicultural.[4] Latinos are already a fusion of many cultures. We celebrate *de colores*—the radiant rainbow of humanity. We are la Raza Cósmica.

# CHAPTER 13

# Building a Diverse and Humanistic Society

STARTING SCHOOL NOT SPEAKING *inglés* was my first foray into the Anglo world. My teachers seemed cold and distant, had strange rules, and did not hug or touch the children. And the food tasted bland. Before the civil rights movement, America was whitebread. I never saw a Latino in any professional position or as a teacher, bus driver, or even a clerk in a nice store. The schools were whitewashing institutions that taught the history, norms, and values of the dominant culture. Like most children I wanted to be accepted, and the path to success was assimilation. I learned to read and write inglés and even forgot most of my *español*.

When I became a teenager, there was no Catholic *escuela* (school) on the outskirts of Tampa, where we lived. My mother boarded a bus with me in tow and journeyed across town. Humbly, she entreated the mother superior at the Academy of Holy Names to give her daughter a scholarship. The mother superior agreed to half a scholarship. Every Sunday, my mother and I would get up at 5 a.m. to babysit children at church during Mass to earn the remaining tuition.

My senior year I found out many of my classmates were going to college. That sounded like a great idea. My parents immigrated here so I could get a good education. But my mother, with a fifth-grade education, thought high school was *una buena educación*. The University of Florida was only 120 miles away, but to my parents, that was as far as their distant homeland. Seeing my determination, however, my parents in their loving and humble way gave me their blessing.

In the early '60s, being a Latina at a university was a Lone Ranger experience. Well, I knew how to fit in—I had learned it in grade school. I started highlighting my father's French ancestry, denied my fabulous *Nicaragüense*-ness, my rich indigenous and Spanish roots, and my immigrant experience. I dressed and acted like the other students and even joined a sorority. *I assimilated.*

Human beings are group oriented—we want to be part of the tribe. I became accepted but had an empty feeling inside. You see, when my *abuela* came to visit, I couldn't talk to her. Many Hispanics in my generation have felt this loss.

What's in a name? A person's identity, culture, and family roots. In my generation many teachers could not pronounce Spanish names. Eduardo became Eddie, Jaime became James, and Marisól became Mary. I was called Jeanne because my parents thought an English name would be easier on me (and more American). They were chagrined when I insisted in my twenties on being called Juana. Whitewashing a child's name was a common practice. (Today, however, García is the eighth-most-common surname in America, and Ángel was the top first name in New York City in 2008.)[1]

Raul Yzaguirre observes: "The road to success that has been offered is to assimilate, change your name, and lose your accent. All those things hold an empty promise that will result in a hollowing out. *Te quita el corazón*—It rips out your heart."

*"The road to success that has been offered is to assimilate, change your name, and lose your accent. All those things hold an empty promise that will result in a hollowing out.* Te quita el corazón—*It rips out your heart."*

—Raul Yzaguirre

# Assimilation—Becoming Homogenized

THE ASSIMILATION WOUND IS not just a Latino phenomenon. Immigrants have always struggled with this conflict. If your *familia* has been here for generations, you might not remember, but European great-grandparents felt this loss as they stepped away from Ellis Island or when they realized their grandchildren did not speak Italian, Russian, or German. Like my parents, they wanted their children to learn inglés and be successful. But cutting one's ancestral roots can leave a psychological scar.

Assimilation melded one people out of the myriad nationalities that came to our shores, integrated our national character, and unified our young country. At the same time, the melting pot set the tone for a country where conformity and homogeneity fed ethnocentricity. This in turn, bred cultural insensitivity and a predisposition to impose our values on others. The understanding that all cultures are unique expressions of the human experience was as lost as the languages our grandparents spoke.

As our country becomes Latinized and multicultural, *assimilation is no longer an adaptive advantage.* Today people need to *acculturate—* to be receptive, skillful, and adaptable to many cultures. Unlike assimilation, where one's culture, language, and background are discarded, acculturation is an *add-on* process. Acculturation increases one's cultural repertoire, adaptability, flexibility, and cross-cultural competency.

But *un momento*—wait a minute! Can people who have assimilated then acculturate and become cultural adaptives? *Sí!* Yes! I know because this happened in my early twenties.

*As our country becomes Latinized and multicultural, assimilation is no longer an adaptive advantage. Today people need to acculturate.*

## Becoming a Cultural Adaptive

FOR A FEMALE IMMIGRANT from a low-income family to obtain a college degree in the early 1960s was as rare as the tiny quetzal bird that floats in the tropical rain forests. Why was I given the prize of a higher education? What was I supposed to do with my life? During my soul searching, President John F. Kennedy was shot. Kennedy was an inspiration to my generation and revered by Latinos as a charismatic, socially responsible leader who resonated with our values.

Inspired by his call to public service, I told my dear *padres*, "I'm joining the Peace Corps." "Ay, Dios mío!" If going 120 miles away to college was a cultural storm, going to the other side of the world was a category 5 hurricane. Telling me I could always come home, mi familia watched their petrified yet excited youngest daughter board a plane for Santiago, Chile.

In my assimilated stupor I thought I was going to help those backward countries south of the border. Imagine my shock to find that Santiago had an old European flavor with flowered *avenidas* surrounding stately museums and government buildings. Chile was the second-oldest democracy in the Western Hemisphere, with highly educated citizens. President Eduardo Frei was Hispanic, as were the senators, mayors, presidents of Chilean universities, TV station directors, the heads of its army and navy, and executives of every business.

Growing up in the good old USA in the '50s, I had no idea someone of my culture could achieve such high-level leadership. In my childhood successful people were without exception White, which is still true for most leaders in top positions. I realized then that while the land of opportunity had given many gifts, my history and culture had been stripped like the lost city of the Inca.

Thus began the redemption of my Hispanic soul. I embraced my Latina heritage. This did not diminish the gratitude I had to my adopted homeland. In fact, it enabled me to make a greater contribution. *I chose the path of acculturation and became a cultural adaptive.* Raul Yzaguirre passionately believes this is essential: "Hispanic success for both practical and pragmatic reasons, as well as for esthetic, self-fulfilling, self-actualizing reasons, the quality and the meaning of life—for all those reasons—needs to be, 'I treasure who I am, I treasure who my parents were, my culture, my language, and I don't have to give any of that up in order to succeed. Indeed, if I keep all those things it will make me more successful in practical terms as well as in self-fulfilling terms.' Latinos have a unique contribution to make to America. We can't do that if we give up our cultural core—that which makes us who we are."

*"Latinos have a unique contribution to make to America. We can't do that if we give up our cultural core—that which makes us who we are."*

—Raul Yzaguirre

## *Bienvenidos*: Latinos by Affinity

YOUNG LATINOS TODAY DO not have to assimilate to be successful. In fact, the Latinization of America implies that adaptation is now a two-way street. Latinos are learning how to be successful in the mainstream culture and at the same time are bringing their cultural assets to enrich America.

For people who are not Latino or multicultural or for those who assimilated as I did, there is the opportunity to acculturate. I am referring to an acculturated person as a cultural adaptive—*a person who adopts beneficial behaviors, values, and reference points from a variety of cultures.*

The Latino culture offers the most user-friendly way to do this because the door is open for a person to become a Latino by corazón, or affinity! Let's look at several reasons why becoming Latino by corazón is the easiest way for learning culture adaptively!

1. Latinos come from many nationalities and races and have learned to acclimate to many subgroups. A Latino group (or extended *familia*) might include a Cuban, a seventh-generation Hispanic from New Mexico, and a newly arrived Venezuelan. In Latino organizations many nationalities and backgrounds work side by side. Numerous organizations have inclusiveness in their mission statements.

2. Cultural adaptability was a survival mechanism for Latinos, who learn at an early age how to succeed in a predominantly alien culture. Latinos who now work in mainstream organizations can model the benefits of knowing how to maneuver in more than one culture.

3. Latinos are Mestizos—cultural hybrids with a long history of integrating other cultures, races, and nationalities. Fusion defines their identity. Latinos are a prototype for cultural adaptability and can show other people how to do likewise.

4. Latinos are a cultural and ethnic group and not a race. Unlike racial groups, a cultural group offers the potential for immersion and the adapting of favorable characteristics. *Y otra vez* (one more time): Latino identification is self-selected and includes people of all races and ethnic groups. (Just check the box.)

5. Inclusiveness and bienvenido are cultural treasures ingrained in values such as being hospitable, *simpático*, and generous. The elastic *familia*, where close friends become "relatives," is an ancient custom. *Comadres, compadres, tías,* tíos*, madrinas,* and *madrinos* become family not due to blood ties but to common experiences, values, and a history of helping one another.

 *I am referring to an acculturated person as a cultural adaptive—a person who adopts beneficial behaviors, values, and reference points from a variety of cultures.*

By becoming a Latino by corazón, therefore, people step out of their cultural conditioning. Jessica Smith served in the Peace Corps in

Guatemala. Heather Tang taught in Chile for two years. Janelle Wilkins was an exchange student in Spain. Reid Lawrence was a Hispanic studies major at William and Mary College. They are all Latinos by corazón and actually have a "Hispanic personality." When speaking español, they wave their hands, talk faster, and are more animated and expressive. Of course, a person doesn't have to go to these lengths; just by reading this book you are immersed in Latino culture and leadership. You are on your way to becoming a Latino by corazón.

And the good news is—once you become a Latino by corazón, you have become a cultural adaptive and can more easily form affinities with other groups.

Let's acknowledge that with changing demographics and growing diversity many people are already cultural adaptives. Cultural fluidity is a defining characteristic of the Millennial generation, who love the music, style, slang, and social values of other cultures.[2] Likewise people who grew up in multiethnic neighborhoods, lived in a foreign country, married into a family from a different tradition, learned a foreign language, or served in the Peace Corps have become cultural adaptives by choosing these types of experiences.

Regardless of their ethnic or racial antecedents, people can acculturate into different cultural modalities. People of color who have mainstreamed can choose to come back to their origins. My own experience in reconnecting to my Latina soul is personal testimony to the power that acculturating brings. The door to partake in the cultural smorgasbord and Latino buffet is a revolving one and remains wide open. *¡Bienvenido!* Come on in!

*Cultural fluidity is a defining characteristic of the Millennial generation, who love the music, style, slang, and social values of other cultures.*

# Ten Strategies to Actualize Latino Destino

**W**E HAVE SURMISED THAT Latino destino is building a humanistic and diverse society and that a strategic way to accomplish this is to redefine inclusiveness. By welcoming people to the familia, leaders can cultivate the critical mass needed to bring our values into the mainstream and to actualize our potential and contributions. Below are ten strategies to further the vision of Latino destino. It is important to recognize that several national Latino organizations have missions to specifically address these issues and can be contacted for additional information and resources.[3]

## 1. Capitalize on Latino inclusiveness, hospitality, and diversity

WHY WOULDN'T PEOPLE WANT to join up? The Latino culture offers community, celebration, hope, and a humanistic vision for the future. We have an international flair and good old-fashioned values. People today are hankering for belonging and meaning. A few generations ago we lived in intact communities and had large extended familias. Latinos can revitalize these traditions. Our inclusiveness, hospitality, and bienvenido spirit welcomes people—they can become Latinos by corazón and participate in our generous culture.

*Latino inclusiveness, hospitality, and bienvenido spirit welcomes people—they can become Latinos by corazón and participate in our generous culture.*

## 2. Strengthen cultural pride

THE PEW STUDY ON Latino Identity found that 69 percent of the Hispanics in the United States believe they come from *many different cultures*, while only 29 percent believe they share a common culture.[4] A

premise of this book is that Latinos are a culture of synthesis. Because
of this complexity, leaders need to create opportunities for conversation
and dialogue so Latinos can identify and share cultural connection
points. This is particularly crucial for emerging and young leaders.

Murguía urges Latinos to bear this in mind: "There's a sense of
connectedness across our ethnic roots, and that connectedness is our
strength. We have common bonds and values that we share. We should
unify around those because when we are separated or divided, we are not
a strong community." A key function of Latino leaders is to assist people
in finding the connecting points of the culture and identifying shared
history and values.

*"There's a sense of connectedness across our ethnic roots,
and that connectedness is our strength. We have common
bonds and values that we share."*

—Janet Murguía

## 3. Keep young people culturally centered

IN 1999, A NEWSWEEK poll indicated that Latinos under thirty-five were
more likely to identify as being Latino or Hispanic than their parents.[5]
Ten years later the Pew Hispanic Center study on Latino youth found that
60 percent are encouraged to speak Spanish by their parents.[6] A cultural
revival is brewing. Young people today are embracing their Latino
identity. However, they know little about their history, and there are few
avenues to learn about and share positive aspects of their culture. Leaders
are charged with creating programs that connect young Latinos with
each other and help them learn about their culture and the contributions
Latinos have made.

## 4. **Integrate immigrants into the Latino community**

US LATINO GROWTH HAS been largely due to immigration. Leaders continue the hard work of integrating the newly arrived. Evidence that this is paying off is that two-thirds (64 percent) of young Latinos say that Latinos from different countries get along well. And more than (52 percent) of young Latinos (aged sixteen to twenty-five) identify themselves first by their family's country of origin, be it México, Cuba, the Dominican Republic, El Salvador, or any of more than a dozen other Spanish-speaking countries.[7] This same tendency was validated for Latino adults, a majority of whom identify with their national origin.[8] Latinos are acculturating and bringing their national identity with them—an asset in our global community and economy.

This identification with people from other countries makes the immigration debate close to the Latino heart. When any person who "looks Hispanic" is discriminated against, immigration becomes an issue of civil rights and human dignity. Leaders have put immigrant reform central to the Latino agenda; this has galvanized and unified Latinos. Leaders must continue reaching out and providing services that bring immigrants into the Latino mainstream.

## 5. **Enhance Latino organizations**

"LATINO LEADERS," NOTES CARLOS orta, are "committed to 'the cause.' They fully engage and bring a passion to their work. The edge we have is that *we are not going to waffle*." As president of the Hispanic Association on Corporate Responsibility, Orta orchestrates a coalition of sixteen of the largest national Latino organizations. He is describing the long-term commitment that its leaders have to building strong organizations that represent Latino interests.

Latinos have advanced because national organizations built their capacity and influence. It is important to note that only two organizations—LULAC (League of Latin American Citizens), founded in 1922, and the American GI Forum, founded in 1948, were precursors to the many Latino organizations founded in the '60s and '70s, This is not surprising since Hispanic identity emerged only at that time. What is surprising are the strength, influence, and number of the organizations that have developed in the last thirty-five years. For a community with many needs and limited resources, organizations have the influence and the power to represent Hispanic interests. Growing and supporting our organizations is the key to Latino empowerment.

*"Latino leaders are committed to 'the cause.' They fully engage and bring a passion to their work. The edge we have is that we are not going to waffle."*

—Carlos Orta

## 6. Galvanize economic power and entrepreneurial strength

LATINOS ARE THE FASTEST-GROWING segment of small businesses in the country. Close to three million Hispanic-owned businesses now generate almost $400 billion in annual revenues. These businesses are using the Latino community model to come together and create local Hispanic chambers of commerce—now numbering in the hundreds—throughout the nation.[9] San Antonio Mayor Julián Castro underscores the benefit to our country: "I believe that Latinos have a wonderful opportunity to renew the entrepreneurialism spirit of our country." And let's not forget small businesses are the backbone of the US economy.

## 7. Grow Latino political power

IF YOU WERE ON the streets for the 2012 presidential campaign, you would have seen a beehive of Latino activity. In the lead-up to Election Day, there were massive efforts to reach the Latino community from candidates, political parties, and community organizations. The National Association of Hispanic Elected and Appointed Officials (NALEO) Educational Fund, along with partners of the *Ya es hora. ¡Ve y vota!*

(It's time. Go and vote!) campaign executed an unprecedented voter-engagement program to provide hundreds of thousands of voters with vital information in both English and Spanish on all aspects of the electoral process.

These efforts paid off—the Latino vote increased to 10 percent of the electorate with an estimated 12.5 million voting.[10] The day-to-day work must continue. Vargas notes, "In 2012 Latinos were responsible for electing the president of the United States, because certain key states, swing states, depended on our vote. Hispanic voters in the United States are projected to surpass whites and other non-Hispanics in the coming decade."

## 8. Create an intergenerational leadership force

THE LATINO POPULATION IS the youngest in the nation and getting younger. One in five schoolchildren and one in four newborns are Hispanic.[11] This presents daunting challenges *and* opportunities for leaders. As noted in the chapter on intergenerational leadership, many organizations serve youth and have leadership programs and internships to develop young people's skills. Due to the growing number of youth, leaders must launch a mobilization movement that utilizes social networking and the Internet to educate and inspire a new generation of Latino activists. Latino organizations must allocate resources to involve and empower youth as partners in Latino advancement.

## 9. Build coalitions and partnerships with other groups

LATINO LEADERSHIP FOCUSES ON coalition and partnership building. Yet lasting coalitions with non-Latino groups have usually been issue oriented and not long-term. It would seem natural that Latinos with their expansive inclusiveness could form strong coalitions with other community and thus leverage the power such unity brings. Some believe that because minority groups compete for scarce resources or scramble to form alliances with Whites, they do not naturally coalesce even though many of the issues they face are the same. Leaders must explore the reasons why coalition building has not succeeded. They must continue to reach out, find common ground, and use their coalition-building skills to bring diverse groups together.

### 10. Bolster connections between Latinas and women in other communities

HAVING WORKED WITH OTHER women for many decades, I understand the difficulties of nurturing organizations that truly represent women's issues from a Latina perspective. Latina feminism has traditionally included the advancement of the familia and the community—and it reflects the social activism and community stewardship of Latino leadership.

The White women's movement, on the other hand, no longer has a unified social or political agenda. Individual success has not centered on improving the general status of women or changing society to reflect women's values. Today, we might say that the White women's movement has stalled. Women make up only 16 percent of the Congress,[12] and wages continue to be 77 percent of what men earn.[13]

Because Latinas and other women of color are still fighting for equality in their communities, they could reignite and reinvigorate the women's movement. Latina leaders are called to cast a more inclusive net. Yet they must ensure that working with other women's groups strengthens their ability to build an equitable society.

## We Will Get There!

WORKING TO REALIZE THESE ten strategies will build a new America—one with inclusiveness and people-centered values as its core. The Latino bienvenido spirit welcomes people to join us in creating this future. Janet Murguía believes we will get there. "Hard work, determination, faith, a good education, and humility helped us get to where we are today," she says, "and these are the same values that will allow us to chart our own course and to realize the American dream."

*"Hard work, determination, faith, a good education, and humility helped us get to where we are today, and these are the same values that will allow us to chart our own course and to realize the American dream."*

—Janet Murguía

# La Bendición—la Raza Cósmica

IN THE EARLY TWENTIETH century a prophetic and far-reaching vision of humankind's future was put forth by the renowned Mexican educator, philosopher, and politician Jóse Vasconcelos. He believed that humanity will evolve into a new familia that combines the best characteristics of all four major racial groups. He envisioned this as *la Raza Cósmica*—the Cosmic Race. While the roots of la Raza Cósmica began with the birth of the Bronze or Mestizo race, it will expand to include all people. Vasconcelos believed that the confluence of many cultures and races will result in a richer and more radiant genetic stream and enrich humanity.[14]

The genesis of this vision can be found in our past. In the beginning there was only one race. Genetic anthropology, which combines DNA and physical evidence to reveal the history of human migration and ancestry, is documenting how people evolved from the same human family. Yes, we all emerged from the same primordial spring! Our common ancestry ties us together.[15]

Writing at a time when American imperialism and the belief in White superiority was on the rise and twenty years before the concept of Germans being a superior race, Vasconcelos was summoning a different vision of human evolution, one that encompassed the beauty and the richness of racial integration. This was almost four hundred years after the appearance of Our Lady of Guadalupe, but his vision embellishes the prophesy first heard on the rocky hill at Tepeyac. La Raza Cósmica is based on the expansive inclusiveness Guadalupe expressed: "I am your merciful Mother, yours and all the people who are united on this land and all other people of different ancestries."[16]

And remember the Aztec black belt she wore? To the Aztec this symbolized pregnancy.[17] Vasconcelos's vision supports the belief that the child that Guadalupe was carrying was the Mestizo, the mixed-race progeny of the future—the first of those who would become today's Latinos and tomorrow's multicultural children—a radiant genetic stream that would integrate the richness of humanity.

The concept of la Raza Cósmica offers an enticing future: the multicultural family. In 2002, the Hopi Indian elders came forth with a similar prophesy. They believed that in these times a universal tribe would be born—a rainbow people who would represent the iridescent beauty of humanity. They would heal the earth, bring peace and understanding, and undo the damage caused by previous generations. Then the elders said, "*The time is now. . .*"[18]

*The concept of la Raza Cósmica offers an enticing future: the multicultural family.*

There is a growing understanding today that we are intricately connected and interdependent, moving us closer to accepting the concept of la Raza Cósmica—the cosmic race and universal tribe. The belief that we belong to one human family is the core of Christianity and most of the other world religions. "Our Father" at the beginning of the Lord's Prayer affirms that people are one spiritual family.

These same sentiments can be found in the song "De Colores," which rejoices in the beautiful colors of the birds, the flowers, the rainbows, and *yes*—our multicolored humanity! The song inspires us to love people and all their many colors.

The emergence of a *de colores* America will be a defining characteristic of the twenty-first century. Latino *destino* because of our inherent diversity is to build the multicultural society. As we embark on the good work of creating this future, we welcome Latinos by corazón into the familia. We commit to creating a society that cares for all people. We celebrate de colores—the incredible beauty of life's diversity.

*The emergence of a* de colores *America will be a defining characteristic of the twenty-first century. Latino destino because of our inherent diversity is to build this multicultural society.*

# Notes

## Preface

1. Genaro C. Armas, "America's Face Is Changing," *CBS News,* February 11, 2009, http://www.cbsnews.com/stories/2004/03/17/national/main607022.shtml.

2. Jeffrey Passel and D'Vera Cohn, "U.S. Population Projections: 2005–2050," in *Pew Social and Demographic Trends*, February 11, 2008, Pew Research Center, http://pewsocialtrends.org/pubs/703/population-projections-united states.

3. Stephanie Siek and Joe Sterling, "Census: Fewer White Babies Being Born," *In America*, CNN, May 17, 2012, http://inamerica.blogs.cnn.com/2012/05/17/census-2011-data-confirm-trend-of-population-diversity.

4. Nia-Malika Henderson, "Julian Castro, Latino Mayor of San Antonio, to Keynote DNC Convention," *Washington Post*, July 31, 2012, http://www.washingtonpost.com/politics/latino-mayor-to-keynote-dnc-convention/2012/07/31/gJQA3fpqNX_story.html.

5. US Census Bureau, "Hispanic Heritage Month 2010: Sept. 15–Oct. 15," *Profile America Facts for Features*, CN 10-FF.17, July 15, 2010, http://www.census.gov/newsroom/releases/archives/facts_for_features_special_editions/cb10-ff17.html./releases/archives/facts_for_features_special_editions/cb10-ff17.html.

6. *New York Times,* "How Obama Won Re-election," http://www.nytimes.com/interactive/2012/11/07/us/politics/obamas-diverse-base-of-support.html (accessed November 12, 2012).

7. Michael Muskal, "Census Bureau: Minority Births Outnumbered Whites for the First Time," *Los Angeles Times*, May 17, 2012, http://articles.latimes.com/2012/may/17/nation/la-na-nn-census-data-20120517.

8. Spanish is the official language in twenty countries. See "Spanish Speaking Countries (Official)," Worldatlas, http://www.worldatlas.com/spanish.htm. In addition, Puerto Rico is often included on that list (although English and Spanish are both spoken). The United States has more Spanish speakers than Spain. Counting both as Spanish-speaking countries brings the total to twenty-two.

## Introduction

1. Jorge Ramos, *The Latino Wave: How Hispanics Are Transforming Politics in America* (New York: HarperCollins, 2005), 97.

2. Ying Lowrey, "Hispanic-Owned Businesses Outpace Overall Business Growth over 10-Year Period," *The Small Business Watchdog,* U.S. Small Business Administration, http://weblog.sba.gov/blog-advo/?p=830 (accessed February 15, 2012).

3. Louis E. V. Nevaer, *Managing Hispanic and Latino Employees* (San Francisco: Berrett-Koehler, 2010), 1–4.

4. Ramos, *Latino Wave*, Prologue, xx.

5. Office of Management and Budget: "Revisions to the Standards for the Classification of Federal Data on Race and Ethnicity," *Federal Register* Notice, October 30, 1997, http://www.whitehouse.gov/omb/fedreg/1997standards.html.

6. Paul Taylor, et al., *When Labels Don't Fit: Hispanics and Their View of Identity*, Pew Hispanic Center, April 4, 2012, http://www.pewhispanic.org/2012/04/04/when-labels-dont-fit-hispanics-and-their-views-of-identity/.

7. US Census Bureau, "Hispanic Origin: Frequently Asked Questions," http://www.census.gov/population/hispanic/about/faq.html (accessed August 1, 2012).

8. US Census Bureau, "Hispanic Heritage Month 2010."

9. US Census Bureau, "Cinco de Mayo," *Profile America Facts for Features*, CB12-FF.10, March 21, 2012, http://www.census.gov/newsroom/releases/archives/facts_for_features_special_editions/cb12-ff10.html.

10. Carlos H. Arce, *The Hispanic Century Is Here: Results and Implications of the 2010 Census* (Austin, TX: EthniFacts, March 24, 2011), http://www.ethnifacts.com/Whitepaper.pdf.

11. The twenty-six countries include Puerto Rico, which actually is a commonwealth of the United States. Except for Spain, these were conquered by the Spanish and therefore share a common language and culture. Central Intelligence Agency, "Spain," *The World Factbook,* https://www.cia.gov/library/publications/the-world-factbook/geos/sp.html.

12. Yesemia D. Acosta and G. Patricia de la Cruz, "The Foreign Born from Latin America and the Caribbean: 2010," *American Community Survey Briefs*, ACSBR/10-15, September 2011, US Census Bureau, http://www.census.gov/prod/2011pubs/acsbr10-15.pdf.

13. Elizabeth Grieco, "Foreign-Born Hispanics in the United States," Migration Policy Institute, http://www.migrationinformation.org/usfocus/display.cfm?ID=95 (accessed February 11, 2012).

14. Acosta and de la Cruz, "Foreign Born: 2010."

15. Lowrey, "Hispanic-Owned Businesses."

16. "Scholarship Connects Chicano, Catholic Identities," *The Free Library*, review of Mario T. Garcia, *The Gospel of César Chávez: My Faith in Action* (New York: Sheed & Ward, 2007), http://www.thefreelibrary.com/ Scholarship+connects+Chicano,+Catholic+identities.-a0209618503 (accessed November 1, 2012).

17. Tom Peters, address to National Association of American Architects, Charlotte, North Carolina, May 2002.

## Part I

1. According to the 2010 US census, 4.7 million Hispanics live in Los Angeles County, California. This equals more than 50 percent of the 8.8 million residents in Mexico City. See "Capital Cities of the World: Population Estimates," *Worldatlas*, http:// www.worldatlas.com/capcitys.htm (accessed November 30, 2011).

2. To view Rocky Mountain Public Broadcasting Station's video *La Raza de Colorado: La Historia*, aired June 4, 2005, go to http://video.rmpbs.org/video/1601211894/.

3. Hispaniola is the second-largest island of the West Indies, where Columbus landed in 1492. It is currently known as the Dominican Republic and Haiti. Called la Española by Columbus, the name was later Anglicized to *Hispaniola*. See *Encyclopaedia Britannica*, s.v. "Hispaniola," http://www.britannica.com/EBchecked/topic/266962/ Hispaniola (accessed October 1, 2012).

## Chapter 1

1. Octavio Paz, *The Labyrinth of Solitude*, 2d ed. (New York: Penguin USA, 1977). First published in Spanish in 1950, *The Labyrinth of Solitude* is considered one of the most enduring and powerful works ever created about México and its people, character, and culture. Paz won the Nobel Prize for literature in 1990.

2. Carlos Fuente, *The Buried Mirror: Reflections of Spain and the New World* (New York: Houghton Mifflin, 1992), 33–43.

3. It should be noted that México is technically considered part of North America but still remains a country with Spanish heritage and language. See Latin American Network Information Center, "Country Directory," http://lanic.utexas.edu/subject/ countries/ (accessed March 12, 2011).

4. Fuentes, *Buried Mirror*, 44.

5. Ibid., 56–73.

6. Trudi Alexy, *The Mezuzah in the Madonna's Foot: Oral Histories Exploring Five Hundred Years in the Paradoxical Relationship of Spain and the Jews* (New York: Simon & Schuster, 1993).

7. Charles C. Mann, *1491: New Revelations of the Americas before Columbus* (New York: Alfred A. Knopf, 2005), 126–27.

8. Jared Diamond, *Guns, Germs, and Steel: The Fate of Human Societies* (New York: W. W. Norton, 1999), 69–74.

9. Ibid., 211, 212, 357, 358.

10. Rodriguez, *Our Lady of Guadalupe* (Austin, TX: University of Texas Press, 1994), 10–13.

11. Franciscan Friars of the Immaculate, *A Handbook on Guadalupe* (Waite Park, MN: Park Press, 1996); part XI, "Nican Mopohua: Original Account of Guadalupe," by Antonio Valerian, translated from the Nahuatl, 194.

12. Virgilio P. Elizondo, et al., *Los Católicos Hispanos en los Estados Unidos* (New York: Centro Católico de Patoral para Hispanos del Norte, 1980), 75–79.

13. Pope Pius XII declared the Virgin of Guadalupe "Queen of México and Empress of the Americas" in 1945 and "Patroness of the Americas" in 1946.

14. José Ignacio Echeagary, et al., *Album Conmemorativo del 450 Aniversario de las Apariciones de Nuestra Señora de Guadalupe* (México: Ediciones Buena Nueva, 1981).

15. Rodriquez, *Our Lady of Guadalupe*, 30.

16. Elizondo, et al., *Los Católicos Hispanos*.

17. Rodriquez, *Our Lady of Guadalupe*, 29.

18. "Our Lady of Charity: Patroness of Cuba," *The Catholic Tradition*, http://www.catholictradition.org/Mary/lady-charity.htm (accessed August 1, 2012).

19. "Virgin of Charity, El Cobre," *Sacred Destinations*, http://www.sacred-destinations.com/cuba/el-cobre.htm.

20. Plinio Corrêa de Oliveira, "Our Lady Aparecida—October 12," *Tradition in Action*, http://www.traditioninaction.org/SOD/j227sd_OLAparecida_10-12.html (accessed August 1, 2012).

21. Octavio Paz, *The Labyrinth of Solitude: The Other México*, 2nd ed. (New York: Grove Press, 1994). Paz delves into the minds of the Spanish-Indian people. He describes them as hidden behind masks of solitude. Due to their history, their identity is lost between a pre-Columbian and a Spanish culture.

22. Rodriquez, *Our Lady of Guadalupe*, 31.

23. Ilan Rachum, "Origins and Historical Significance of Día de la Raza," *Revista Europea de Estudios Latinoamericanos y del Caribe*, 76, April 2004), 61, http://www.cedla.uva.nl/50_publications/pdf/revista/76RevistaEuropea/76Rachum.pdf.

## Chapter 2

1. Raul Yzaguirre, "Liberty and Justice for All," in *Latinos and the Nation's Future*, ed. Henry Cisneros, (Houston: Arte Publico Press, 2009), 28–29.

2. Nicholás Kanellos, "The Latino Presence: Some Historical Background," in *Latinos and the Nation's Future*, ed. Henry Cisneros (Houston: Arte Publico Press, 2009), 15–19.

3. Ibid., 21.

4. Ibid., 20.

5. Paul A. Janson, "Manifest Destiny and Mission in the 21st Century," *George Mason University's History News Network*, July 8, 2002, http://hnn.us/articles/534.html.

6. William Earl Weeks, *Building the Continental Empire: American Expansion from the Revolution to the Civil War* (Chicago: Ivan R. Dee, 1996), 61.

7. Stephen L. Hardin, *The Alamo 1836: Santa Anna's Texas Campaign*, Osprey Campaign Series 89 (Oxford, England: Osprey Publishing, 2001).

8. Bill Groneman, *Battlefields of Texas* (Plano, TX: Republic of Texas Press, 1998).

9. S. C. Gwynne, *Empire of the Summer Moon* (New York: Scribner, 2010), 162, 164–5, 167.

10. "The White Man's Burden," a poem by the English poet Rudyard Kipling, was originally published in the popular magazine *McClure's* in 1899, with the subtitle *The United States and the Philippine Islands*. It justified imperialism as a noble enterprise.

11. Coretta Scott King, *The Words of Martin Luther King Jr.* (New York: Newmarket Press, 1983), 67.

12. Passel and Cohn, "Population Projections: 2005–2050" (see preface, n. 2).

13. Cristina Benitez and Marlene González, *Latinization and the Latino Leader* (Ithaca, NY: Paramount Market Publishing, 2011), 1–3.

14. See Central Intelligence Agency, "Spain" (see introduction, n. 11).

15. The White House, Office of the Press Secretary, "Fact Sheet: The U.S. Relationship with Central and South America," March 15, 2011, http://www.whitehouse.gov/the-press-office/2011/03/15/fact-sheet-us-relationship-central-and-south-america.

16. Deborah Sharp, "Si usted no habla español, puede quedarse rezagado—If You Don't Speak Spanish, You Might Be Left Behind," *USA Today*, May 9, 2001, http://www.spain.uga.edu/resources/articles/usa_today.pdf.

17. Larry Rohter, "Learn English, Says Chile, Thinking Upwardly Global," *New York Times*, December 29, 2004, http://www.nytimes.com/2004/12/29/international/americas/29letter.html?_r=1&scp=1&sq=%22english%20opens%20doors%22&st=cse.

18. *Languages of the World*, http://www.nationsonline.org/oneworld/languages.htm (accessed May 4, 2011).

19. Taylor, et al., *When Labels Don't Fit* (see introduction, n. 6).

20. Nations Online Project, "Most Widely Spoken Languages in the World," last modified May 27, 2011, http://www.nationsonline.org/oneworld/most_spoken_languages.htm.

21. "Hispanic Buying Power to Reach 1.3 Trillion in 2013," *Hispanic Digital Media*, February 26, 2009, http://hispanicdigital.blogspot.com/2009/02/hispanic-buying-power-to-reach-13-bill.html.

22. The International Monetary Fund, *Report for Selected Countries and Subjects*, http://www.imf.org/external/data.htm (accessed July 15, 2012).

23. US Department of Commerce, "Hispanic-Owned Businesses Grow by More than Double the National Rate," September 21, 2010, http://www.commerce.gov/blog/2010/09/21/hispanic-owned-businesses-grow-more-double-national-rate.

24. Evangeline Gomez, "Latino-Owned Businesses: Leading the Recovery," *Forbes Magazine*, December 28, 2011, http://www.forbes.com/sites/evangelinegomez/2011/12/28/latino-owned-businesses-leading-the-recovery/.

25. Elizabeth Llorente, "Election 2012: Obama Wins Re-election, Clinches Latino Vote," Fox News Latinos, November 6, 2012, http://latino.foxnews.com/latino/politics/2012/11/06/election-2012-obama-wins-re-election-after-clinching-ohio/.

26. *LatinoDecisions.com*, "Latinos Pivotal to the National Election," 2012 Election Eve Poll, http://www.latinodecisions.com/files/4113/5241/8534/StateComparisonLEE.pdf (accessed November 18, 2012).

27. National Association of Latino Elected and Appointed Officials, "A Profile of Latino Elected Officials in the United States and Their Progress since 1996," http://www.naleo.org/downloads/DirecSummary2010B.pdf (accessed August 1, 2012).

28. Lance Gay, "Mexican Food Becoming America's Favorite Ethnic Treat," *Hispanic Trending*, February 28, 2006, http://www.hispanictrending.net/2006/02/mexican_food_be.html.

29. Ibid.

30. Jesse Sanchez, "Latinos Have Come a Long Way in Baseball," *MLB.com*, September 21, 2010, http://mlb.mlb.com/news/article.jsp?ymd=20100920&content_id=14886934&vkey=news_mlb&c_id=mlb.

**Part II**

1. Lao Tzu, "The Ripple Effect," in *Tao Te Ching* (New York: Vintage Press, 1989).

2. Charles Manz and Henry Sims, *The New Superleadership: Leading Others to Lead Themselves*, 1st ed. (San Francisco: Berrett-Koehler, 2001).

3. Stephen Covey, *7 Habits of Highly Effective People* (New York: Simon & Schuster, 1989).

4. Lee Bowman and Terrence Deal, *Leading with Soul: An Uncommon Journey of Spirit*, 3rd ed. (San Francisco: John Wiley & Sons, 2011).

5. Robert K. Greenleaf, *The Servant as Leader* (Newton Center, MA: The Robert Greenleaf Center, 1970).

**Chapter 3**

1. National Alliance for Hispanic Health, *Quality Health Services for Hispanics: The Cultural Competency Component*, DHHS Publication No. 99-21 (Washington, DC: Department of Health and Human Services, 2000).

2. Miguel Corona, "Inspiring Hispanic Interns through Personalismo," *Intern Matters*, March 4, 2010, http://internmatters.wordpress.com/2010/03/04/empowering-hispanic-interns-through-personalismo/.

3. National Community for Latino Leadership, *Reflecting an American Vista: The Character and Impact of Latino Leadership* 1, no. 1, January 2001. NCLL is a national organization founded in 1989 whose mission is to develop ethical, responsible, and accountable leaders on behalf of the U.S. Latino population. See http://www.latinoleadership.org/.

4. Common Ground International, "From Personalismo to Confianza: Building Relationships with Latinos," January 26, 2009, http://commongroundinternational.com/from-personalismo-to-confianza-building-relationships-with-latinos/.

5. Greenleaf, *Servant as Leader*. (see part II, n. 5).

6. Norma Carr-Ruffino, *Managing Diversity: People Skills for a Multicultural Workplace* (Andover, UK: International Thomson Publishing, 1996), 337.

7. Nilda Choy, MD, *The Latino Patient: A Cultural Guide for Health Professionals* (Yarmouth, ME: Intercultural Press, 2002), 24, 25, 29.

**Chapter 4**

1. Greenleaf, *Servant as Leader* (see part II, n. 5).

2. National Community for Latino Leadership, *Reflecting an American Vista* (see chap. 3, n. 3)

3. Rodolfo "Corky" Gonzales, "I Am Joaquin," http://www.latinamericanstudies.org/latinos/joaquin.htm (accessed November 11, 2010). See also the YouTube video "I Am Joaquin (part one of two)," http://www.youtube.com/watch?v=U6M6qOG2O-o.

4. Peggy McIntosh, *White Privilege and Male Privilege: A Personal Account of Coming to See Correspondences through Work in Women's Studies* (Wellesley, MA: Wellesley College, 1988).

5. Paulo Freire, *The Pedagogy of the Oppressed*, trans. Myra Bergman Ramos, special anniversary edition (New York: Continuum, 2000).

6. Lerner Stores Corporation, http://www.stocklobster.com/1892.html (accessed November 15, 2011).

7. California Department of Education, "César E. Chávez: Middle School Biography," http://chavez.cde.ca.gov/ModelCurriculum/Teachers/Lessons/Resources/Biographies/Middle_Level_Biography.aspx (accessed December 1, 2011).

## Chapter 5

1. Covey, *7 Habits* (see part II, n. 3).

2. Carr-Ruffino, *Managing Diversity* (see chap. 3, n. 6), 41–45.

3. Ibid., 42–43.

4. Juana Bordas, "Passion and Power: Finding Personal Purpose," self-published, 2nd ed., 2009, http://www.mestizaleadership.com/articles-publications/index.php.

5. Shirley Griggs and Rita Dunn, "Hispanic-American Students and Learning Styles," *Emergency Librarian*, November-December 1995, no. 2, accession number 9511291097, http://educationinaminute.com/bogota/Resources/Articles/Griggs%20and%20Dunn%202.pdf.

6. Zev Chafets, "The Post-Hispanic Politician," *New York Times Magazine*, May 6, 2010, http://www.nytimes.com/2010/05/09/magazine/09Mayor-t.html?pagewanted=all.

7. US Census Bureau, "State & County QuickFacts: San Antonio, Texas," last revised June 6, 2012, http://quickfacts.census.gov/qfd/states/48/4865000.html.

8. "Hilda L. Solis," Times Topics, *New York Times*, July 6, 2009, http://topics.nytimes.com/topics/reference/timestopics/people/s/hilda_l_solis/index.html.

9. Lisa Quiroz, interview, "Focused Efforts," How to Make a Difference, *Leaders* 33, no. 2, 64, April 2010, http://www.leadersmag.com/issues/2010.2_Apr/Making%20a%20Difference/Quiroz.html.

10. Greenleaf, *Servant as Leader* (see part II, n. 5).

11. Joseph Jaworski, *Synchronicity: The Inner Path of Leadership,* 2nd ed. (San Francisco: Berrett-Koehler, 2011).

12. Joseph Campbell, *The Hero's Journey: Joseph Campbell on His Life and Work*, 3rd (centennial) ed., ed. and introduction Phil Cousineau (Novato, CA: New World Library, 2003).

13. Greenleaf, *Servant as Leader* (see part II, n. 5).

14. Covey, *7 Habits* (see part II, n. 3), 147.

**Part III**

1. Carr-Ruffino, *Managing Diversity* (see chap. 3, n. 6), 32–38.

**Chapter 6**

1. Burt Nanus, "What Is Vision—and Why It Matters," chap. 1 in *Visionary Leadership* (San Francisco: Jossey-Bass, 1992).

2. Juana Bordas, *Salsa, Soul, and Spirit: Leadership for a Multicultural Age*, 2nd ed. (San Francisco: Berrett-Koehler, 2012), 50–55.

3. C. E. Ross and J. Mirowsky, "Socially Desirable Responses and Acquiescence in a Cross-Cultural Society," *Journal of Health and Social Behavior* 25 (1984): 189–97.

4. Robert Rodriguez, *Latino Talent: Effective Strategies to Recruit, Retain and Develop Hispanic Professionals* (Hoboken, NJ: John Wiley & Sons, 2008), 39.

5. Yolanda Nava, *It's All in the Frijoles* (New York: Fireside, 2000), 40–42.

6. Cristina Benitez, *Latinization: How Latino Culture Is Transforming the U.S.* (Ithaca, NY: Paramount Marketing, 2007), 28.

7. James M. Kouzes and Barry Z. Posner, *The Leadership Challenge*, rev. ed. (San Francisco: Jossey-Bass, 2003).

8. Kanellos, "The Latino Presence" (see chap. 2. n. 2), 20.

9. US Census Bureau, "Hispanic Heritage Month 2010" (see preface, n. 5).

10. Taylor, et al., *When Labels Don't Fit* (see introduction, n. 6).

11. Randall B. Lindsey, et al., *Cultural Proficiency: A Manual for School Leaders*, 2nd ed. (Thousand Oaks, CA: Sage Publications), 48.

12. Pew Research Center: "Millennials: A Portrait of Generation Next," February 24, 2010, http://pewresearch.org/millennials/.

**Chapter 7**

1. "Economic Treaty: The Financial Autonomy of Navarre," *Navarra.Es*, http://www.navarra.es/home_en/Navarra/Asi+es+Navarra/Autogobierno/ El+convenio+economico.htm (accessed November 5, 2011).

2. As related to the author by Leobardo Estrada, professor at University of California at Los Angeles, whose focus is on ethnic and racial demographic trends, particularly in the Latino population. The US Bureau of the Census has asked Estrada to provide his knowledge on methodologies related to ethnic and racial groups.

3. US Census Bureau, "Directive No. 15: Race and Ethnic Standards for Federal Statistics and Administrative Reporting," as adopted on May 12, 1977, http://wonder.cdc.gov/ wonder/help/populations/bridged-race/Directive15.html.

4. Office of Management and Budget, "Data on Race and Ethnicity" (see introduction, n. 5).

5. F. James Davis, *Who Is Black? One Nation's Definition* (University Park, PA: Penn State Press, 2001).

6. Interview with LaDonna Harris, Comanche, president of Americans for Indian Opportunity. In Bordas, *Salsa, Soul, and Spirit*, 168.

7. Elizabeth M. Hoeffel, et al., *The Asian Population: 2010*, 2010 Census Briefs, C2010BR-11, March 2012, US Census Bureau, http://www.census.gov/prod/cen2010/briefs/c2010br-11.pdf.

8. Karen R. Humes, Nicholas A. Jones, and Roberto R. Ramirez, *Overview of Race and Hispanic Origin: 2010*, 2010 Census Briefs, C2010BR-02, March 2011, US Census Bureau, http://www.census.gov/prod/cen2010/briefs/c2010br-02.pdf.

9. *Océano Pocket Diccionario* (Barcelona, España: Grupo Oceano Editorial, 1952); s.v. "bienvenido"; trans. as "to welcome, receive, or accept with pleasure, to approve or appreciate or even to embrace."

10. Cuban American National Council, "CNC History," http://www.cnc.org/ (accessed November 10, 2011).

11. Betsy Guzman, *The Hispanic Population,* Census 2000 Brief, May 2001, US Census Bureau, http://www.census.gov/prod/2001pubs/c2kbr01-3.pdf.

12. National Council of La Raza, "Governance and History," http://www.nclr.org/ (accessed November 11, 2011).

13. Scott Keeter and Paul Taylor, Pew Research Center: "The Millennials," December 11, 2009, http://pewresearch.org/pubs/1437/millennials-profile.

14. Pew Hispanic Center, *Between Two Worlds: How Young Latinos Come of Age in America*, December 2009, http://www.pewhispanic.org/2009/12/11/between-two-worlds-how-young-latinos-come-of-age-in-america/.

15. Newsmax: The Associated Press, "10,000 Boomers to Retire Each Day for 19 Years," December 27, 2010, http://www.newsmax.com/Newsfront/RetirementCrisis/2010/12/27/id/381191.

16. US Hispanic Leadership Institute, "Mission," http://www.ushli.org/about/mission.php (accessed January 5, 2012).

17. Thom S. Rainer and Jess W. Rainer, *The Millennials: Connecting to America's Largest Generation* (Nashville, TN: B & H Publishing Group, 2011), 59.

18. *Merriam-Webster's Online*, s.v. "ally," http://www.merriam-webster.com/dictionary/ally (accessed January 5, 2012).

19. Eric Greenberg and Karl Weber, *Generation We: How Millennial Youth Are Taking over America and Changing the World* (Emeryville, CA: Pachatusan, 2008).

20. Email response from Ron Blackburn on June 9, 2012, regarding youth representation on ASPIRA's board.

21. Rainer and Rainer, *The Millennials,* 37.

22  Ibid., 7.

23. Hilary Doe and Zachary Kolodin, eds., *Blueprint for the Millennial America,* presented by the Roosevelt Campus network; available at http://www.scribd.com/doc/44487427/Blueprint-for-Millennial-America.

24. There is a precedence for having a national anthem in communities of color. In 1919, the NAACP adopted "Lift Ev'ry Voice and Sing" as the "Negro national anthem."

25. US Census Bureau, "Census of Population and Housing—1790 Census," http://www.census.gov/prod/www/abs/decennial/1790.html (accessed October 1, 2012).

26. Susan Saulny, "Census Data Presents Rise in Multiracial Population of Youths," *New York Times*, March 24, 2011, http://www.nytimes.com/2011/03/25/us/25race.html.

27. "Lift Ev'ry Voice and Sing," National Association for the Advancement of Colored People, http://www.lounaacp.org/lifthistory.html (accessed July 30, 2012). In 1919, the NAACP adopted the song as the Negro national anthem, thus enhancing the identity of Black Americans. I propose Latinos follow in this tradition and that "De Colores," which reflects the culture and community's great diversity, be adopted as the Hispanic national anthem.

## Chapter 8

1. Norma Carr-Ruffino, *Managing Diversity* (see chap. 3, n. 6), 232.
2. Greenleaf, *Servant as Leader* (see part II, n. 5).
3. National Community for Latino Leadership, *Reflecting an American Vista: The Character and Impact of Latino Leadership* 1, no. 1, January 2001; see http://www.latinoleadership.org/.
4. Greenleaf, *Servant as Leader.*
5. Latino Policy Form, *An American Agenda from a Latino Perspective*, April 2008, http://www.latinopolicyforum.org/assets/C0589015_LatinosUnited_v3_FINAL_VERSION.pdf.
6. Ibid.
7. The League of United Latin American Citizens, founded in 1929, is the oldest Hispanic civil rights organization in the United States. http://lulac.org/about/history/ (accessed December 11, 2011).
8. In 1954, LULAC brought *Hernandez v. Texas* to protest the fact that Mexican Americans had been barred during jury selection. The US Supreme Court ruled this exclusion unconstitutional. See Public Broadcasting Service, "A Class Apart: A Mexican American Civil Rights Story," *American Experience,* 2009.
9. Mark Hugo Lopez and Gabriel Velasco, *A Demographic Portrait of Puerto Ricans*, Pew Hispanic Center, June 13, 2011, http://pewhispanic.org/reports/report.php?ReportID=143.
10. Organización Auténtica, "US Census Bureau: Facts about Cuban Americans," http://www.autentico.org/oa09629.php (accessed October 2, 2012).
11. US Census Bureau, "Hispanic Heritage Month 2010" (see preface, n. 5).
12. Joey Bunch, "Survey Tabs Denver as Best City to Call Home," *Denver Post*, January 29, 2009, http://www.denverpost.com/breakingnews/ci_11578103.

## Chapter 9

1. Just over 18 million, or 47 percent of the foreign-born population, were of Hispanic origin. Elizabeth Grieco, *Race and Hispanic Origin of the Foreign-Born Population in the United States: 2007*, American Community Survey Reports ACS -11, US Census Bureau, January 2010, http://www.census.gov/prod/2010pubs/acs-11.pdf.
2. Merage Foundation for the American Dream, *Becoming an American: The Immigrant Experience*, a video in the American Dream series.
3. US Census Bureau News, "Hispanic Heritage Month 2011: Sept. 15–Oct. 15," *Profile America Facts for Features: 2011*, CB11-FF.18, August 26, 2011, http://www.census.gov/newsroom/releases/pdf/cb11ff-18_hispanic.pdf.

4. Acosta and de la Cruz, "Foreign Born" (see introduction, n. 12).

5. Kathleen Kennedy Townsend, "Renewing the U.S.-Latin American Alliance For Progress, 50 Years Later," *The Atlantic,* September 15, 2011, http://www.theatlantic.com/international/archive/2011/09/renewing-the-us-latin-american-alliance-for-progress-50-years-later/245169/.

6. McKee, David L. "Some Specifics on the Brain Drain from the Andean Region," *International Migration/Migrations Internationales/ Migraciones Internacionales* 21, no. 4 (1983): 488–99.

7. Acosta and de la Cruz, "Foreign Born."

8. Taylor, et al., *When Labels Don't Fit* (see introduction, n. 6).

9. Acosta and de la Cruz, "Foreign Born."

10. Quoted in Burton Bollag, "Immigrants' Entrepreneurial Spirit Helps U.S. Economy," *US Policy,* US Embassy, Brussels, Belgium, January 2009, http://www.uspolicy.be/headline/immigrants%E2%80%99-entrepreneurial-spirit-helps-us-economy.

11. Taylor, et al., *When Labels Don't Fit* (see introduction, n. 6).

12. Jeffrey Passel and D'Vera Cohn, "Immigration to Play Lead Role in Future U.S. Growth," Pew Research Center, February 11, 2008, http://pewresearch.org/pubs/729/united-states-population-projections.

13. Ibid.

14. Ibid.

15. Passel and Cohn, "Population Projections: 2005–2050" (see preface, n. 2).

16. Ernest Gundling, Terry Hogan, and Karen Cvitkovich, *What Is Global Leadership? 10 Key Behaviors That Define Great Global Leaders* (Boston: Nicholas Brealey Publishing, 2011).

17. Ibid.

18. Ibid.

19. Ibid.

20. Walter Link, Thais Corral, and Mark Gerzon, eds., *Leadership Is Global: Co-Creating a More Humane and Sustainable World* (Shinnyo-en Foundation, 2006). The Global Leadership Network website is at http://www.gln-online.org/.

21. Taylor, et al., *When Labels Don't Fit* (see introduction, n. 6).

22. Pew Hispanic Center, *Between Two Worlds* (see chap. 7, n. 14).

23. "U.S. Troops Land in the Dominican Republic," This Day in History (April 28, 1965), *History.com,* http://www.history.com/this-day-in-history/us-troops-land-in-the-dominican-republic (accessed January 15, 2012).

24. Raul Yzaguirre, speech to Dominican American Round Table, October 8, 2011, Lehman College, City University of New York.

25. Passel and Cohn, "Population Projections: 2005–2050."

26. Pew Hispanic Center, *Between Two Worlds* (see chap. 7, n. 14).

27. Arizona Senate Bill 1070 was the most stringent antiillegal immigration measure passed in decades. The act "directs law enforcement officers who possess 'reasonable suspicion' that an individual is unlawfully present to make reasonable attempts to determine the immigration status of that person and makes the unlawful presence of a foreign national a criminal offense" (Legal Information Institute, "Support Our Law Enforcement and Safe Neighborhoods Act of 2010," August 19, 2010, http://www .law.cornell.edu/wex/support_our_law_enforcement_and_safe_neighborhoods_act _of_2010).

28. US Department of Justice, FBI, "Hate Crime Statistics," http://www.fbi.gov/about-us/ cjis/ucr/hate-crime/2010/narratives/hate-crime-2010-victims (accessed December 12, 2011).

29. Llorente, "Election 2012" (see chap. 2, n. 25).

**Chapter 10**

1. Antonia Pantoja, *Memoir of a Visionary* (Houston, TX: Arte Público Press, 2002), 61.

2. Kouzes and Posner, *Leadership Challenge* (see chap. 6, n. 7), 28–33.

3. Warren Bennis and Burt Nanus: *Leaders: The Strategies for Taking Charge*, 2nd ed. (New York: Harper Collins, 1997).

4. James McGregor Burns, *Leadership* (New York: Harper & Row, 1978).

5. "Immigrants Protest across the U.S.," *PBS News Hour,* May 1, 2006, http://www.pbs .org/newshour/bb/law/jan-june06/immigration2_05-01.html.

6. Leslie Berestein Rojas, "Beyond May Day and Marches: An Evolving Immigrant Rights Movement," Southern California Public Radio, May 1, 2012, http:// multiamerican.scpr.org/2012/05/beyond-may-day-and-marches-an-evolving -immigrant-rights-movement/.

7. John Gardner, as listed in *Direct Quotes: Contemporary Consultants* (1966; a printed workbook available from Mary Jo Clark and Pat Heiny, P.O. Box 52, Richmond, IN 47375). From a speech delivered by John Gardner to Leadership USA, November 18, 1995, Pomona, CA.

8. Hispanic Association on Corporate Responsibility, "About," http://www.hacr.org/ about/ (accessed July 15, 2012).

9. Eugene Robinson, *Disintegration: The Splintering of Black America* (New York: Doubleday, 2010).

10. Barbara Epstein, "What Happened to the Women's Movement?" *Monthly Review* 5, no. 1, May 2001, http://monthlyreview.org/2001/05/01/what-happened-to-the -womens-movement.

11. Mark Hugo Lopez and Paul Taylor, "Latino Voters in the 2012 Election," Pew Hispanic Center, November 7, 2012, http://www.pewhispanic.org/2012/11/07/ latino-voters-in-the-2012-election/.

12. Lara Birnback, et al., "Public Engagement and the Growing Latino Population," Center for Advances in Public Engagement, working paper, Summer 2011, http:// www.publicagenda.org/files/pdf/CAPE_Public_Engagement_and_Americas _Growing_Latino_Population.pdf.

13. Rainer and Rainer, *The Millennials*, 7 (see chap. 7. n. 17).

14. US Census Bureau, "Hispanic Heritage Month 2010" (see preface, n. 5). See also: Rakesh Kochhar, Ana Gonzalez-Barrera, and Daniel Dockterman, *Through Boom and Bust: Minorities, Immigrants and Homeownership*, Pew Hispanic Center, May 12, 2009, http://www.pewhispanic.org/2009/05/12/through-boom-and-bust/.

15. New York Times/CBS News poll based on telephone interviews conducted July 13 to 27, 2003, with 3,092 adults throughout the United States, http://www.nytimes.com/packages/html/politics/20030806_poll/20030806poll-results.html.

## Chapter 11

1. Richard Gould, *The Life and Times of Richard Castro* (Denver: Colorado Historical Society, 2007).

2. MC Marketing Charts, "Hispanics Create More than Half of Food Growth," April 9, 2010, http://www.marketingcharts.com/topics/behavioral-marketing/hispanics-create-more-than-half-of-food-growth-12546/latinum-hispanic-food -growth-apr-2010.

3. National Community for Latino Leadership Inc. (NCLL), *Reflecting an American Vista: The Character and Impact of Latino Leadership* 1, no. 1, January 2001.

4. Sobre la Asociación Española de Personalismo. "¿Que Es Personalismo?" (What Is Personalismo?) http://www.personalismo.org/ (accessed August 1, 2012).

5. *Internet Encyclopedia of Philosophy*, s.v. "René Descartes (1596-1650): Overview," http://www.iep.utm.edu/descarte/ (accessed February 10, 2012).

6. Carr-Ruffino, *Managing Diversity* (see chap. 3, n. 6).

7. Mona Reaume, "Hiding Our Feelings Can Impact Our Health and Longevity," http://www.alive.com/1806a5a2.php?subject_bread_cramb=5 (retrieved August 20, 2012).

8. Daniel Goleman, *Emotional Intelligence* (New York: Bantam Books, 1995).

9. Kouzes and Posner, *Leadership Challenge* (see chap. 6. n. 7).

## Chapter 12

1. Goleman, *Emotional Intelligence*.

2. New York Times/CBS News poll (see chap. 10, n. 15).

3. Nicole Ibarra, "Survey: Hispanic Professionals Say Future Looks Bright," *Hispanic Trending*, July 19, 2007, http://www.hispanictrending.net/2007/07/survey-hispanic .html.

4. Chávez, "Farm Workers Prayer" (see introduction, n. 15).

5. *Education of the Heart: Quotes by César Chávez (Commitment)*, http://www.fsu .edu/~flserve/resources/Chavez/Education-of-the-Heart.pdf (accessed August 1, 2012).

6. Federico Peña, "We Are America," speech delivered in Denver, CO, May 1, 2006.

7. *Education of the Heart: Quotes by Cesar Chavez (Organizing)*, http://www.fsu .edu/~flserve/resources/Chavez/Education-of-the-Heart.pdf (accessed August 1, 2012).

8. Nava, *All in the Frijoles* (see chap. 6, n. 5), 150–52.

9. Ibid., 173.

10. Greenleaf, *Servant as Leader* (see part II, n. 5).

**Part V**

1. Article 1, section 2, clause 3 of the US Constitution, http://law2.umkc.edu/faculty/projects/ftrials/conlaw/thirteenthamendment.html (accessed August 15, 2012).
2. Office of Management and Budget, "Data on Race and Ethnicity" (see introduction, n. 5).
3. Frances Hesselbein, "Managing in a World That Is Round," *Leader to Leader Journal*, no. 2, Fall 1996, http://www.hesselbeininstitute.org/knowledgecenter/journal.aspx?ArticleID=136.
4. Saulny, "Multiracial Population of Youths" (see chap. 7, n. 26).

**Chapter 13**

1. Sam Roberts, "New Favor for a Name That Straddles Cultures," *New York Times*, January 20, 2007, http://www.nytimes.com/2007/01/20/nyregion/20angel.html.
2. Greenberg and Weber, *Generation We* (see chap. 7, n. 19), 12.
3. Rodriguez, *Latino Talent* (see chap. 6, n. 4), 191–99.
4. Taylor, et al., *When Labels Don't Fit* (see introduction, n. 6).
5. PR Newswire, "Newsweek: Latin U.S.A.: How Young Hispanics Are Changing America," July 3, 1999, http://www2.prnewswire.com/cgi-bin/stories.pl?ACCT=104&STORY=/www/story/07-03-1999/0000975520&EDATE.
6. Pew Hispanic Center, *Between Two Worlds* (see chap. 7, n. 14).
7. Ibid.
8. Taylor, et al., *When Labels Don't Fit*.
9. United States Hispanic Chamber of Commerce, http://www.ushcc.com/ (accessed August 1, 2012).
10. Paul Taylor, Ana Gonzalez-Barrera, Jeffrey Passel, and Mark Hugo Lopez, "An Awakened Giant: The Hispanic Electorate Is Likely to Double by 2030," Pew Hispanic Center, November 14, 2012, http://www.pewhispanic.org/2012/11/14/an-awakened-giant-the-hispanic-electorate-is-likely-to-double-by-2030/.
11. Pew Hispanic Center, *Between Two Worlds*.
12. Center for American Women and Politics, Rutgers University, "Facts on Women in Congress 2011," http://www.cawp.rutgers.edu/fast_facts/levels_of_office/Congress-CurrentFacts.php (accessed July 31, 2012).
13. National Women's Law Center, "Women Can't Afford Unfair Pay Today," April 2012, http://www.nwlc.org/sites/default/files/pdfs/womenunfairpayfactsheet.pdf.
14. José Vasconcelos, *La Raza Cósmica* (México D.F., Espasa Calpe, S.A., 1948), 47–51.
15. Natalie Angier, "DNA Shows Humans Are All One Race," *New York Times*, August 22, 2000, http://www.nytimes.com/2000/08/22/science/do-races-differ-not-really-genes-show.html?pagewanted=all&src=pm. Updated information supports the 2000 studies. Studies by the Human Genome Project indicate that all modern humans share a common female ancestor who lived in Africa about 140,000 years ago, and all men share a common male ancestor who lived in Africa about 60,000 years ago. See Human Genome Project Information, "Genetic Anthropology, Ancestry, and Ancient Human Migration," http://www.ornl.gov/sci/techresources/Human_Genome/elsi/humanmigration.shtml (accessed January 12, 2012).

16. Franciscan Friars of the Immaculate, *A Handbook on Guadalupe* (see chap. 1, n. 11), 194.

17. Mary Fong and Rueyling Chuang, eds., *Communicating Ethnic and Cultural Identity* (Lanham, MD: Rowman & Littlefield, 2004), 112.

18. "A Message from the Hopi Elders: The Hopi National Elders at Oraibi, Arizona," March 2002, http://www.matrixmasters.com/takecharge/hopi-prophecy.html (accessed January 15, 2012).

# Glossary

*Abriendo Caminos*—"Opening Pathways" (title of the film about Antonia Patoja)

*abrazos*—embraces

*abuela*—grandmother

*abuelos*—grandparents

*ahora*—now

*Alemania*—Germany

*aliados*—allies

*amigos*—friends

*¡ándale!*—go quickly

*antepasados*—ancestors

*aspira*—to aspire

*a sus órdenes*—at your service

*¡Ay, chihuahua!*—expression of surprise or shock

"Ay, mi hijita, nunca olvides quien eres y de donde venistes"—Oh my dearest little daughter, never forget who you are and where you came from

*Ay, no hay que llorar, porque la vida es un carnival*—No need to cry, because life is a carnival

*banda*—band

*barrio*—neighborhood

*bendición*—blessing

*bien educado*—well-educated

*bienvenido*—welcome

*¡caramba!*—wow!

*cariño*—affection

*carisma*—charisma

*caudillo*—boss

*charlar*—chat

*Chicano*—American of Mexican descent

*chico*—kid

*comadre*—female friend of the family

*compadre*—male friend of the family

*compartir*—to participate

*comunidad*—community

*con gotas se llena el valde*—the barrel fills up drop by drop

*con permiso*—with permission

*conciencia*—conscience, self-awareness

*confianza*—confidence

*conjunto*—set

*conquistadores*—conquerors

*consejo*—counsel

*consistencia*—consistency

*corazón*—heart

*cultura, la*—the culture

*de colores*—of many colors

*de*—of *or* from

*destino*—destiny

*días de fiestas*—days of festivities

*dicho*—saying

*dinero*—money

*echando flores*—giving flowers

*el*—the (masculine)

*el Día de la Raza*—the day of the race (new Latino people of the world)

*el Golfo de México*—the Gulf of México

*el Pueblo de Nuestra Señora la Reina de Los Angeles*—the Village of Our Lady, the Queen of the Angels of the River Porziuncola

*¿Entiende Ud. español?*—Do you speak Spanish? (asked formally)

*es tu primo*—he's your cousin

*España*—Spain

*español*—Spanish

*esperanza*—hope

*está en las manos de Dios*—it is in the hands of God

*estoy*—I am (temporary)

*familia*—family

*fe y esperanza*—faith and hope

*fuerza*—force

*igualdad*—equality, fairness, and justice

Fidelistas—supporters of Fidel Castro of Cuba

*fiesta*—party

*finca*—farm

*flores*—flowers

*frijoles*—beans

*ganas*—desire

*gente*—people

*gozar la vida*—to savor life

*gracias*—thank you

*gusto*—taste or liking

*hacienda*—estate

*hágalo con orgullo*—do it with pride

*hermanos*—brothers; *hermanas*—sisters

*hombre de palabra*—man of his word

*inglés*—English

*in Lak'ech*—You are in me and I am in you (Mayan)

*jamón*—ham

*juntos*—union, we are together

*la*—the (feminine singular)

La Raza Unida— organization whose name means "the united race"

*Latinismo*—Latinism

*lengua*—language

*libro*—book

*los*—the (masc. plural); *las* (fem. plural)

*los que no trabajan no comen*—those that don't work don't eat

*madrina*—godmother

*maestro*—master

*maíz*—corn

*mande*—tell me what you want me to do

*más*—more

*mestizaje*—experience of Mestizo mix

Mestizo —mixture of European (predominantly Spanish) and Indian

*mi*—my

*mi casa es su casa*—my house is your house

*milagro*—miracle

*mucho*—much

*música*—music

*muy contento/a*—very happy

*niños*—children

*no importa*—it's not important

*¡Orale!*—Keep it up! Right on! or Way to go!

*padres*—parents

*padrino*—godfather

*palabras*—words

*para servirle*—to serve you

*partera*—midwife

*pasión*—passion

*paso a paso*—step by step

Peronistas—supporters of Juan Perón of Argentina

*personalismo*—persona

*pico de gallo*—a diced chunky salsa; literally, "beak of the rooster"

*por favor*—please

*primos*—cousins

*problema*—problem

*¡Que viva el español!*—Long live the Spanish language!

*¿Que es destino?*—What is destiny?

*¡Que simpatico!*—How easygoing!

*rancheros*—ranchers

*Raza, la*—the race; best defined as "the new Latino people of the world"

*Raza Cósmica, la*—the cosmic race

*respeto*—respect

*rico*—rich

*salsa*—sauce

*sentimentos*—feelings

*ser*—to be (permanent)

*ser honesto*—to be honest

*sí, es la hora*—yes, it's the hour

*Si quieres hablar español, oprima el número*—If you speak Spanish, press the number

*sí se puede*—yes, we can

*simpático*—easy to get along with

*soy*—I am (permanent)

*soy como soy*—I am the way I am

*te quita el corazón*—it rips your heart out

*tilma*—a traditional Indian poncho

*tía abuela*—grandmother aunt

*tías*—aunts

*tíos*—uncles

*trabajar*—to work

*último, el*—the best, the last

*un*—a

*único*—unique

*unidos*—united

*vámonos*—let's go

Valle del Sol—Hispanic organization, literally, "valley of the sun"

*vaqueros*—cowboys

*vida*—life

*vida Latina, la*—the Latin life

*yo decido*—I decide

*yo siento, ergo soy*—I feel, therefore I am

# Index

# About the Author

JUANA BORDAS LEARNED LEADERSHIP from her immigrant parents especially her mother, Maria, who cooked food and scrubbed floors in the school lunch room so Juana could get a scholarship to a Catholic school. "Their vision for the future, determination, and sacrifice taught me the very essence of Servant Leadership."

The first in her family to go to college, she joined the Peace Corps and worked in the barrios of Santiago, Chile. Juana later received the U.S. Peace Corps' Franklin Williams Award for her life-long commitment to advancing communities of color.

Juana was a founder and executive director of Denver's Mi Casa Resource Center recognized today as a national empowerment model. She was founding President of the National Hispana Leadership Institute, the only program in America that prepares Latinas for national leadership. In 2001, she launched the Circle of Latina Leadership in Colorado "to prepare the next generation of Latina leaders." For her extensive work with Latinas, she was commended by *Latina Style Magazine* for creating "a Nation of Latina Leaders."

A former faculty member at the Center for Creative Leadership—the most highly utilized executive program in the world—Juana served as advisor to Harvard's Hispanic Journal on Public Policy and the Kellogg National Fellows Program. She was vice-chair of the Greenleaf Center for Servant Leadership's board and a trustee of the International Leadership Association.

Her best-selling book *Salsa, Soul and Spirit—Leadership for a Multicultural Age* was awarded the 2008 International Latino Book Award for leadership. In 2008, Juana received Denver's Martin Luther King Jr. Award for Social Responsibility and the Wise Woman Award from the National Center for Women's Policy Studies. She is in the Colorado Women's Hall of Fame. In 2009 the Denver Post and the Colorado Women's Foundation named her the Colorado Unique Woman of the Year.

Today, Juana is President of Mestiza Leadership International (MLI)—a company that focuses on leadership, diversity, and organizational change. MLI'S mission is to prepare collaborative and inclusive leaders for our multicultural and global age.

To learn more and to exchange ideas with Juana, contact JuanaBordas.com.

Friend Me on Facebook: facebook.com/JuanaBordas

Follow Me on Twitter: twitter.com/JuanaBordas

Also by Juana Bordas

# Salsa, Soul, and Spirit
## Leadership for a Multicultural Age, Second Edition

One of America's historic strengths is the ability to incorporate aspects from many different cultures to create a stronger whole. But current leadership approaches are overwhelmingly written by white males and remain distressingly Eurocentric. Juana Bordas has set out to change this. In this influential book, she shows how incorporating Latino, Black, and American Indian approaches can enrich leadership practice.

Bordas identifies nine core leadership principles common to all three cultures. Using a lively blend of personal reflections, interviews with leaders from each community, historical background, and insightful analysis, Bordas illustrates the creative ways these principles have been put into practice in communities of color. The multicultural leadership model developed in this book offers a more flexible and inclusive way to lead and a new vision of the role of the leader in organizations and in our increasingly diverse world.

Paperback, 256 pages, ISBN 978-1-60994-117-8
PDF ebook, ISBN 978-1-60994-118-5

Berrett–Koehler Publishers, Inc.
*www.bkconnection.com*                                      **800.929.2929**

# Berrett–Koehler
## Publishers

**Berrett-Koehler** is an independent publisher dedicated to an ambitious mission: *Creating a World That Works for All*.

We believe that to truly create a better world, action is needed at all levels—individual, organizational, and societal. At the individual level, our publications help people align their lives with their values and with their aspirations for a better world. At the organizational level, our publications promote progressive leadership and management practices, socially responsible approaches to business, and humane and effective organizations. At the societal level, our publications advance social and economic justice, shared prosperity, sustainability, and new solutions to national and global issues.

A major theme of our publications is "Opening Up New Space." Berrett-Koehler titles challenge conventional thinking, introduce new ideas, and foster positive change. Their common quest is changing the underlying beliefs, mindsets, institutions, and structures that keep generating the same cycles of problems, no matter who our leaders are or what improvement programs we adopt.

We strive to practice what we preach—to operate our publishing company in line with the ideas in our books. At the core of our approach is stewardship, which we define as a deep sense of responsibility to administer the company for the benefit of all of our "stakeholder" groups: authors, customers, employees, investors, service providers, and the communities and environment around us.

We are grateful to the thousands of readers, authors, and other friends of the company who consider themselves to be part of the "BK Community." We hope that you, too, will join us in our mission.

### A BK Business Book

This book is part of our BK Business series. BK Business titles pioneer new and progressive leadership and management practices in all types of public, private, and nonprofit organizations. They promote socially responsible approaches to business, innovative organizational change methods, and more humane and effective organizations.

# Berrett–Koehler
## Publishers

A community dedicated to creating
a world that works for all

### Visit Our Website: www.bkconnection.com

Read book excerpts, see author videos and Internet movies, read our authors' blogs, join discussion groups, download book apps, find out about the BK Affiliate Network, browse subject-area libraries of books, get special discounts, and more!

### Subscribe to Our Free E-Newsletter, the *BK Communiqué*

Be the first to hear about new publications, special discount offers, exclusive articles, news about bestsellers, and more! Get on the list for our free e-newsletter by going to **www.bkconnection.com**.

### Get Quantity Discounts

Berrett-Koehler books are available at quantity discounts for orders of ten or more copies. Please call us toll-free at (800) 929-2929 or email us at bkp .orders@aidcvt.com.

### Join the BK Community

BKcommunity.com is a virtual meeting place where people from around the world can engage with kindred spirits to create a world that works for all. BKcommunity.com members may create their own profiles, blog, start and participate in forums and discussion groups, post photos and videos, answer surveys, announce and register for upcoming events, and chat with others online in real time. Please join the conversation!

Certified

Corporation

bcorporation.net